Discipline and Discharge in Arbitration

2001 Supplement

BNA Books Authored by the ABA Section of Labor & Employment Law

Covenants Not to Compete: A State-by-State Survey

The Developing Labor Law

Discipline and Discharge in Arbitration

Elkouri & Elkouri: How Arbitration Works

Employee Benefits Law

Employee Duty of Loyalty: A State-by-State Survey

Employment Discrimination Law

Equal Employment Law Update

The Fair Labor Standards Act

How to Take a Case Before the NLRB

International Labor and Employment Laws

Labor Arbitration: A Practical Guide for Advocates

Labor Arbitration: Cases and Materials for Advocates

Labor Arbitrator Development: A Handbook

Occupational Safety and Health Law

The Railway Labor Act

Trade Secrets: A State-by-State Survey

Discipline and Discharge in Arbitration

2001 Supplement

Editor-in-Chief

Anne L. Draznin
Arbitrator and Attorney
Professor of Legal Studies and Labor Relations
University of Illinois—Springfield
Springfield, IL

Chapter Reviewers

Lynne Hicks
MacDonald & Hicks, P.C.
Denver, CO

Charles W. Kohler
Arbitrator and Attorney
Columbus, OH

Thomas Y. Mandler
Michael, Best & Friedrich, LLP
Chicago, IL

Committee on ADR in Labor and Employment Law
Section of Labor and Employment Law
American Bar Association

The Bureau of National Affairs, Inc., Washington, D.C.

Second Printing, February 2006

Library of Congress Cataloging-in-Publication Data
(Revised for supplement)

Discipline and discharge in arbitration / editor in chief, Norman Brand ; associate editors, Patricia Thomas Bittel . . . [et al.] ; Assistant editor, Henry G. Stewart.
p. cm.
ISBN 1-57018-060-1
1. Arbitration, Industrial—United States. 2. Labor disputes—United States. I. Brand, Norman. II. Bittel, Patricia Thomas.
KF3424.D57 1998
344.7301'89143—dc21 98-42447
CIP

Published by BNA Books
1231 25th St., NW, Washington, D.C. 20037
http://www.bnabooks.com

ISBN: 1-57018-232-9; 978-1-57018-232-7

BOARD OF EDITORS

Chapter 3

Chapter Editor

HARRY R. GUDENBERG
Attorney & Arbitrator
Oradell, NJ

Topic Authors

GENNARO BIZZARRO
Murtha Cullina, LLP
Hartford, CT

THOMAS M. CLOHERTY
Murtha Cullina, LLP
Hartford, CT

WESLEY KENNEDY
Allison, Slutsky & Kennedy, P.C.
Chicago, IL

WILLIAM M. LAMOREAUX
Law Offices of William Lamoreaux
Dallas, TX

LIZA REYNOLDS
Allison, Slutsky & Kennedy, P.C.
Chicago, IL

Chapter 4

Chapter Editor

JERALD A. HOCHSZTEIN
Newburger & Vossmeyer, LLC
St. Louis, MO

Topic Authors

JOHN BOLONOVICH
Stokes & Murphy, P.C.
Atlanta, GA

KENNETH R. CASS
Attorney
Dunedin, FL

MARTIN J. CRANE
Sherman Dunn Cohen Leifer & Yellig, P.C.
Washington, DC

MELVA HARMON
Attorney
Little Rock, AR

FREDRIC R. HOROWITZ
Arbitrator
Santa Monica, CA

ARCH STOKES
Stokes & Murphy, P.C.
Atlanta, GA

Chapter 5

Chapter Editor

DEBRA S. NEVEU
Attorney & Arbitrator
New Orleans, LA

Topic Authors

RUSSELL M. GUTTSHALL, III
Exxon-Mobil Corp.
Houston, TX

DEBRA S. NEVEU
Attorney & Arbitrator
New Orleans, LA

JEFFREY D. HANSLICK
Blackwell Sanders Peper Martin LLP
Kansas City, MO

Chapter 6

Chapter Editor

WILLIAM M. EARNEST
Elarbee, Thompson & Trapnell, LLP
Atlanta, GA

Topic Authors

SCOTT E. ATWOOD
Elarbee, Thompson & Trapnell, LLP
Atlanta, GA

WEN-SHIN CHENG
Tressler, Soderstrom, Maloney & Priess
Chicago, IL

LYNNE HICKS
MacDonald & Hicks, P.C.
Denver, CO

LAURA K. JOHNSON
Elarbee, Thompson & Trapnell, LLP
Atlanta, GA

MARK P. JOHNSON
Sonnenschein Nath & Rosenthal
Kansas City, MO

JEFFREY B. KENT
Elarbee, Thompson & Trapnell, LLP
Atlanta, GA

STACEY A. MEYERS
Schuchat, Cook & Werner
St. Louis, MO

ALISA LORETTA PITMAN
Elarbee, Thompson & Trapnell, LLP
Atlanta, GA

NANCY F. REYNOLDS
Elarbee, Thompson & Trapnell, LLP
Atlanta, GA

JOHN S. SCHAUER
Seyfarth, Shaw, Fairweather & Geraldson
Chicago, IL

Chapter 7

Chapter Editor

LAWRENCE M. OBERDANK
Arbitrator & Mediator
Savannah, GA

Topic Author

LAWRENCE M. OBERDANK
Arbitrator & Mediator
Savannah, GA

Chapter 8

Chapter Editor

ANNE L. DRAZNIN
Arbitrator & Professor
Chicago, IL

Topic Authors

ANNE L. DRAZNIN
Arbitrator & Professor
Chicago, IL

CHARLES F. IPAVEC
Arbitrator
Cleveland, OH

JOHN J. MICHELS, JR.
McGuire Woods, LLP
McLean, VA

LUELLA E. NELSON
Attorney
Portland, OR

Chapter 9

Chapter Editor

STEVEN M. BIERIG
Arbitrator
Highland Park, IL

Topic Authors

FRANK T. MAMAT
Clark Hill PLC
Detroit, MI

SUSANNAH MUSKOVITZ
Faulkner, Sackett & Muskovitz
Cleveland, OH

GEORGE T. ROUMELL, JR.
Riley, Roumell, & Connolly, P.C.
Detroit, MI

Chapter 10

Chapter Editor

RICHARD K. ZUCKERMAN
Rains & Pogrebin, P.C.
Mineola, NY

Topic Authors

JOSEPH J. ALLOTTA
Allotta & Farley
Toledo, OH

SHARON N. BERLIN
Rains & Pogrebin, P.C.
Mineola, NY

JOHN KAGEL
Arbitrator
Redwood City, CA

WAYNE J. SCHAEFER
Certilman Balin Adler & Hyman, LLP
East Meadow, NW

DAVID WORLEY
Jacobs & Slawsky
Atlanta, GA

Chapter 11

Chapter Editor

SUSAN GRODY RUBEN
Arbitrator & Mediator
Cleveland, OH

Topic Authors

BRENT R. BAUGHMAN
Greenebaum Doll & McDonald PLLC
Louisville, KY

JOHN HAMLIN
Paul, Hastings, Janofsky & Walker, LLP
Stamford, CT

SINCLAIR KOSSOFF
Arbitrator
Chicago, IL

WILLIAM SCOTT HINCKLEY
Union Pacific Railroad
Omaha, NE

MICHELLE PEAK
Union Pacific Railroad
Omaha, NE

CATHERINE SOSSO
Union Pacific Railroad
Omaha, NE

Chapter 12

Chapter Editor

EDWIN S. HOPSON
Wyatt, Tarrant & Combs, LLP
Louisville, KY

Topic Authors

JEROLD E. GLASSMAN
Grotta, Glassman & Hoffman, P.A.
Roseland, NJ

KURT M. GRAHAM
Varnum, Riddering, Schmidt & Howlett, LLP
Grand Rapids, MI

MARY L. KNOBLAUCH
Anthony Ostlund & Baer, P.A.
Minneapolis, MN

PETER A. MILIANTI
Ross & Hardies
Chicago, IL

STEVE D. OLSON
Fruth & Anthony, P.A.
Minneapolis, MN

CHRISTIAN M. POLAND
Ross & Hardies
Chicago, IL

HERBERT L. SEGAL
Segal, Stewart, Cutler, Lindsay, Janes & Berry, PLLC
Louisville, KY

DAVID J. SILBERMAN
Grotta, Glassman & Hoffman, P.A.
Roseland, NJ

CARL E. VER BEEK
Varnum, Riddering, Schmidt & Howlett, LLP
Grand Rapids, MI

Chapter 13

Chapter Editor

THOMAS Y. MANDLER
Michael, Best & Friedrich LLC
Chicago, IL

Topic Authors

JOSH M. FRIEDMAN
New Legal Media
Chicago, IL

THOMAS Y. MANDLER
Michael, Best & Friedrich LLC
Chicago, IL

VICKI R. KAHANER
New York City Health & Hospitals Corporation
New York, NY

Chapter 14

Chapter Editor

HOWARD STEINMAN
Tallan, A CMGI Company
Arlington, VA

Topic Author

JANET MCENEANEY
Arbitrator
Bayside, NY

Foreword

Since 1945 the ABA Section of Labor and Employment Law has had as its stated purposes (1) to study and report upon continuing developments in the field of labor and employment law, (2) to assist the professional growth and development of practitioners in the field of labor and employment law, and (3) to promote justice, human welfare, industrial peace, and the recognition of the supremacy of law in labor-management relations and the employment relationship.

Through the publication of books such as *Discipline and Discharge in Arbitration* and through annual and committee meeting programs designed to provide a forum for the exchange of ideas, the Section has pursued these stated goals. Gradually, the Section has built a library of comprehensive legal works intended for the use of the Section membership as well as the bar generally.

The Section of Labor and Employment Law is pleased to provide this supplement to the treatise on discipline and discharge in arbitration as part of its library of books published by BNA Books, a Division of The Bureau of National Affairs, Inc. The combined efforts of many individual authors recruited by the Committee on ADR in Labor and Employment Law are reflected in this work.

The Section wishes to express its appreciation to the committee, and in particular to the editor-in-chief, Anne L. Draznin; to the chapter reviewers, Charles W. Kohler, Lynne Hicks, and Thomas Y. Mandler; to the chapter editors, Steven M. Bierig, William M. Earnest, Harry Gutenberg, Jerald A. Hochsztein, Edwin S. Hobson, Thomas Y. Mandler, Debra S. Neveu, Lawrence M. Oberdank, Susan Grody Ruben, Howard Steinman, Henry G. Stewart, and Richard K. Zuckerman; and to the topic authors. This group has tried to accomplish two primary objectives: (1) to be equally balanced and nonpartisan in its viewpoints, and (2) to ensure the book is of significant value to the practitioner, student, and sophisticated nonlawyer.

The views expressed herein do not necessarily represent the views of the American Bar Association, or its Section of Labor and Employment Law, or any other organization, but are simply the collective, but not necessarily the individual, views of the authors. Information on the affiliation of government employees who contributed to this work is for informational purposes and does not constitute any official endorsement of the information provided herein. Individual views, when expressed, are identified as such.

MARK S. DICHTER
Chair

SORRELL LOGOTHETIS
Chair-Elect
Section of Labor
and Employment Law
American Bar Association

July 2001

Preface

This book is a supplement to the 1998 first edition of Discipline and Discharge in Arbitration edited by Norman Brand. It is intended to update the material in the original edition. For that reason, the original chapter divisions and subheadings have been retained. If there was nothing new to report, the heading is not listed.

This supplement covers the period from 1996 through January, 2000. Judicial precedents or arbitral decisions of note that occurred after that time will be included in subsequent editions or supplements. In the original edition, Chapter 1, "Arbitration Advocacy," was an essay on the mechanics of the process of labor arbitration by the editor of that edition, Norman Brand. It provided a context for the use of the substantive descriptions and case references of the subsequent chapters. As such it stands on its own and is not updated in this supplement.

Growth in arbitration comes in uneven bumps and spurts. This uneven territory is reflected in the varying length and depth of the various chapter additions. The differences in the chapter commentaries are not intended to reflect any editorial emphasis or designation of importance. Rather they are indicia that in some areas more than others there has been considerable published activity or significant legal or theoretical developments.

At the end of this volume, we have included some useful supplementary materials. For those participating—or planning to participate—in a non-union workplace grievance dispute resolution, we have included as Appendix A a copy of the 1995 Due Process Protocol for Mediation and Arbitration of Statutory Disputes Arising Out of the Employment Relationship. We have also included a complete set of cross-reference tables: Table of Arbitration Decisions, Table of Arbitrators, and Table of Court Cases. These tables are provided for ease of access to the materials cited in the supplement. Because such materials were absent from the Main Edition, we have also included similar tables for the Main Edition. Thus, this supplement offers both updated substantive materials and a full set of finding aids for both the Main Edition and this supplement. We hope that these expanded reference resources enhance the usefulness of both volumes.

As the board of editors table reflects, many people worked on this volume. Some had worked on the original volume, others are new to the task with this supplement. New or old, all of the contributors to this supplement had to devote considerable effort to preparing their contributions. Assessing formative materials can be considerably harder and often more time consuming than amassing similar decisions citable in a string following a broad general summative statement. Unlike the task in the main edition, these contributors had to do more than find new additions to their assigned substantive areas. They had to assess the potential of each new case they found, determining the possible importance and value of the new decisions they reviewed in order to decide what to include. The efforts of these authors and editors is thus deserving of particular recognition and thanks.

In addition, of special note are the efforts of Renee Brown, of BNA, truly an "editor's editor," Marilyn Stahl, project legal assistant, and Sandra Bristow, the department secretary, for their hard work and attention to detail, their extraordinary ability to decipher my cryptic notations and directions, and their patience and good humor throughout. My thanks and deep appreciation to these people and to all who supported, assisted, and otherwise collaborated with me on this project!

ANNE L. DRAZNIN
Editor-in-Chief

Springfield, IL
December 2000

Summary Table of Contents

Detailed Table of Contents

Chapter 1

Arbitration Advocacy

Advocacy is a skill and was not subject to review for new developments.

Chapter 2

Just Cause

I. Theories of Just Cause

C. Standards of Proof [New Topic]

One of three different standards of proof are usually imposed: (1) "preponderance of the evidence," (2) "clear and convincing evidence," and (3) "beyond a reasonable doubt." However, legalistic formulations of the standard of proof in arbitration proceedings have been labeled misplaced and without value.[1]

1. Preponderance of the Evidence [New Topic]. "Preponderance of the evidence" is the standard of proof traditionally imposed in arbitration proceedings.[2] It is the lowest standard of proof applied to most noncriminal disputes. An employer generally only needs to show that it was more probable than not that the alleged misconduct occurred.[3] Mitigating factors, such as length of employment, may be considered in assessing how much evidence must be produced. For instance, proof of misconduct for an employee who only worked for a company for a few years required only a preponderance of the evidence, whereas clear and convincing evidence was required to show misconduct of an employee who was with a company for 15 years.[4]

Because the point of the grievance procedure is to enable parties to resolve disputes, there are salient policy reasons for applying a less stringent standard of proof than that used in judicial proceedings. More relaxed proof requirements tend to enhance the agreement/facilitative function of grievance processes.[5]

---

[1]Norton Cmty. Hosp., 106 LA 970, 974–75 (Hart, 1996).

[2]Fermco Envtl. Restoration Mgmt. Co., 104 LA 596, 598 (Cocalis, 1995).

[3]Nabisco Brands, Inc., 106 LA 422, 426 (Wolff, 1996).

[4]Milwaukee Bd. of Sch. Dirs., 110 LA 566, 573 (Winton, 1998).

[5]Fermco Envtl. Restoration Mgmt. Co., 104 LA 596, 598 (Cocalis, 1995).

2. Clear and Convincing Evidence [New Topic]. The "clear and convincing evidence" standard is lower than the "beyond a reasonable doubt" standard but is significantly higher than the preponderance standard. It is sometimes defined as the "preponderance standard plus an opprobrium."[6] A more rigorous clear and convincing standard is often used when the penalty of discharge is imposed so that it is clearly shown that "more than just a slight tilt in the scale of justice," as required by the preponderance standard, was produced to show that the employee committed the offense charged.[7]

Proof of an employee's misconduct must be clear for discharge to be upheld.[8] Witness credibility is important in this context. For example, when an employer attempted to prove that an employee was involved in illegal drug activity on the job, the reports of an undercover agent whose identity was never revealed were not enough to meet the clear and convincing standard.[9] Corroborating testimony that indicated the employee was a potential suspect before the undercover agent's purchase of drugs from him was necessary to support the discharge.

3. Beyond a Reasonable Doubt [New Topic]. Higher standards of proof are required for serious offenses because of the potential ramifications of a discharge for conduct that could be criminal or involves moral turpitude.[10] Prospective employers may be adverse to hiring someone who already has been found to have acted illegally and, as a consequence, an employee might be unable to find another job.[11]

The "beyond a reasonable doubt" standard is used in criminal cases but it is not invoked in all arbitrations where the activity has criminal overtones.[12] Generally, the more rigorous reasonable doubt standard is only used where the alleged offense is both criminal and involves an element of moral turpitude.[13]

Arbitrators have also declined to apply the criminal reasonable doubt standard because arbitration proceedings do not give rise to a risk of unreasonable government action.[14] One arbitrator explained that the degree of proof should be what "the arbitrator considers necessary based on her own evaluations and weighing the evidence presented."[15] Under this reasoning, arbitrators should make decisions

[6]J. R. Simplot Co., 103 LA 865, 867 (Tilbury, 1994).

[7]Id.

[8]Manor West Health Care & Retirement Ctr., 106 LA 344 (Oberdank, 1996). See also Norton Cmty. Hosp., 106 LA 970 (Hart, 1996).

[9]Indianapolis Plant of Carrier Corp., 103 LA 891 (Lipson, 1994).

[10]Manor West Health Care & Retirement Ctr., 106 LA 344, 347 (Oberdank, 1996).

[11]Id.

[12]Id.

[13]Id. at 348.

[14]Ken Meyer Meats, Inc., 107 LA 1017, 1020 (Sergent, 1996).

[15]US West Communications, Inc., 107 LA 791, 795 (Yehie, 1996).

consistent with the standards of fairness ordinarily followed in industrial relations.[16]

II. Due Process as an Element of Just Cause

A. Elements of Due Process

1. Timely Employer Action. Timely action by employers in imposing discipline is important because it permits an employee to respond to the discipline at a time when memories are fresh.[17] An employer's failure to act promptly has resulted in the setting aside or reduction of discipline. For example, while the employer otherwise met the just cause standard for termination, an almost 4-month delay in imposing discipline violated the contract's requirement that discipline be imposed "as soon as possible."[18] The employee was reinstated with back pay. In another case, a termination was reduced to a suspension when the employer waited 3 weeks to notify the employee of the infraction when the contract required notice of wrongdoing "as soon as possible."[19]

2. Fair Investigation. Discharges were overturned in two cases involving heated exchanges between an employee and company officials because the employer accorded no weight to the grievant's version and failed to consider the context in which the statements were made.[20] A discharge of an employee for making racial and ethnic slurs was reduced to a suspension because the employer failed to consider the workplace problem that prompted the complaints or the veracity of the complaints.[21]

Discharges have also been overturned in separate cases involving walking off the job[22] and violation of a no-smoking policy[23] where employer decisions either were made without an investigation or were designed to support a decision already made: "[S]uch a one-sided investigation, which tends to lead to an overblown assessment of the seriousness of the circumstances and a marshalling of the facts to substantiate a foregone conclusion that the grievant is guilty as

---

[16]Nevada Power, 110 LA 949, 952 (Ross, 1998).

[17]King Soopers, Inc., 110 LA 242 (Snider, 1998) (termination 12 days after incident held timely).

[18]University of Ill., Chicago, 109 LA 680, 688 (Jacobs, 1997).

[19]Marriott Servs. Corp., 109 LA 689, 692 (Kaufman, 1997).

[20]Handchy Indus., 109 LA 1019 (Cerone, 1998); Ken Meyer Meats, Inc., 107 LA 1017 (Sergent, 1996). See also Levi Straus & Co., 109 LA 255 (Eisenmenger, 1997) (discharge reduced to suspension because employee had reasonable belief that comments made to employee assistance program counselor investigating alleged threat as part of employer's Threat Response Team would be held confidential).

[21]Firestone Synthetic Rubber & Latex Co., 107 LA 276 (Koenig, 1996).

[22]Rexam Graphics, 111 LA 1176 (Gangle, 1998).

[23]Western Sugar Co., 109 LA 944 (DiFalco, 1997).

charged, violates the notion of fair play and therefore violated just cause."[24]

In another case, however, discharge was upheld even though the employer's investigation was not exhaustive: "An employer is free, at the risk of making an expensive error, to act on the basis of a reasonable judgment, bolstering its case later with more evidence if that later proves necessary."[25]

3. Precise Statement of Charges. An employer's failure to provide an employee with a clear statement of charges at the time of discipline caused a suspension to be reduced to a written reprimand.[26] The employee had cursed a supervisor, refused a work assignment, and walked off the job. The employer's suspension letter charged the grievant with "abusive language" and "leaving his work area without authorization." The more serious charge of insubordination was not raised until the arbitration hearing. The arbitrator refused to consider the charge of insubordination because it was not raised in a timely manner and reduced the suspension to a written reprimand, discipline that was consistent with the employer's policies related to the less serious charges communicated to the grievant. In another case, a demotion for alleged inconsistent performance was overturned when the employer neither told the employee the reason for the demotion nor admonished him at the time for the alleged conduct that led to the demotion.[27]

4. Employee Right to be Heard. Failure to seek the grievant's side of the story before imposing discipline may be considered a per se violation of due process.[28] Finding no just cause for discharge, one arbitrator opined that "[d]ischarge and disciplinary actions must include basic notions of fairness and due process which includes the right of an employee to have the opportunity to be heard . . . before 'sentence is carried out'."[29] Other arbitrators consider the omission only when the employee was prejudiced by not being permitted to respond to the charges before being disciplined.[30]

In another case, discharge of an employee for punching another employee's time card was upheld even though the employer did not discuss the incident with him prior to discharge. Because the grievant had nothing new to add at the arbitration hearing, the arbitrator

[24]Rexam Graphics, 111 LA 1176, 1185 (Gangle, 1998).

[25]Southwestern Bell Tel. Co., 109 LA 274, 279 (Nolan, 1997) (employer made discharge decision without contacting grievant's physicians, who subsequently did not support grievant's testimony).

[26]University of Fla., 106 LA 510 (Nolan, 1996).

[27]GES Exposition Servs., 108 LA 311 (Levy, 1997).

[28]Jefferson Partners, 109 LA 335, 339 (Bailey, 1997).

[29]Buttrey Food & Drug Co., 110 LA 641, 646 (Prayzich, 1998).

[30]Napco, Inc., 111 LA 77, 83 (Franckiewicz, 1998).

said that the employer was not missing any relevant information when it made its termination decision.[31]

5. Double Jeopardy. An employer was held not to have just cause to discharge the driver of a vehicle used to transport patients to and from the hospital whose negligence was a significant cause of a patient's death because it had issued the employee a written warning shortly after the accident but before learning of the patient's condition.[32] The arbitrator held that the failure of the employer to condition the written warning on further investigation or the condition of the patient constituted a classic example of double jeopardy.

An employee suspended pending an investigation into alleged misconduct who is subsequently discharged on the basis of the investigation is not considered to have been disciplined twice for the same offense and is not subjected to double jeopardy, especially if the employer specifically states that the suspension is to allow the employer to investigate the "alleged misconduct."[33]

Double jeopardy has been held not to occur when the employer imposes a suspension pending further investigation[34] or imposes a "cooling off" period to allow an employee to reconsider her conduct,[35] even if the employer subsequently imposes additional discipline when all relevant information becomes available.

6. Weingarten Rights. In one case it was held that, in the absence of NLRB deferral, the arbitrator lacked authority to make the factual determination of whether the employee's request for union representation at an investigatory meeting had been denied.[36] In the absence of contract language or a past practice, the arbitrator declined to hold that the denial of union representation at an investigatory conference constituted a per se due process violation under standards of industrial justice.[37]

III. Progressive Discipline as an Element of Just Cause

A. Other Employer Communications Distinguished

1. Counseling. As counseling is generally considered "nondisciplinary," it has been held that evidence of one of these sessions is not

---

[31]Goodmark Foods, Inc., 112 LA 1191, 1194 (Nolan, 1999). See Yellow Freight Sys., Inc., 106 LA 1062 (Briggs, 1996). But see Chicago Transit Auth., 110 LA 403 (Wolff, 1997) (arbitrator questioned whether employee's due process rights were violated by removal from job in nonsafety situations before hearing employee's side of story).

[32]Metropolitan Tulsa Transit Auth., 112 LA 146 (Jennings, 1999).

[33]Portland Water Dist., 111 LA 673, 676 (Shieber, 1998); JPC Corinth Div., 111 LA 973, 979 (Nicholas, 1998).

[34]Portland Water Dist., 111 LA 673 (Shieber, 1998); City of Rogers City, 110 LA 92 (Daniel, 1997).

[35]Northwest Publ'ns, Inc., 104 LA 91 (Bognanno, 1994).

[36]Norfolk Shipbldg. & Drydock Corp. (NORSHIPCO), 105 LA 529 (Hockenberry, 1995).

[37]Id. at 533.

proof of the offense that prompted it.[38] In other words, the employer may offer such evidence to show that the employee was on notice that certain behavior was unacceptable but not that the employee committed a particular infraction.

B. *Sources of Progressive Discipline*

Contractual disciplinary provisions may be interpreted in light of standards of due process and fairness.[39]

The issue of notice to an employee is important. In one case, an employee's suspension was reduced because the employee did not have adequate forewarning of the possible consequences of breaking a no-smoking policy.[40] In another case, discharge was ruled to be inappropriate for an employee who had been terminated for tardiness on 35 out of 69 days because the employer provided no notice to its employees that excessive tardiness could lead to discharge.[41]

C. *Steps of Progressive Discipline*

When circumstances warrant, progressive discipline can be combined with preliminary steps where there are multiple separate acts of misconduct.[42] Contractual requirements of notice as to proposed discharge or suspension may invalidate a discharge if not followed, even when the company rule would otherwise support discharge.[43] While progressive disciplinary policies must be consistently applied, in at least one case a suspension without pay pending investigation was permitted when the employer's policy stated that the step just prior to discharge was suspension with pay.[44]

3. Suspension. When deciding whether a previous act of misconduct or discipline is material or superfluous to a suspension case,

---

[38]Phillips Pipeline Co., 110 LA 335, 338 (Simon, 1998).

[39]Oregon State Police Officer's Ass'n, 99-1 ARB ¶ 5547 (Nelson, 1999) (employer violated contract by not documenting stated reasons for personal investigation of grievant).

[40]Jamison Door Co., 99-1 ARB ¶ 5553 (Sergent, 1999).

[41]Contempo Designs, 111 LA 1141, 99-1 ARB ¶ 5516 (Rothstein, 1999).

[42]See United States Ceramic Tile Co., 99-1 ARB ¶ 5457 (Franckiewicz, 1998). The company policy said disciplinary action "may, but will not necessarily follow" the pattern of a verbal warning for the first offense, with a written warning for the second. The company issued verbal and written warnings simultaneously for two proximate, separate offenses. Denying the grievance, the arbitrator ruled there was no violation of the contractual requirement, but added the dictum that combining a written warning with a suspension or discharge might well be excessively harsh and a denial of the opportunity for corrective action after the warning.

[43]Penske Truck Leasing, 110 LA 833, 837 (Bumpass, 1998) (discharge violated collective bargaining agreement where employee did not receive required initial written warning before discipline).

[44]Modine Mfg. Co., 109 LA 349, 352 (Byars, 1997) (employee's outburst considered serious breach of conduct and not minor one covered by progressive discipline rules where employee left work floor without permission and struck and broke Plexiglas cover when confronted by supervisor).

the corrective and rehabilitative purpose of progressive discipline is often stressed.[45] A suspension should comply with the terms of the collective bargaining agreement and, according to one arbitrator, should not be imposed if the agreement specifies that a written warning must be given before an employee is suspended.[46]

In general, a suspension will not be overturned because of an employer's delay in suspending the employee as long as the employer puts forth a reasonable basis for the delay, but a 25-day delay has been found to be too long.[47] It has also been found that a suspended employee may be awarded back wages for lost overtime where the suspension deprived the employee of the opportunity to elect to work premium hours.[48]

"Conditional" suspensions lasting until the employee satisfies a condition imposed by the employer may be upheld as not violating the collective bargaining agreement. If it is equated with an indefinite suspension, however, a conditional suspension may be an excessive penalty if it is unduly burdensome to the employee.[49]

Employers may deviate from progressive disciplinary policies when confronted with a serious act of misconduct. For example, an employer suspended an employee without pay, even though the employer's progressive policy stated that a suspended employee would receive full straight-time pay for the time missed, stating that the purpose of the policy was to "eliminate the unacceptable behavior, rather than to punish."[50] However, it depends on the misconduct at issue.[51] This has been held to be true even where an employee entered a guilty plea to a criminal misdemeanor.[52]

When there has been a longstanding practice of having a verbal warning as a first step, it may not be ignored.[53] When an employer

---

[45]City of Wooster, 111 LA 1167, 1174 (Richard, 1999) (employee's previous progressive disciplinary penalties—written warnings and suspensions—were directly relevant and material to suspension in question; the arbitrator said that "[p]rogressive discipline has two purposes: to correct employee misconduct at the lowest possible level of discipline, and to provide both warning of the severity of future discipline for repetition of that [or *similar*] misconduct and a foundation to support the propriety of more severe discipline for subsequent [*similar*] offenses").

[46]Lane County, 111 LA 481, 487 (Downing, 1998).

[47]Safeway Stores, Inc., 109 LA 817, 820 (Watkins, 1997) (delay because store manager was busy because of end of labor dispute and holiday weekend held to be unreasonable).

[48]General Mills, Inc., 97-2 ARB ¶ 3206 (Feldman, 1997) (employee must be paid 16 hours of wages at normal rate when suspension fell on days routinely used to sign up for overtime and, as result, 3-day suspension actually resulted in loss of additional premium pay).

[49]Fourslides, Inc., 97-2 ARB ¶ 3247 (Kelman, 1997).

[50]Modine Mfg. Co., 109 LA 349, 352 (Byars, 1997) (employee left work floor without permission, then became angry and struck and broke Plexiglas cover of sandblaster when confronted by supervisor).

[51]U.S. Steel Corp., 111 LA 52, 56 (Neyland, 1998) (two employees' efforts to use their positions as union officials in manipulative manner to miss mandatory employee meeting did not give employer right to disregard progressive discipline and suspend for 5 days where employees otherwise had clean disciplinary records and substantial lengths of service).

[52]Cook County Sch. Serv. Dep't, 111 LA 417 (Doering, 1998) (1-week suspension more reasonable than discharge for social service caseworker who pled guilty to possession of small amount of marijuana).

[53]Ralphs Grocery Co., 112 LA 449 (Gentile, 1999).

implements a new policy, a suspension for violating the policy may be overturned if the violator did not receive adequate forewarning of the consequences of breaking the policy.[54]

4. Discharge. Depending on the circumstances, summary discharges may be upheld if based on single contractually specified incidents[55] or where very serious conduct, such as violation of a critical safety rule, precludes imposition of progressive discipline.[56] If misconduct is not serious but repeatedly occurs, discharge still may be unwarranted if the employee has not been given notice that multiple occurrences of the minor misconduct could lead to discharge.[57]

Discharge for absenteeism may be upheld, even though the employee was not at the stage of discharge in the progressive discipline scheme, where the employee lied to cover an unauthorized absence.[58] "Last straw" discharge may be approved where a relatively minor offense triggers the final step in the progressive discipline process.[59]

A discharge has been held to be unreasonable where the employee was "put on notice" for an excessive length of time.[60] If a policy specifies a time limit on the life of the warnings for the purpose of progressive discipline, then the frequency of previous disciplinary notices of violation of rules may be given no weight.[61]

5. Demotion and Transfer as Alternatives to Progressive Discipline. A standard of reasonableness and fairness rather than the just cause standard may apply to demotions and transfers.[62] In some instances transfer to another job may not be permissible as a form of discipline.[63] Where an employer presented clear and convincing evidence that an employee was guilty of sexual harassment on earlier occasions, however, demotion was upheld for subsequent misconduct

---

[54]Jamison Door Co., 99-1 ARB ¶ 5553 (Sergent, 1999) (employee did not receive adequate forewarning of consequences of breaking no-smoking policy).

[55]Union Tank Car Co., 110 LA 1128 (Lalka, 1998) (what amounts to serious violation cannot be readily predicted). See Safelite Glass Corp., 111 LA 561 (Bain, 1998) (threatening a supervisor did not warrant summary discharge).

[56]Cleveland-Cliffs Iron Co., 110 LA 314, 320 (Vonhof, 1997) (reasonable to discharge employee for refusal to open his lunch bucket for inspection where agreement explicitly stated that failure to do so would result in discharge).

[57]Sign Display & Allied Crafts, 99-1 ARB ¶ 5516 (Rothstein, 1999).

[58]Merck-Medco RX Servs. of Tex., 110 LA 782 (Baroni, 1998).

[59]CBPO of Am., Inc., 98-1 ARB ¶ 5083 (Silver, 1997) (discharge appropriate for unsafe driving, although no accident occurred, where employee previously given oral reprimand for safety, a written warning for serious violation, and an opportunity to correct problems); Andex Indus., 111 LA 615 (Allen, 1998) (1-day absence).

[60]Empire Dist. Elec. Co., 110 LA 348, 352 (Murphy, 1997) (telling employee that another infraction at any time would result in discharge considered "perilous state regarding employment").

[61]Marriott Servs. Corp., 109 LA 689, 691 (Kaufman, 1997).

[62]GES Exposition Servs., 108 LA 311, 313 (Levy, 1997) (demotion based on unexplained "inconsistent performance" or unsubstantiated incidents of misconduct could be considered capricious or arbitrary under standard of reasonableness).

[63]Miami Beach Fraternal Order of Police, 98-1 ARB ¶ 5160 (Kravit, 1997) (right to transfer as a form of discipline may be limited).

of the same nature in a situation where discharge of the employee would not have been warranted.[64]

Because of the seniority rights of employees, disciplinary demotions may be unenforceable. However, an employee may choose a voluntary demotion where the contract said that a promoted employee could voluntarily return or be returned by the employer to a former job.[65]

IV. Arbitral Concepts of Fairness

A. *Making and Communicating Rules*

In testing the reasonableness of a rule, factors to be considered include the subject matter of the rule, whether the rule is consistent with the existing collective bargaining agreement, whether the employee had notice of the rule,[66] the consistency of the rule's enforcement, the appropriateness of the penalty, and whether progressive discipline was applied.[67]

1. Content. To meet the reasonableness requirement, a rule must relate to the orderly and efficient operation of the plant[68] and must not be arbitrary, capricious, or inconsistent.[69] There is a need for work rules even though they may limit an employee's freedom.[70]

Rules that govern the safety and health of employees are routinely deemed reasonable and related to the orderly and efficient operation of business.[71] This includes antiviolence and no-weapons rules when they are necessary to protect the health and safety of employees.[72]

---

[64]City of Orlando, Fla. Police Dep't, 98-1 ARB ¶ 5142 (Sweeney, 1998) (police officer was properly demoted from rank of sergeant to position of probationary officer).

[65]Tetra Pak, Inc., 108 LA 470, 475 (Fowler, 1997) (seniority is at heart of collective agreements).

[66]Champion Int'l Corp., 111 LA 100, 105 (Duda, 1998) (employee conclusively presumed to have notice of new work rule posted on company bulletin board).

[67]Wynn's Precision, Inc., 111 LA 669, 671 (Kilroy, 1998) (employee reinstated where rule was patently arbitrary, capricious, and invidious).

[68]Cajun Elec. Power Coop., 111 LA 769, 773–74 (O'Grady, 1998).

[69]Wynn's Precision, Inc., 111 LA 669, 671 (Kilroy, 1998) (work rule that required employee to use toilet nearest work station was arbitrary, capricious, and invidious). But see Southwest Airlines, 107 LA 270, 274 (Jennings, 1996) (airline's grooming standard not arbitrary, capricious, or inconsistent where rule preserved employer's image with customers with whom attendants came into contact).

[70]Clarion Sintered Metals, Inc., 110 LA 770, 773 (Cohen, 1998) (work rule prohibiting indecent dress).

[71]Cajun Elec. Power Coop., 111 LA 769, 773–74 (O'Grady, 1998) (drug testing rule reasonably related to efficient and safe operations).

[72]Navistar Internat'l Transp. Corp., 109 LA 796, 799 (Kessler, 1997) (work rule prohibiting weapons at employer's facility "designed to prevent an employee, in the heat of a dispute, from getting a weapon to enforce their personal perception of what is right"); Golden States Food Corp., 108 LA 705, 707–08 (Gentile, 1997) (employee's discharge for violation of "zero tolerance" policy for "actual or threatened violence in the workplace" upheld based on rationale that touching of another employee in anger without permission constitutes "just cause" to sustain serious level of discipline).

In addition, rules and policies to prevent sexual harassment have been routinely found to be reasonable.[73] The need for drug and alcohol policies has also been acknowledged.[74] Rules, including those that govern health and safety, however, must still meet the other tests for reasonableness.

2. Consistency With Collective Bargaining Agreement. Management may establish reasonable rules as long as they do not contravene the collective bargaining agreement.[75] Policies that are not covered by the collective bargaining agreement[76] may be established without ratification by the union.[77] An employer may discipline an employee for violating a policy that was unilaterally implemented after an impasse in negotiations over the policy was reached and after notice of unilateral implementation was given to all employees.[78] However, unilateral promulgation and implementation may be limited by past practice.[79]

A work rule may be held invalid because it causes a unilateral change in mandatory subjects of collective bargaining. For example, a casual dress code implemented by the employer was held to be reasonable because it was made known to employees by being universally enforced.[80] The employer, however, was required to bargain with the union over the cost of clothing mandated by the policy because the policy had the effect of reducing wages.[81]

3. Employee Notice of Rules. In assessing discipline, principles of fairness require that the employee has notice of the rule. Learning about work rules from other employees is not the proper manner in which employees should learn about company requirements.[82] The

---

[73]American Safety Razor Co., 110 LA 737, 744 (Hockenberry, 1998) (upholding sexual harassment policy); ABTCO, Inc., 104 LA 551, 554 (Kanner, 1995).

[74]PPG Indus., Inc., 109 LA 399, 404 (Grenig, 1997) (purpose of work rules prohibiting employees from being under influence of or impaired by drugs or alcohol is to protect safety of employees and others).

[75]Crown Cork, 112 LA 749 (Cohen, 1999).

[76]Alpena Power Co., 112 LA 1008, 1010 (Coyne, 1999).

[77]Crown Cork, 112 LA 749, 754 (Cohen, 1999) (absenteeism policy properly implemented even though union never ratified it or agreed to add it to collective bargaining agreement).

[78]Congreso de Uniones Indus. de P.R. v. Bacardi Corp., 156 LRRM 2600, 2601–02 (D.P.R., 1997) (discharge of employee for alcohol consumption at work place upheld where employer had inherent right to establish drug and alcohol policies after employer had unsuccessfully attempted to negotiate matter with union and where due notice was given to employees).

[79]Flowserve Corp., 111 LA 813, 819–20 (Jennings, 1998) (employer violated collective bargaining agreement by unilaterally instituting new plant rules where there was longstanding past practice of negotiating changes to safety shoe policies).

[80]Aerospace Cmty. Credit Union, 112 LA 58, 68 (Kelly, 1999).

[81]Id. at 69.

[82]Memphis Publ'g Co., 112 LA 432, 437 (Hart, 1999) (reprimand of newspaper reporter for violating work rule requiring approval for outside employment that had been in effect for 13 years overturned on finding reporter may not have known rule applied to him, where grievant was not employed by newspaper when notice of applicable rules last given to staff).

employer should provide new employees with copies of, and a familiarization with, its expectations in employee handbooks, collective agreements, work rules, and policies in order to substantiate with certainty that employees are aware of what is expected of them.

Acquiescence in the grievant's past conduct is equivalent to condoning it and can result in a finding that the employee did not have notice that his or her conduct violated the rule.[83] Failure to discipline an employee within a reasonable period of time may result in a similar situation.[84]

a. Unwritten and Unpublished Rules. Disciplinary action may be warranted for actions that have not been published or otherwise communicated to employees where common sense dictates that the action is unreasaonble.[85]

b. Clarity of Rules. Rules must clearly and unambiguously establish the scope of prohibited conduct. Overly broad policies may be unenforceable.[86] For example, a "clean-shaven" policy has been held to be overly broad where it unnecessarily applied to all employees.[87] In another case, an absenteeism work rule was deemed invalid where the number of occurrences between each step was different for each employee and the rule failed to set forth the number of episodes necessary to trigger the next step.[88]

Lack of clarity, however, does not excuse an employee from determining for herself how a rule applies:

> If an employee has any question or concern about the application of a well publicized rule of conduct, he has an obligation to determine for himself how the rule is applied. He cannot simply "lay behind the log" and claim ignorance of the details of the policy as a defense to enforcement of discipline against him for violation of the policy.[89]

An employer may also further clarify rules by direct communication with employees.[90]

---

[83]Clarion Sintered Metals, Inc., 110 LA 770, 776 (Cohen, 1998) (grievant cannot be disciplined for work rule violation for wearing clothing she had no reasonable basis to believe violated indecent dress rule where company had permitted grievant to wear "Hooters" T-shirt for 2 months).

[84]Safeway Stores, Inc., 109 LA 817, 820 (Watkins, 1997) (suspension of employee overturned where employer took 25 days to take disciplinary action and employee reasonably believed he had been excused from discipline).

[85]K&D Indus. Servs., Inc., 112 LA 820 (Allen, 1999) (employer had just cause to discipline employee who urinated on co-worker while off-duty; employee need not be notified through published rule or otherwise that such misbehavior is punishable because common sense dictates urinating on another person is unreasonable, offensive, and wrong).

[86]The Fitzpatrick Co., 108 LA 686, 691 (Briggs, 1997).

[87]Mission Foods, 111 LA 501, 505–06 (Snider, 1998).

[88]Toledo Liberty Glass Plant, 109 LA 1007, 1011 (Feldman, 1997).

[89]Exxon Pipeline Co., 109 LA 951, 952 (Abercrombie, 1997) (employee discharged for just cause for violating alcohol policy even though employer did not specifically tell employee .04% blood alcohol content would be positive result, where grievant was aware positive alcohol test would result in discipline).

[90]Southwest Airlines, 107 LA 270, 274 (Jennings, 1996) (grooming standards held not vague where managers had told grievant rules required him to wear long hair under cap).

B. Consistency of Enforcement

1. Uniform Enforcement. Consistent enforcement of a rule by an employer helps to justify the imposition of severe discipline such as discharge. For example, where an employer consistently adhered to its rule prohibiting fighting in any form, the discharge for fighting of an employee with 18 years of service was upheld.[91] In some instances, inconsistent rule enforcement may not be fatal to the imposition of discipline.[92]

2. Lax Enforcement. In general, an employer's failure to consistently enforce plant rules may result in the discipline being overturned at arbitration.[93] Laxity in the enforcement of plant rules, however, may be rectified by the employer. For example, an arbitrator found that placing the union and its members on notice that further violations would not be tolerated and that employees would be disciplined in accordance with stated rules rendered the plant rule enforceable even though the employer had been lax enforcing the rule in the past.[94]

3. Unequal or Discriminatory Enforcement. Disparate treatment or discriminatory enforcement is an affirmative defense. To prove disparate treatment, one must show that the circumstances surrounding the cases offered for comparison were similar. The party alleging disparate treatment bears the burden of proving it by a preponderance of the evidence.[95]

C. Appropriateness of the Penalty

When determining the appropriateness of the penalty for violation of a work rule, certain actions justify more serious penalties. For example, allegations of sexual harassment or assault are viewed far more critically today than in the past.[96] In fact, sexual harassment

---

[91]Aladdin Indus., Inc., 111 LA 361, 363 (Jewett, 1998).

[92]Cumberland Elec. Membership Corp., 109 LA 60, 64 (Cantor, 1997).

[93]Coos-Curry Elec. Coop., Inc., 111 LA 47 (Calhoun, 1998) (employer did not have just cause to discharge employee who drank alcohol on the job where employer had never previously enforced rule).

[94]Crown Cork & Seal Co., Inc., 111 LA 141 (Goldberg, 1998) (employee violated plant rule for leaving workplace to go to tavern). See also Golden States Foods Corp., 108 LA 705, 707–08 (Gentile, 1997) (employer had just cause to discharge employee who grabbed fellow employee where 6 weeks before incident a "zero tolerance" "anti-violence" policy had been distributed and implemented); Carter Corp., 110 LA 1064, 1067 (Ipavec, 1998) (even though employer had been lax in past in enforcing work rule requiring employees to wear safety glasses, employer had just cause to discharge employee where employer had impressed on employees need to wear glasses for several months before discharge).

[95]Beta Steel Corp., 112 LA 877, 881 (Brookins, 1998) (employee discharged for writing vulgar graffiti on forklift not subject to disparate treatment where another employee who possessed "sailor's tongue" not disciplined).

[96]American Safety Razor Co., 110 LA 737 (Hockenberry, 1998).

and assault may warrant severe discipline, including discharge, even where the prohibition against sexual harassment and assault is not codified in a written rule.[97] Similarly, other cases have upheld discharge for violations of violence and no-weapon rules.[98]

The penalty, though harsh, may be upheld unless the penalty itself is unreasonable or the employee was treated in a disparate manner.[99] However, it is appropriate for an arbitrator to reduce a penalty "when the penalty assessed by management is so severe in relation to the offense as to shock the conscience."[100]

Aggravating or mitigating circumstances may also influence the penalty. For example, an employee's years of service, work record, and previous misconduct have influenced penalties.[101] Where the grievant recognizes his misconduct and makes sincere apologies, that may also be considered.[102]

D. *Fair Administration of the Progressive Discipline System*

Where an employer has a progressive discipline system in place, whether the system was followed—and, if not, whether the employer was justified in failing to follow it—will be considered. In determining whether an employer is warranted in failing to follow its progressive discipline system, the seriousness of the violation, previous related discipline, and previous steps in the progressive discipline have been included in the balance.

Proceeding directly to termination requires the employer to satisfy the following two-prong test:

> First, imposition of immediate discharge in lieu of progressive discipline can only be justified when the employee's conduct substantially imperils the orderly, efficient and safe operation of [the] business. Second, if the

[97]ABTCO, Inc., 104 LA 551, 554 (Kanner, 1995); International Mill Serv., 104 LA 779, 782 (Marino, 1995) (although sexual jokes, posters, propositions, and like were loosely tolerated as workplace norm 20 years ago, they are unacceptable and illegal today).

[98]Toledo Libbey, 109 LA 1010 (Feldman, 1997); San Diego Trolley, 112 LA 323, 327 (Prayzich, 1999).

[99]Exxon Pipeline Co., 109 LA 951 (Abercrombie, 1997) (decision to discharge for positive alcohol test upheld where there was no evidence of disparate treatment even though procedure followed was harsh and abrupt).

[100]Sandusky Cabinets, Inc., 112 LA 373, 377 (Morgan, 1999).

[101]Nabisco, Inc., 109 LA 547, 553 (Hayford, 1997) (discharge of employee for fighting rescinded and changed to 6-week suspension based on employee's 20 years of satisfactory service and mitigating circumstances of delivery truck driver's unprovoked hostile and aggressive conduct toward grievant); Pioneer Flour Mills, 107 LA 379, 383–84 (Bankston, 1996) (employee who violated work rule when he did not report on-the-job back injury discharged for just cause where he had 3 written warnings on file, had currently been counseled for a similar offense, and possessed dismal employment record).

[102]Will-son Corp., 108 LA 920, 924 (Nadelbach, 1997) (discharge of union steward who used profanity after dispute with management too severe where he recognized misconduct and apologized several times).

> first test is met, the employer must then make a showing that progressive discipline has been adequately and unsuccessfully applied, or alternatively, that the magnitude of the employee's bad act justifies immediate discharge.[103]

Where violation of a safety rule creates a potentially hazardous situation, it has been recognized that progressive discipline may be precluded where to hold otherwise would put employees at serious risk of death or serious injury.[104]

---

[103]Albertson's, Inc., 109 LA 194, 200 (McCurdy, 1997) (analyzing employer's policy of automatic discharge of employees consuming product before payment).

[104]Union Tank Car Co., 110 LA 1128, 1134 (Lalka, 1998) (employee properly discharged for first-time violation of safety rule that required employees to properly read flashpoints on tags before welding).

Chapter 3

Attendance

I. Absence as a Cause For Discipline

A. Employers' Policies

1. Collectively Bargained Versus Unilaterally Imposed Policies. Arbitrators continue to affirm an employer's authority to unilaterally modify attendance policies if the relevant collective bargaining agreement authorizes the employer to modify rules reasonably. Previous negotiations between the union and the employer on the issue of attendance policies may not necessarily impose an additional bargaining obligation if the collective bargaining agreement allows the employer to make unilateral modifications to the policy.[1]

3. Due Process Issues. Discharge has been overturned where an employee was unaware that absence could lead to discipline. In *Missouri Gas Energy*,[2] an employer who did not provide proper notification of the company's new attendance policy was found to have improperly disciplined an employee for absenteeism. Similarly, in another case it was held that an employer who wished to discharge a habitually tardy employee for "absenteeism" must first put the employee on notice that such misconduct could potentially lead to serious discipline such as termination.[3]

4. Conflicts Between Just Cause and the Employer's Policy. Whether strict adherence to its attendance policy relieves an employer from the burden of proving just cause continues to be an unsettled

---

[1]National Gypsum Co., 112 LA 248 (Nicholas, Jr., 1999).

[2]110 LA 164 (Madden, 1998).

[3]Contempo Designs, 111 LA 1141 (Rothstein, 1999).

issue. Some arbitrators uphold discipline by finding just cause if an employer simply complies with its attendance policy.[4]

B. The Employee's Work Record

Just cause has been found for discipline of habitually absent employees, especially when attendance is related to job performance.[5]

C. Mitigating and Aggravating Circumstances

1. Illness of Employee. a. Mental Illness. Severe stress and other emotional problems, as opposed to severe mental illness, may be the basis for overturning a termination for absenteeism. In *General Mills, Inc.*,[6] no just cause was found for terminating an employee whose poor attendance record would otherwise have warranted dismissal because the employee was in extreme mental and emotional distress after the death of his parents, the breakup of his marriage, and the vandalization of his car.

2. Drugs, Alcohol, and Related Issues. An employer may terminate an employee for misconduct, such as absenteeism, even if the absences are caused by alcoholism, when the employee has been previously reprimanded and warned about excessive or unexcused absenteeism.[7]

8. Employee Dishonesty. Employees who give false information regarding the reason for absence may be discharged. In *Merck-Medco RX Services of Texas*,[8] it was held that the employer properly discharged an employee who lied about being sick when in fact she was participating in a union demonstration. Although the employee had not yet progressed to the discharge stage of the contractual progressive discipline scheme, her misconduct was deemed sufficient to warrant discharge because it involved dishonesty, abuse of time, and the receipt of pay under false or misrepresented circumstances.

10. Impact on the Employer's Operations. Just cause for discipline may exist where absenteeism affects the employer's operators and imposes a significant harm or burden on an employer. Thus, for instance, just cause was found where an employee's absenteeism interrupted the flow of work and assignments had to be adjusted to

---

[4]See Napco, Inc., 111 LA 77 (Franckiewicz, 1998).

[5]Professional Med Team, Inc., 111 LA 457 (Daniel, 1998).

[6]112 LA 152 (Bailey, 1998).

[7]Andex Indus., Inc., 111 LA 615 (Allen, 1998).

[8]110 LA 782 (Baroni, 1998).

her absence.[9] In another case, just cause was found for discipline where attendance was directly related to job performance.[10]

II. Tardiness and Leaving Early

Arbitrators continue to require employers to follow progressive discipline in response to tardiness.[11] In one case, where the grievant had a long history of unexcused absences but had never received a written warning, the employee's termination for tardiness was reversed.[12] Where an employer's policy called for a written warning or suspension before an employee could be terminated for tardiness, chronically late employees who were discharged without first being given such a warning or suspension were reinstated.[13] In one such case, the arbitrator noted that the company's tolerance of the grievant's chronic lateness conveyed an impression that the tardiness policy would not be enforced.[14] Conversely, where the grievant had previously been suspended for violating the attendance policy, the employee's claim that he had never been told the rules was rejected, and his discharge for a leave-early absence was upheld.[15]

Point systems for tardiness and absenteeism may support discipline if they are clearly defined and fairly administered.[16] There is a potential for inconsistency between a no-fault point system and a just cause standard, however.[17] An employer that uses a point system may not discipline an employee for habitual tardiness as an offense separate and independent from the point system, because doing so would constitute double jeopardy.[18]

Where the contract provides rules that govern attendance, the employer may not unilaterally impose a point system under the label of management rights.[19] However, where the management rights clause expressly permitted the employer to "unilaterally implement reasonable rules," the employer could unilaterally impose a no-fault point system when faced with severe absenteeism that was hindering

---

[9]Knoll, Inc., 112 LA 438 (Borland, 1998).

[10]Professional Med Team, Inc., 111 LA 457 (Daniel, 1998).

[11]Albertson's, Inc., 96-1 ARB ¶ 6077 at 6390 (Kaufman, 1995).

[12]Albertson's, Inc., Store No. 916, 99-1 ARB ¶ 5451 at 7624–25 (Eisenmenger, 1998).

[13]Contempo Designs, 111 LA 1141, 1142, 99-1 ARB ¶ 5516 at 7976 (Rothstein, 1999); James Hardie Gypsum, 111 LA 210, 214 (Olson, 1998).

[14]Contempo Designs, 11 LA 1141, 1142, 99-1 ARB ¶ 5516 at 7976 (Rothstein, 1999).

[15]Rexnord Corp., 96-2 ARB ¶ 6262 (Doering, 1996).

[16]Taber Metals Gulfport, L.P., 99-2 ARB ¶ 3067 at 3453 (Moreland, 1999) (listing 7 characteristics of acceptable point systems).

[17]Kirk & Blum Mfg. Co., 112 LA 327, 331–32 (Duff, 1999); James Hardie Gypsum, 111 LA 210, 214 (Olson, 1998).

[18]Kirk & Blum Mfg. Co., 112 LA 327, 333 (Duff, 1999).

[19]Cargill Inc., 99-1 ARB ¶ 5468 at 7694–95 (Moreland, 1998).

operations.[20] In one case, it was held that a management rights clause permitted an employer to begin enforcing a longstanding but previously unenforced unilateral work rule against early quits after notice to employees, even though the employer had tried and failed to add early quits to the attendance and tardiness provision of the most recent collective bargaining agreement.[21]

A. *Defining "Tardiness"*

Leaving work early may be treated as the equivalent of a tardy.[22] Returning late from lunch may likewise be penalized as a tardy.[23] However, discharge was found not warranted where the employee had punched in on time but was not at his assigned work station at the beginning of the shift, where he was at his work area within 2 or 3 minutes thereafter, and there was no forklift available for him to use when he arrived. In the same case, the arbitrator said the fact that the grievant arrived at work in street clothes was not grounds for discipline because there was no rule against working in street clothes.[24] In another case, the employer improperly cited a bus driver for tardiness when the dispatcher knew that the grievant was standing outside the drivers' room smoking a cigarette at the designated time for reporting to work.[25]

Where the grievant reported to work on time following a medical leave of absence but the company would not permit him to begin work until his physician faxed a medical release, the grievant could not be assessed a tardy.[26] In a case where the grievant phoned in 4 hours late after oversleeping and offered to work the rest of his shift but the employer told him not to bother coming in for the rest of the day, however, the occurrence was properly treated as a tardy rather than a no-show.[27]

B. *Factors Used by Arbitrators in Evaluating Discipline*

1. Automobile Breakdowns and Inclement Weather. In one case, the arbitrator stated that he would have given more weight to the grievant's claim that he was late because his car had recently been

---

[20]National Gypsum Co., 112 LA 248 (Nicholas, Jr., 1999). See also Georgia-Pac. Corp., 108 LA 438, 440 (Moore, 1997).

[21]Michigan Hanger Employees Ass'n, 97-1 ARB ¶ 3008 (Smith, 1996).

[22]Taber Metals Gulfport, L.P., 99-2 ARB ¶ 3067 at 3454 (Moreland, 1999); Rexnord Corp., 96-2 ARB ¶ 6262 (Doering, 1996).

[23]Lucky Stores, Inc., 96-2 ARB ¶ 6246 at 7270 (Grabuskie, 1995).

[24]Vogt Valve Co., 98-2 ARB ¶ 5215 at 6252 (Florman, 1998).

[25]North County Transit Dist., 107 LA 73, 76–78 (Kaufman, 1996).

[26]Tecumseh Prods. Co., 106 LA 369, 370–71 (Flaten, 1996).

[27]Albertson's, Inc., Store No. 916, 99-1 ARB ¶ 5451 at 7623 (Eisenmenger, 1998).

totaled if the grievant had had a good record for punctuality. However, because the grievant had repeatedly been disciplined for tardiness before the car accident, he was obligated to find a way to get to work on time.[28]

2. Oversleeping. The fact that the grievant's alarm clock did not go off was held not to be a valid excuse for tardiness.[29] In another case, the grievant's claim that medication caused him to oversleep did not excuse 3 tardies. The arbitrator commented in a footnote that the grievant appeared to be in robust health.[30] Another grievant's excuse of oversleeping because of medication was rejected because his testimony was not credible and his doctor's notes were ambiguous.[31]

3. Prior Record. Where the grievant had already been rewarded for good attendance under a point system by having some of his points erased, the arbitrator claimed that he had no authority to give additional consideration to the grievant's previous work record, and the discharge was upheld.[32] An employee was held to be properly discharged for being 7 minutes late where he had a history of tardiness and had received a "final warning" for lateness 2½ months earlier.[33] In one case, the arbitrator held that the grievant's previous record of frequent tardiness outweighed his otherwise valid excuse that his car had recently been totaled.[34]

4. Miscellaneous Excuses. Arbitrators have rejected excuses for tardiness or equivalent infractions, such as early departures, in the following circumstances: an employee who was absent 26 times and tardy 16 times in 17 months because of family problems and depression;[35] an employee restricted to light duty by doctor's orders who left work early because the light-duty assignment offered to him was outside his usual department;[36] and an employee who received a point for leaving work 7½ hours early at the request of the police because his house had been broken into.[37] Where the grievant's repeated tardiness and absences were because of "extreme emotional and mental turmoil" (his parents died, his wife left him, and his car was broken into), discharge was deemed an excessive penalty.[38]

---

[28]Lucky Stores, Inc., 96-2 ARB ¶ 6246 at 7270 (Grabuskie, 1995).

[29]Albertson's, Inc., Store No. 916, 99-1 ARB ¶ 5451 at 7623 (Eisenmenger, 1989); Albertson's, Inc., 96-1 ARB ¶ 6077 at 6391 (Kaufman, 1995).

[30]State Univ. of N.Y., 110 LA 44, 47 n.5 (Babiskin, 1998).

[31]St. Vincent Med. Ctr., 106 LA 117, 121 (Richard, 1996).

[32]Fort James Corp., 99-1 ARB ¶ 5519 at 7994 (Specht, 1998).

[33]Albertson's, Inc., 106 LA 753 (Kaufman, 1996).

[34]Lucky Stores, Inc., 96-2 ARB ¶ 6246 at 7270 (Grabuskie, 1995).

[35]Knoll Inc., 112 LA 438 (Borland, 1998).

[36]Taber Metals Gulfport, L.P., 99-2 ARB ¶ 3067 at 3454 (Moreland, 1999).

[37]Fort James Corp., 99-1 ARB ¶ 5519 at 7993 (Specht, 1998).

[38]General Mills, 112 LA 152, 157–58 (Bailey, 1998).

5. Inconsistent Application. Where the employer's allegedly dissimilar treatment of similar offenses had occurred under earlier versions of the attendance program but where the employer was consistent in its application of the existing point system, the grievant's discharge for tardiness was upheld.[39]

7. Improvement. Where, after the grievant had been warned that she could be terminated if she were tardy again, she went 10 months without a single late arrival, an isolated tardy was not sufficient to support just cause for discharge.[40]

8. De Minimis Doctrine. Arbitrators continue to apply the de minimis doctrine. For example, where the grievant checked in on time and arrived at his work station only 2 or 3 minutes late and there was no forklift available for his use when he arrived, the discharge was reversed.[41] However, one arbitrator has stated that tardies of even 1 to 3 minutes may warrant discipline if they occur repeatedly or in conjunction with longer tardies.[42]

9. Notification. Where employees were expected to call in if they were going to be absent or late, the grievant's failure to call in on 3 different days when he arrived 30 to 45 minutes late was just cause for discipline.[43]

10. Last-Chance Agreements [New Topic]. Where the grievant was subject to a "last-chance agreement" based on past infractions including absenteeism, his discharge for accumulating enough tardies and absences to merit a warning under the attendance point system was upheld. The grievant's attendance violation, regardless of fault, was a disciplinary offense for purposes of the last-chance agreement.[44] Similarly, where an employee was working under a last-chance agreement because of chronic tardiness and absenteeism, one 18-minute tardy was just cause for discharge because the employee understood that the last-chance agreement covered tardiness.[45] In one case, the arbitrator expressed the view that the company engaged in direct dealing in violation of Section 8(a)(5) of the National Labor Relations Act when it offered the grievant a last-chance agreement that modified the company's tardiness policy without first notifying the union.[46]

C. Alternative Consequences

1. Withholding Work as Discipline. Where the attendance policy did not provide for sending tardy employees home but the contract

[39]Fort James Corp., 99-1 ARB ¶ 5519 at 7993 (Specht, 1998).
[40]Albertson's, Inc., 96-1 ARB ¶ 6077 at 6391 (Kaufman, 1995).
[41]Vogt Valve Co., 98-2 ARB ¶ 5215 at 6252 (Florman, 1998).
[42]Lucky Stores, Inc., 96-2 ARB ¶ 6256 at 7270 (Grabuskie, 1995).
[43]State Univ. of N.Y., 110 LA 44 (Babiskin, 1998).
[44]Omatsu Dresser Co., 96-1 ARB ¶ 6018 (Berger, 1995).
[45]Reliant Fastener, 96-1 ARB ¶ 6172 (Briggs, 1995).
[46]James Hardie Gypsum, 111 LA 210, 215 (Olson, 1998).

authorized the company to schedule and assign overtime to employees, the company properly assigned other employees to work in place of the grievants who arrived several hours late for an overtime shift, sent the grievants home, and charged them with an absence.[47]

3. Withholding Overtime and Holiday Pay. Where the collective bargaining agreement provided that employees absent the day before a holiday would not receive holiday pay, the company could not withhold holiday pay from an employee who was 1½ hours late the day before a holiday.[48]

4. Undesirable Assignments as Discipline [New Topic]. Where the employer unilaterally imposed a policy of assigning tardy truck drivers to the least desirable run, the arbitrator held that the policy was disciplinary and violated the collective bargaining agreement's provision on discipline for attendance.[49]

III. Requiring Medical Examinations and Certifications

B. Elements of a Valid Doctor's Note

The opinion of a psychiatrist was rejected where the arbitrator found, among other things, that the opinion lacked meaningful foundation.[50]

C. Employer's Authority to Require Medical Examinations

There is lack of agreement as to whether requiring physical examinations is always a mandatory subject of bargaining. In one case it was held that, in general, physical examinations are a mandatory subject of bargaining, and an employer frustrates the purpose of bargaining by mandating physical examinations that have not been agreed to with the union.[51] It also has been held that an employer violated the collective bargaining agreement by requiring medical evaluations for respirator users, despite claims that the evaluation was required by an Occupational Safety and Health Act standard, because the evaluations were presumptively within the purview of a contractual joint health and safety committee and the evaluations

---

[47]Whirlpool Corp., Lavergne Div., 108 LA 1098, 1099 (Modjeska, 1997).
[48]Jostens Printing & Publ'g Div., 97-1 ARB ¶ 3049 (Berger, 1996).
[49]Bakerstown Container Corp., 99-2 ARB ¶ 3071 (Paolucci, 1999).
[50]East Ohio Gas Co., 91 LA 366 (Dworkin, 1988).
[51]TCI Gen. Contractor, Inc., 93 LA 281 (Christenson, 1989).

had not been considered by the committee.[52] In another case it was held that where a collective bargaining agreement is silent on the issue of mandated physical examinations, a company may unilaterally establish a physical fitness evaluation program without bargaining as part of its right to establish reasonable rules to ensure the health and safety of employees.[53] One arbitrator opined that an employer's authority to require medical examinations may include periodic follow-up medical evaluations, such as periodic evaluations to determine that an employee's diabetic condition remained under control.[54]

An employer's policy regarding medical exams must be communicated to employees to be enforceable. One arbitrator refused to enforce a policy requiring a drug test as part of a return-to-work physical because the policy was unwritten, unpublished, and not communicated to the employees.[55]

Physical examinations may be mandated before termination of an employee, at least where the employee appears to be attempting to deal with a medical problem. An employer's termination of an employee without a medical examination to determine the effect of the grievant's medical condition on his or her conduct may violate the contract.[56] However, it has also been held that an accident-prone employee was not entitled to a physical examination before termination where a record of 4½ years of illness and numerous accident-related absences "speaks for itself" and where an examination could not possibly reveal when his next accident would occur.[57]

E. *The Employee's Right to Privacy*

Privacy claims continue to be fact-specific. It has been held that an employee may not resort to self-help such as refusal to take a drug test on the basis of a violation of privacy or other individual right where the employer had a right to insist on the test.[58]

A bus driver was properly discharged for refusing to release results of his Department of Motor Vehicles–mandated physical examination (including a drug screen) to his employer on privacy grounds where the driver had previously released the results of his medical examination and agreed to do so in the future.[59]

---

[52]Sohio Oil Co., 92 LA 201 (Strasshofer, 1988).

[53]Mason & Hanger-Silas Mason Co., 92 LA 131 (McKee, 1989).

[54]U.S. Steel Corp., 96 LA 567 (Petersen, 1990).

[55]Donaldson Mining Co., 91 LA 471 (Zobrak, 1988).

[56]Rohr Indus., 95 LA 1212 (Harkless, 1990).

[57]Mead Paper, 91 LA 52, 57 (Curry, 1988).

[58]Crescent Metal Prods., Inc., 91 LA 1129 (Coyne, 1989).

[59]San Diego Transit Corp., 96 LA 137 (Christopher, 1991).

Mandatory blood testing in a unilaterally established wellness program was held to have unreasonably invaded employees' privacy without justification where there was no showing of any substantial basis for requiring all employees to submit to a blood test and there was no direct evidence relating the blood test to the jobs of the employees.[60]

[60]Southern Champion Tray Co., 92 LA 677 (Williams, 1988).

Chapter 4

Job Performance Problems

II. Incompetence

A. "Pure" Incompetence

A "pure" incompetent employee has been defined as one who, despite his or her best efforts, cannot meet the employer's expectations.[1] Employers are not required to retain employees who do not or cannot meet the employer's performance requirements.[2] For example, if an employee's illiteracy prevents him from completing a state-mandated training course, he may be terminated.[3] Failure to obtain state certification[4] or to pass mandated training requirements can also provide sufficient cause for discharge.[5]

It is important to note, however, that failure to meet basic job performance standards is often coupled with charges of negligence or misconduct.[6] Such discharges have been upheld under the theory of reserved rights, where the management rights clause required that a reasonable production standard be met.[7]

---

[1]Wayne County, 108 LA 879, 882 (Babiskin, 1997); Cardinal Health, Inc., 108 LA 1039, 1047 (LaRocco, 1997).

[2]Arizona Opera Co., 105 LA 1126, 1131 (Wyman, 1996); Pacific Offshore Pipeline Co., 106 LA 79 (Kaufman, 1996); Samaritan Health Sys., 106 LA 927 (White, 1996); Cardinal Health, Inc., 108 LA 1039 (LaRocco, 1997); Stevens Graphics, Inc., 109 LA 1100 (Statham, 1998); BMW of Manhattan, 111 LA 525, 534 (Gregory, 1998).

[3]Levy County, 109 LA 1184 (Hoffman, 1998). Note that just cause did not exist to justify the termination in this case because the employer failed to give the employee 1 year to complete a training course.

[4]City of Key West, 110 LA 609 (Greef, 1998).

[5]Pacific Offshore Pipeline Co., 106 LA 79 (Kaufman, 1996) (employee properly discharged when he failed training rquirements).

[6]Putnam County Sheriff's Dep't, 106 LA 528 (Nelson, 1996); Office of Sheriff, Jacksonville, Fla., 107 LA 972 (Cornelius, 1996); Ken Meyer Meats, 107 LA 1017, 1021–22 (Sergent, 1996).

[7]Cummins Cumberland, Inc., 106 LA 993, 996 (Heekin, 1996); City of Naples, 109 LA 147, 151 (Bressler, 1997).

B. Conduct as an Element of Incompetence

When evaluating the merits of a discharge on the grounds of incompetency, many arbitrators require that employers follow progressive discipline.[8] Fair treatment of the employee prior to discharge continues to be important. Such fairness factors include, but are not limited to, clear notice of the standards expected of the employee and clear notice that failure to meet the employer's standards can lead to discipline; adequate training and instructions about how to correct the employee's job performance problems; adequate time and opportunity for the employee to improve; and the option of taking alternative assignments, if at all possible.[9] In addition, whether production quotas or standards are reasonable and are enforced in a fair, nondiscriminatory manner also may be at issue where the discharge is due to failure to meet production standards.[10]

In some instances, employers have been required to show specific examples of incompetence in order to establish just cause.[11] Hearsay testimony and unsubstantiated allegations have been held to be insufficient as sole bases for employer action.[12] Seniority or substantial tenure may be a mitigating factor. A long-term employee may be given the benefit of the doubt and the employer ordered to provide either another period of training or a demotion to another job in lieu of discharge.[13] Stress, temporary disability, and psychiatric problems have sometimes been given weight as mitigating factors when considering an employee's unsatisfactory job performance. In these circumstances, the employer may be required to give the employee a reasonable opportunity to demonstrate recovery before being labeled unable

---

[8]Albertson's, Inc., 105 LA 913, 917 (Kaufman, 1995); Consolidated Drum Reconditioning, 108 LA 523 (Richman, 1997). See also Bermuda Dunes Country Club, 104 LA 1082, 1084–85 (Darrow, 1995) (arbitrary and capricious standard applied because contract did not contain just cause provision).

[9]Peoples Natural Gas, 105 LA 37 (Murphy, 1995) (discharge reversed because training inadequate); County of Hennipen, 105 LA 391, 395, 397 (Imes, 1995) (discharge reversed where employee given inadequate training and inadequate warning of possible consequences of continued poor performance); Hilshire Farm & Kahn's, 105 LA 988, 992 (Nathan, 1995) (discharge sustained because employee previously given adequate training, assistance, and alternative job assignments); Cummins Cumberland, Inc., 106 LA 993, 996 (Heekin, 1996) (notice to employee of what was expected inadequate); GTE of Fla., Inc., 108 LA 1115, 1120 (Cohen, 1997) (employer failed to give clear notice and adequate training); Marriott Servs. Corp., 109 LA 689, 692 (Kaufman, 1997) (discharge reversed where employee not given adequate notice and chance to explain errors); Bonar Packaging, 112 LA 370, 372 (Moore, 1999) (discharge reversed because company failed to offer adequate supervision or assistance); Glacier County Sch. Dist., 112 LA 700, 703 (Prayzich, 1999) (discharge reversed where employer gave mixed messages rather than clear notice that job was in jeopardy).

[10]See Watts Health Care Found., 112 LA 780, 782 (Cloke, 1999) (employee's termination lacked just cause because it was based on unreasonable standard). See also Wayne County, 108 LA 879, 882 (Babiskin, 1997).

[11]Johnson Controls World Servs., Inc., 105 LA 1994, 1999 (Poole, 1996); Ken Meyer Meats, 107 LA 1017, 1020 (Sergent, 1996). See also Milwaukee Bd. of Sch. Dirs., 110 LA 566, 573 (Winton, 1998) (different standard would apply to short-term employee).

[12]Albertson's, Inc., 105 LA 913, 918 (Kaufman, 1995); U.S. Dep't of Justice, Border Patrol, 106 LA 1175, 1180–81 (Rezler, 1996).

[13]Peoples Natural Gas, 105 LA 37, 40 (Murphy, 1995); Sena-Kean Manor, 104 LA 369 (Franckiewicz, 1995); J.L. Clark, 108 LA 1012 (Gordinier, 1997); Glacier County Sch. Dist., 112 LA 700, 704 (Prayzich, 1999).

to do the job.[14] However, it has also been held that disability does not require the lowering of performance standards, and an employer is not required to employ a worker who is so disabled that she demonstrates incapacity to consistently carry out essential job duties.[15]

III. Failure to Meet Quality or Quantity Standards

The employer has a right to impose reasonable and realistic quality or quantity standards[16] and to raise those standards when necessary to make operations more competitive or efficient.[17] Where the basic competence of the employee is not at issue, discipline for failure to meet quality standards is possible under the concept of just cause.[18] Critical to the just cause determination is the substantive and procedural reasonableness of the standard. Thus, when an employer fails to provide employees with reasonable notice of the expected performance standard,[19] provides insufficient or inadequate training,[20] requires an unreasonable quantity of work under the circumstances, or fails to impose similar discipline when other employees failed to meet production standards, no just cause for discipline has been found.

IV. Loss of Qualifying Status

A. *Driver's License*

The loss or suspension of an employee's driver's license when licensure is necessary to operate a vehicle while on the job may result in termination, suspension, or reassignment to a nondriving job. For example, in *ATC / Vancom of California*,[21] the discharge of a bus driver who was convicted of driving his personal vehicle off-duty under the

---

[14]See Mine Workers (UMW) Dist. 6, 110 LA 84, 90–91 (Ruben, 1997) (case of neglectful or incompetent employee distinguishable from that of temporarily disabled employee because disabled employee not "at fault" for nonperformance). See also Dial Corp., 107 LA 879 (Robinson, 1997).

[15]Wayne County, 108 LA 879, 886 (Babiskin, 1997). See also Wayne County, 110 LA 1157 (Babiskin, 1998); National Linen Supply, 107 LA 4 (Ross, 1996). In the latter case, it was held that, although the grievant's misconduct was a symptom of his disability and not subject to his control, he could be terminated because improved performance was unlikely.

[16]Watts Health Care Found., 112 LA 780, 782 (Cloke, 1999) ("[i]n the absence of clear evidence that unrealistic or unreasonable standards or workloads have been adopted by an employer, even unusual or difficult rules should be upheld").

[17]See Arizona Opera Co., 105 LA 1126 (Wyman, 1996) (acknowledging employer's right to increase number of selections auditioners must sing and new musical director's right to impose higher quality standards).

[18]Watts Health Care Found., 112 LA 780 (Cloke, 1999); Cummins Cumberland, Inc., 106 LA 993 (Heekin, 1996).

[19]Consolidated Drum Reconditioning, 108 LA 523 (Richman, 1997).

[20]GTE of Fla., Inc., 108 LA 1115 (Cohen, 1997); Peoples Natural Gas, 105 LA 37 (Murphy, 1995).

[21]111 LA 244 (McKay, 1998).

influence of alcohol was sustained, even though the driver's license was suspended for only 1 month. It was held that (1) the collective bargaining agreement provided for discipline up to and including termination for a driving under the influence (DUI) violation; (2) historically, the employer had always terminated employees convicted of DUI, even when off duty; and (3) the employees and the union were well aware of that fact. However, in *J.F. Cassidy, Inc.*,[22] the termination of an over-the-road driver convicted of an off-duty DUI was overturned because (1) the incident occurred while the grievant was off duty driving his personal vehicle; (2) the employer had a rule providing for termination if an employee was convicted of DUI but it had never been made known to the employees; and (3) the convicting court had specifically permitted the grievant to retain his driving privilege solely for the purpose of driving to and from work and while on the job.

Discipline based on drug and alcohol abuse while driving has been overturned where it was found to be indefinite or excessive. In *L.F. Widmann, Inc.*,[23] the indefinite suspension of a driver convicted of DUI and his permanent reassignment to a lower-paying warehouse job was held to be excessive discipline. The arbitrator made the discipline and reassignment coincide with the 2-month suspension of the grievant's driver's license. In *Lockheed Missiles & Space Co.*,[24] the grievant, a launch technician who was occasionally required to operate a vehicle on the job, tested positive for marijuana during a random U.S. Department of Transportation (DOT) drug test. Following a suspension pending investigation, the employee was discharged for being under the influence of drugs. The DOT regulations were clear that having once tested positive for drug use, the grievant could not be recertified to drive a vehicle on the job. For this reason, the grievant's initial suspension was upheld. However, the termination was overturned. The arbitrator reasoned that a positive drug finding at the level in the grievant's test did not, standing alone, establish that the grievant was under the influence of drugs.

B. Security Clearance

Suspension or loss of a government security clearance, when it is a prerequisite for a job, may result in termination. In *Westinghouse Hanford Co.*,[25] the grievant, a security guard at a nuclear facility, was reassigned to a nonguard position when his security clearance

---

[22]97 LA 801 (Oberdank, 1991).
[23]99 LA 1172 (Dunn, 1992).
[24]101 LA 804 (Gentile, 1993).
[25]101 LA 46 (Nelson, 1993).

was suspended by the U.S. Department of Energy because of alcoholism. Following several failed attempts at rehabilitation, the grievant was found to be unfit for duty by the health facility named in the collective bargaining agreement to make fitness determinations. Because he could not maintain his medical clearance, he was discharged. Declaring that the employer was entitled to follow the advice of the contractually recognized health professionals, the arbitrator upheld the discharge.

C. Insurance

The inability to obtain, or retain, adequate liability insurance coverage can expose the employer to severe financial and legal exigencies in the event of an accident. For this reason, it has been held that an employee with such a poor driving record that he is uninsurable may be terminated. In *Ernst Enterprises*,[26] a grievant's termination from his cement delivery driving job was upheld after the employer received a letter from its insurer that it would not continue to insure the employer unless the grievant was removed from coverage under the policy. The arbitrator accepted the employer's argument that to retain the grievant in that position would make the company exceptionally vulnerable in the event of an accident. Because no other jobs were available and no alternative insurance coverage was feasible, the termination was upheld, but the employer was required to record it as nondisciplinary in nature.

In *Central Arkansas Transit Authority*,[27] the employer discharged a school bus driver after receiving notification from its insurance company that it would not insure the driver after he was convicted of driving while intoxicated while off duty. The discharge was upheld. The arbitrator noted that Arkansas law required bus operators carry a minimum level of insurance. The company had given the union notice of its intent to follow this practice 10 years earlier in a letter stating that it would discharge drivers for this reason, and the company had been consistent in discharging drivers for this reason. By contrast, in *Yellow Cab Cooperative Association*,[28] although uninsurability was found to be a valid basis for termination, the arbitrator concluded that the employer could not terminate 7 drivers for uninsurability because it did not meet two conditions precedent: (1) the employer did not conduct its own investigation of the drivers' records; and (2) the employer did not take all reasonable steps to protect the employees' jobs. The employer was ordered to put the discharged drivers back on the payroll with back pay while it reasonably explored

---

[26]103 LA 782 (Doering, 1994).
[27]107 LA 219 (Allen, 1996).
[28]102 LA 848 (Watkins, 1993).

alternative sources of insurance coverage. If, at the end of 40 days after release of the decision the company could not obtain insurance without increasing its costs or the grievants were unwilling to absorb any increased costs, the discharges would be upheld.

V. Negligence or Carelessness

F. Defenses to Discipline

A mental lapse of a quality control inspector with many years of service that was attributed to heightened anxiety about a spouse's serious medical condition was deemed sufficient mitigation to reduce termination for culpable negligence to reinstatement without back pay.[29]

VI. Demotion for Inability to Perform

The employer's right to impose nondisciplinary demotions for ineptitude or incompetence has been denied where the employee had been demoted from a supervisory position for failure to perform because the employer failed to provide sufficient training in the new position.[30] In cases involving discharge for consistent failure to meet production standards or for other incompetence, arbitrators have reinstated an employee and ordered demotion to the next highest-ranking job within her capabilities as a remedy.[31]

Disciplinary demotions are usually not allowed unless expressly permitted by contract. Thus, a disciplinary demotion was disallowed where demotion was not listed as a possible penalty. The demotion was held to contravene contractual seniority rights; moreover, the demotion amounted to a permanent form of discipline that was inconsistent with progressive disciplinary concepts in that the demotion failed to provide the employee with time to rehabilitate or take corrective action.[32]

VII. Loafing and Extending Breaks

In two separate cases, discharge for sleeping on the job was reduced to a suspension following a finding that the company or the

---

[29]Dial Corp., 107 LA 879 (Robinson, 1997).

[30]Klauser Corp., 102 LA 381 (McCurdy, 1994).

[31]See J.L. Clark, 108 LA 1012 (Gordinier, 1997).

[32]Gaylord Container Corp., 107 LA 1138 (Allen, 1997).

job contributed to the employee's inability to remain awake while performing the job.

In *Basin Electric Power Cooperative*,[33] an employee was discharged for sleeping at his computer terminal while monitoring the 35-minute operational phase of a water control operational change. The discharge was reduced to a 1-day suspension with a written warning and notice of reprimand, based on the finding that the nature of the job contained a serious drowsiness inducement factor.

In *Contico International*,[34] an employee was discharged for sleeping during slack time following an electrical outage. This company's rules provided for automatic termination for sleeping on the job. However, the employee had been scheduled to work more than 60 hours per week for over a month, often working 7 days per week. During this period, the employee did not have a helper working on his shift, as did the utility men working the other two shifts. The discharge was reduced to a 30-day suspension without pay, based on reasoning that, given the large number of hours worked in the previous month, it was almost inevitable that the employee would fall asleep during slack time where she had little or nothing to do. The arbitrator found that the company contributed to the condition that caused the sleepiness.

Notice or publication of new work rules is important for a violation of the rule to be upheld. In *Bayshore Concrete Products, Co.*,[35] the notice provided of a new rule was found to be insufficient where it was communicated to employees solely through a paycheck attachment. The contract required the company to send a copy to the union and to post a copy on the bulletin board, neither of which the company did.

Religious convictions of employees may override an employee's responsibility to notify the employer before leaving the workplace. In *Public Service Co. of New Mexico*,[36] an employee left work early without permission during a power outage emergency. His failure to notify his supervisor that he was leaving was connected to several severe personal problems and his basic tribal or religious convictions. His Navajo background precluded him from sharing personal problems with non-Navajo people. Analyzing it as a freedom of religious expression and practice issue, the arbitrator reduced the employee's discharge to a disciplinary suspension.

---

[33] 91 LA 443 (Jacobowski, 1988).
[34] 93 LA 530 (Cipolla, 1989).
[35] 92 LA 311 (Hart, 1989).
[36] 98 LA 23 (Sartain, 1991).

Chapter 5

Refusal to Perform Work or Cooperate

I. "Work Now, Grieve Later"

The adage "work now, grieve later" (also expressed as "obey now, grieve later") continues to be the norm. This means employees must follow orders given by a supervisor, although the employee may later challenge the propriety of the order through established grievance procedures.

II. Insubordination: Refusal to Do Work Required by Superior

A. *General Principles*

To be insubordinate, an employee's refusal to work or obey must be knowing, willful, and deliberate. The willful and deliberate requirement may be negated by evidence of depression,[1] personal problems,[2] hospitalization,[3] or high blood pressure,[4] even though the condition did not prevent the grievant from complying with the order. Lack of personal control over the subject of the order has also been recognized as a valid excuse for lack of compliance with an order.[5]

---

[1]Laidlaw Transit, Inc., 104 LA 302 (Concepcion, 1995); Mine Workers (UMW) Dist. 6, 110 LA 84 (Ruben, 1997).

[2]Danaher Tool Group Mass. Operations, 109 LA 497 (Alleyne, 1997).

[3]Citgo Petroleum Corp., 112 LA 594 (Nicholas, 1999).

[4]St. Louis County, Duluth, Minn., 112 LA 487 (Daly, 1999).

[5]Clermont County Bd. of Mental Retardation, 110 LA 1178 (Murphy, 1998) (grievant ordered to provide medical information found not insubordinate where doctor having control of requested record caused delay).

The order in question must be explicit and clearly given so that the employee understands both its meaning and its intent as a command. However, arbitrators differ about what constitutes a direct order.[6] Moreover, in at least one case it was held that a direct order was not necessary where the grievant understood the instruction.[7]

The order itself must be reasonable[8] and work-related.[9] In addition, it must have been given by someone with appropriate authority who is understood by the employee to be an appropriate person to give such an order.[10] Further, the employee must be made aware of the consequences of failing to follow the order[11] and, if practical, must be given time to correct the purportedly insubordinate behavior.[12]

---

[6]General Mills, Inc., 107 LA 886 (Ipavec, 1997) (grievant's refusal to refeed product constitutes insubordination even if supervisor did not say that his direction was a direct order); Borough of Bellevue, 112 LA 577 (Parkinson, 1999) (grievant's refusal of vaccination not insubordination where supervisor asked if grievant wanted the shot); City of Decatur, Ill., 112 LA 385 (Kubie, 1999) (grievant's counteroffer in response to demand to sign proferred document not refusal of unequivocal direction by supervisor); City of Kittitas, 108 LA 833 (Smith, 1997) (grievant using best judgment about conflicting directions from two superiors not insubordinate).

[7]Paladin Packaging & Display, Inc., 109 LA 285 (Franckiewicz, 1997).

[8]School Dist. of Springfield Twp. v. Springfield Twp. Educ. Support Personnel Ass'n, 711 A.2d 602 (Pa. Commw. Ct., 1998) (award upheld in finding no insubordination where rule forbidding grievant to appear for his shift more than 15 minutes early was unreasonable); U.S. Steel Corp., 109 LA 321 (Antoine, 1997) (direction to work inside water treatment column, which required use of full face mask, held unreasonable where grievant provided medical opinion that he could not work in those conditions because of claustrophobia); Bunge Corp., 111 LA 1201 (Hilgert, 1998) (direction to report for call-in instantaneously not reasonable where grievant told supervisor that he had to finish hair treatment before reporting); Liberty Med. Ctr., 109 LA 609 (Harkless, 1997) (order to tuck in shirt immediately without opportunity to bring evidence of religious tenet requiring coverage of private parts unreasonable where employer had permitted practice for number of years); Wynn's Precision, Inc., 111 LA 669 (Kilroy, 1998) (instruction to use toilet nearest work station unreasonable where that toilet was chronically unclean, unsanitary, and hot and an alternate was only 137 feet away from work station); Toledo Hosp., 105 LA 310 (Feldman, 1995) (not insubordinate where resolution of dispute between professionals depends on reasonable but conflicting interpretations of policy).

[9]Health Care & Retirement Corp., 105 LA 449 (Duff, 1995) (refusal to attend nondisciplinary instruction not gross insubordination warranting discharge where order did not involve work direction and there was denial of union representation); USCP-Wesco, Inc., 109 LA 225 (Grabuskie, 1997) (no warrant for discharge despite employee's refusal to remove head scarf that was found to offend black co-workers, where instruction was not work direction).

[10]Horizon Tech. Group Westland, 111 LA 1027 (Ellman, 1998) (grievant insubordinate for refusing direction of supervisor not in grievant's direct chain of command where his foreman had not given inconsistent instructions and employer had practice of shifting employees from one area to another).

[11]E.B. Eddy Paper, Inc., 111 LA 620 (Brodsky, 1998); Mid-Am. Packaging, 111 LA 129 (Bankston, 1998); Lucky Stores, Inc., 112 LA 481 (Gentile, 1999); Adams TV v. Electrical Workers (IBEW) Local 474, 932 S.W.2d 932, 155 LRRM 2871 (Tenn. Ct. App., 1996) (arbitral award upheld in finding employer must warn employee that his conduct could result in dismissal before discharging him for insubordination). But see City of Danbury v. Teamsters Local 677, 1998 WL 253937 (Conn. Super. Ct., 1998) (arbitrator's decision reinstating grievant because he was not warned before discharge for insubordination vacated).

[12]Mid.-Am. Packaging, 111 LA 129 (Bankston, 1998).

B. Specific Conduct Constituting Insubordination

Conduct that has been held to be disciplinable insubordination includes refusal to take a drug test;[13] refusal to comply with a mandatory referral to rehabilitation where the grievant exhibited extremely threatening behavior;[14] sticking a finger in a supervisor's face, coupled with derisive comments and insistence that the employee would not take directions directly from that supervisor;[15] refusal to speak with the supervisor's superior unless the supervisor provided a letter to the employee's attorney describing the reason for the meeting;[16] unsubstantiated allegations of a supervisor's criminal conduct by the grievant;[17] refusal to return to work after filing a grievance about pay;[18] disregard of an order to cease discussing the grievant's transfer at a safety meeting;[19] repeated interruptions of the company president in an information meeting;[20] refusal to work because the grievant unilaterally decided that switching back and forth between assignments was not cost-effective;[21] and refusal to move to a new crane during a shift.[22]

C. Exceptions

Exceptions to the "work now, grieve later" rule have been found in a number of identifiable categories.

1. Safety and Health. If a refusal to follow an order is safety- or health-related, the question is whether the employee's fear was reasonable under the circumstances.[23]

2. Union Rights. Although the general rule permits an employee to refuse to participate in an investigatory interview without union representation, just cause for discharge was found in one case

---

[13]Cincinnati Metro. Hous. Auth., 109 LA 427 (Sergent, 1997) (refusal to take drug test deemed insubordinate where employee exhibited profuse sweating, glassy eyes, slow and incoherent speech, nervousness, anxiety, and loss of control); Integrated Distrib. Sys., 108 LA 737 (Neas, 1997) (grievant's refusal to take drug test unless he could speak beforehand with union representative who was out of town deemed insubordinate).

[14]Raytheon Aircraft Co., 105 LA 1081 (Thornell, 1996).

[15]Hussman Corp., 109 LA 833 (Crider, 1997).

[16]University of Cal., 108 LA 804 (Staudohar, 1997).

[17]City of Wooster, 111 LA 1167 (Richard, 1999).

[18]Monitor Sugar Co., 111 LA 32 (Sugerman, 1998).

[19]Natco Ltd. P'ship, 110 LA 17 (Ables, 1997).

[20]Converters Paperboard Co., 108 LA 149 (Brodsky, 1997).

[21]Danaher Tool Group, 109 LA 497 (Alleyne, 1997).

[22]Armco Corp., 105 LA 773 (Lalka, 1996).

[23]Bargar Metal Fabricating Co., 110 LA 119 (Oberdank, 1998) (concern for safety insufficient to justify refusal to work where work had always been performed that way and grievant never mentioned safety as reason for refusing work assignment); Health Olus, Inc., 110 LA 618 (Duff, 1998) (employer's knowledge of grievant's painful physical problems excused break taken in defiance of supervisor order).

for refusal to take a drug test where the contract authorized the employer to conduct a drug test "any time an employee is involved in an accident" and did not give the employee a right to talk to a union representative before taking the test.[24] Similarly, an employee who refused to open his lunch bucket for inspection during a routine search was not entitled to union representation before complying.[25]

3. Contract Rights. Noncompliance with an order that directly conflicts with a clear right of the employee may not be considered actionable insubordinate conduct if the employee has no time to resort to the grievance process and no remedy is available. This exception was interpreted very broadly in *Hugo Neu-Proler Co.*,[26] where the arbitrator ruled that, if an employer knowingly ordered a breach of contract, an employee's refusal to obey was not insubordination. Nevertheless, reliance on a contract interpretation, however erroneous and regardless of whether a remedy is available, generally has not been recognized as an exception to the "work now; grieve later" rule.[27]

4. Other. Orders that violate statutory rights continue to be recognized as an exception to the "obey and grieve" rule,[28] but like contract rights, interpretations of statutes offer no protection.[29] In one case involving a government employee, it was found that the employee was not required to make statements that would criminally incriminate him even though the state employer had granted legal immunity, where the immunity document was subject to an alternative interpretation.[30] In contrast, an arbitrator upheld the discharge of a city employee who distributed a pamphlet to fellow workers that made unsubstantiated claims of criminal conduct by city officials and by management.[31]

Where past practice gave discretion to police officers to make confidentiality decisions about informants and the officer had assured the informant of confidentiality, there was no just cause for discharge for refusal to disclose the identity of that confidential informant.[32]

Although awards that reinstate individuals who test positive for alcohol or drugs have frequently been vacated as against public policy, the U.S. Court of Appeals for the Third Circuit has enforced an award

---

[24]Integrated Distrib. Sys., 108 LA 737, (Neas, 1997).

[25]Cleveland-Cliffs Iron Co., 110 LA 314 (Vonhof, 1997).

[26]109 LA 880 (Richman, 1997).

[27]Goodman Beverage Co., 108 LA 37 (Morgan, 1997); Freeman Decorating Co., 110 LA 331 (Allen, 1998).

[28]Lithibar Matik, Inc., 109 LA 446 (Hodgson, 1997) (refusal to take drug test where employer violated National Labor Relations Act by implementing discipline for refusing to test without giving notice to union or opportunity to bargain).

[29]Colletti Trucking, 105 LA 507 (White, 1995) (driver refusing to operate truck because of alleged violation of U.S. Department of Transportation regulations properly discharged where employer accurately informed him that truck was too small to be covered by those regulations).

[30]Ohio Bureau of Workers' Comp., 110 LA 986 (Nelson, 1998).

[31]City of Wooster, 111 LA 1167 (Richard, 1999).

[32]City of Madrid, Iowa Police Dep't, 109 LA 837 (Cohen, 1997).

that reinstated an employee who refused to take a drug test.[33] The court held that, where the contract did not define "cause" for a test, the arbitrator was authorized to interpret the term and acted within his authority when he concluded that finding marijuana in the seaman's suitcase on the vessel was not sufficient basis to require him to take a drug test.

D. Discipline Imposed

In an insubordination case, limits to arbitral authority to ensure that the penalty imposed by the employer is appropriate may be made only by explicit contract language.[34] In one case, a federal district court in New York emphasized that if the employer wished to limit the arbitrator's authority to modify a penalty, it should negotiate that into the contract.[35] Similar holdings have recently been issued by other federal district courts in New York and Puerto Rico.[36] In one case it was held that the contract foreclosed an arbitrator from reviewing the penalty if the offenses charged were established and the contract provided that "the arbitrator shall have no power to modify or reduce any disciplinary sanctions selected by the Company."[37]

Other courts have not followed this line of reasoning. Despite the fact that the contract authorized the company to unilaterally develop and post only disciplinary procedures, not substantive penalties, a federal court in North Carolina found that posted work rules providing for termination of an employee for refusing a drug test foreclosed arbitral modification of the penalty.[38] Similarly, a state court in Pennsylvania held that where the question submitted to the arbitrator was whether there was just cause for termination, the arbitrator exceeded his authority when he concluded that there was not just cause for termination after determining that there was just cause for discipline.[39]

---

[33]Exxon Shipping Co. v. Exxon Seamen's Union, 73 F.3d 1287, 151 LRRM 2161 (3d Cir., 1996).

[34]Federal Packaging Corp. v. Paperworkers Local 150, 940 F. Supp. 1155, 156 LRRM 2122 (N.D. Ohio, 1996); IMC-Agrico Co. v. Chemical Workers Council, 171 F.3d 1322, 160 LRRM 2961 (11th Cir., 1999); Sykel Enters., Inc. v. Teamsters Local 819, 1996 WL 1088210, at 7 (E.D.N.Y., 1996) (upholding arbitrator's reduction of penalty even though contract provided that "[i]n cases of . . . insubordination . . . the employer may discharge the employee and thereupon notify the union in writing of the cause of such discharge" because it also allowed union to "contest such discharge").

[35]VAW of Am., Inc. v. Steelworkers, 53 F. Supp. 2d 187 (N.D.N.Y., 1999).

[36]Teamsters Local 819 v. Sykel Enters., Inc., 1997 WL 160666 (S.D.N.Y., 1997); Telemundo of P.R., Inc. v. Union de Periodistas y Artes Graficas y Ramas Anexas, 1997 WL 170577, 1997 U.S. Dist. LEXIS 4274 (D.P.R., 1997).

[37]Carter Healthcare Ctr., Inc., 104 LA 89, 90–91 (Duff, 1995).

[38]Bandag, Inc. v. Steelworkers Local 922, 157 LRRM 2673, 2676 (E.D.N.C., 1996), aff'd without op., 121 F.3d 697, 157 LRRM 2704 (4th Cir., 1997).

[39]Township of Penn v. State, County & Mun. Employees Dist. Council 89, 713 A.2d 1218 (Pa. Commw. Ct., 1998).

Myriad circumstances peculiar to the individuals and circumstances involved have been found to mitigate in favor of a reduction of penalty,[40] including diminished employee capacity, previous employer knowledge, and circumstances that aggravate an offense.[41]

III. Refusals to Work Overtime

With respect to overtime, employees cannot avoid the "work now, grieve later" rule unless there is a reasonable basis to believe it would be unsafe or unhealthy to obey.[42] Further, arbitrators are generally loathe to second-guess management's choice of discipline for an employee's refusal or failure to work the required overtime.[43]

A. *Management Rights Versus Personal Needs*

Management is generally free to set work schedules, including scheduling overtime, even at the last minute; this has been held to be true regardless of whether the collective bargaining agreement specifically provides such.[44] Absent specific collective bargaining

---

[40]Owens-Brockway Plastic Prods., Inc., 109 LA 655 (Bailey, 1997) (discipline for making statement that secretary found threatening and calling supervisor a liar mitigated by previous psychiatrist advice that grievant's actions could become unpredictable); Health Plus, Inc., 110 LA 618 (Duff, 1998) (employer's knowledge of painful physical problems mitigated insubordination by grievant who took break in violation of supervisor's orders); Vista Chem. Co., 104 LA 584 (Nicholas, 1995) (24 years' service and partial fault of employer that communications broke down mitigated failure to report for medical exam necessitated by injury on job); Citgo Petroleum Corp., 112 LA 594 (Nicholas, 1999) (diminished capacity from depression mitigated discipline but does not excuse insubordination); Norfolk Shipbldg. & Drydock Corp. (NORSHIPCO), 105 LA 529 (Hockenberry, 1995) (stress brought on in part from crisis involving grievant's child mitigated use of phone without permission); Bryan Foods, Inc., 109 LA 633 (Baroni, 1997) (fact that supervisor who once threatened to beat up another employee may have followed grievant and screamed, "Give me your I.D." mitigated grievant's discipline for profane and abusive language); Safelite Glass Corp., 111 LA 561 (Bain, 1998) (statement to supervisor—"I'd better not see you in church on Sunday or I will get you"—mitigated by circumstances).

[41]Pratt & Whitney, N. Berwick, Me., 112 LA 461 (Chandler, 1999) (grievant did not acknowledge role in altercation); City of Stockton, 112 LA 696 (Riker, 1999) (aggravation found to negate usefulness of progressive discipline: discharge of camp supervisor for failure to acknowledge inappropriateness of tying two children to pole, singing derogatory song while dancing around them, and allowing other children to ridicule them upheld).

[42]Stone Container Corp., 106 LA 475, 479 (Gentile, 1996) (employee cannot avoid "work now, grieve later" rule even if she or he believes overtime order violates collective bargaining agreement); Pacific Power & Light Co., 103 LA 824, 831 (DiFalco, 1994) (dicta that employee must reasonably believe overtime work to be unsafe to avoid "obey now, grieve later" rule). See also Land-O-Sun Dairies, Inc., 105 LA 740, 743 (Draznin, 1995) (explaining that "if an employee believes a managerial determination to enforce a rule is unjustified, s/he has two choices: comply with the Employer's decision and grieve later, placing the onus of responsibility on the Employer, or refuse to comply with the determination, force the Employer to follow through with its policy enforcement, and grieve the consequences, an action which places the onus of responsible action on the employee").

[43]Powdertech Corp., 110 LA 880, 884 (Doering, 1998); Toledo Edison, 106 LA 813, 822 (Imundo, 1996); Piedmont Airlines, Inc., 103 LA 751, 758 (Feigenbaum, 1994).

[44]Jefferson Smurfit Corp., 110 LA 276, 280 (Goldstein, 1997) ("The vast majority of reported awards support the position that overtime is compulsory, in the absence of a contractual prohibition in the collective bargaining agreement, as an inherent right of management." (citations omitted.)); Fruehaug Corp., 46 LA 15 (Dworkin, 1996).

agreement language to the contrary, the only limitation on management's ability to schedule overtime, either in advance or at the last minute, is that of reasonableness.[45] Refusal or failure to work required overtime, even overtime scheduled at the last minute, is tantamount to insubordination and is a "serious" offense.[46]

Management's determination of what constitutes appropriate discipline for an employee's refusal or failure to work required overtime, as with management's ability to schedule overtime, is only subject to a reasonableness limitation,[47] regardless of whether the employee has a valid reason for refusing the overtime. An employee's refusal of overtime usually has been upheld when (1) he or she reasonably believed that the overtime work was not required,[48] or (2) when an "emergency" prevented them from working the overtime.[49]

C. Discipline Examples

Although arbitrators may reduce the degree of discipline imposed for an employee's refusal or failure to work overtime for personal reasons, arbitrators increasingly require that the employee's personal reasons amount to an "emergency" to avoid discipline altogether. For example, in *Jefferson Smurfit Corp.*,[50] the employee challenged as unreasonable his 3-day suspension for failing to work required overtime, claiming that he had to leave work to assist his wife in caring for their sick infant. The imposition of discipline was nevertheless affirmed. The arbitrator applied Shulman's "rule of reason":

> I think that, on balance, it was not sufficient to warrant [the employee's] refusal to work the overtime. Employees obviously must try to satisfy their parental and family obligations without interfering with the [e]mployer's business. If there is a crisis or emergency, certainly the responsibility of a family come [sic] first. But employees may not refuse to

---

[45]Volz & Goggin, eds., Elkouri & Elkouri, How Arbitration Works, 5th ed., 739–40 (BNA Books, 1997) ("the essence of most decisions is that where the agreement is silent on the subject management has the right to make reasonable demands for overtime work from employees"); McConway & Tolery Corp., 55 LA 31 (Cohen, 1970); Michigan Seamless Tube Co., 48 LA 1077 (Keefe, 1967); Link-Belt Co., 48 LA 570 (Cayton, 1966).

[46]Sonoco Prods. Co., 107 LA 782 (Baroni, 1996) (describing employee's refusal to work overtime as "insubordination" and "serious"); Pacific Power & Light Co., 103 LA 824, 832–33 (DiFalco, 1994) (describing employee's refusal to work overtime as "insubordination" and "serious").

[47]Hercules Mach. Tool & Die Co., 108 LA 258, 265 (Brown, 1997) (3-day suspension for refusal to work overtime "reasonable under the circumstances"); Sonoco Prods. Co., 107 LA 782, 786 (Baroni, 1996) ("a three day suspension for ignoring a supervisor's directive to work overtime is not at all, under the circumstances, unreasonable").

[48]Federal Mogul Corp., 109 LA 1123, 1125 (Daniel, 1997) (no refusal to work overtime where employee reasonably believed because of miscommunication he was not scheduled to work overtime).

[49]Piedmont Airlines, Inc., 103 LA 751, 756–58 (Feigenbaum, 1994) (rejecting employee's challenge to her 7-day suspension for refusing to work overtime because neither of employee's claimed excuses, that she could not work overtime because of personal illness and inability to secure child care, constituted "emergency").

[50]110 LA 276 (Goldstein, 1997).

> work overtime and then stand behind the shield of family as a defense in the absence of a real need.[51]

An employee further risks discipline for refusing or failing to work overtime because of her own illness, particularly when the employee claims illness for the first time at the end of working a regular shift in response to the notice that overtime will be required. In that circumstance, management's imposition of discipline is likely to stand, especially if it specifically advised the employee of the consequences of her refusal or failure to work the required overtime. For example, in *Land-O-Sun Dairies, Inc.*,[52] management's imposition of discipline in response to the employee's claim that he was sick and unable to work overtime was appropriate because he had already completed almost his full shift, the illness was "generic" in nature, and it was neither serious nor constituted an emergency. Management told him at the time that "if he did not take the overtime it would be considered a voluntary quit."[53] In rejecting the employee's challenge to his discharge, the arbitrator opined that

> [T]he [employee] knew or should have known that if he refused to work the mandatory overtime his action would be considered a voluntary quit. * * * [Further,] a claim of illness is not in itself, alone, sufficient to negate the enforcement of a clearly announced and understood policy. * * * The [employee] would have had to make some effort to indicate the extent and type of his illness when he claimed it to allow [management] to make a determination whether or not to allow the [employee] an exception to the rule. He did not do this.[54]

IV. Refusals to Work With Other Employees

C. *Exception for "Intolerable Affronts"*

Management may consider the wishes of individuals who have been sexually harassed when disciplining the alleged harasser. For example, in *Renton School District*,[55] the school district demoted one of its custodians for sexually harassing several female teachers and aides. In upholding the employee's challenge to the demotion, which involved a transfer to a post that put him in less contact with the

---

[51]Id. at 278. Under Shulman's rule of reason, "[a]lthough an employee's refusal to work overtime may be a breach of duty for which he may properly be disciplined, his refusal may be justified, and if justified, is not a ground for disciplinary penalty." Ford Motor Co., 11 LA 1158, 1160 (Shulman, 1948). See also PQ Corp., 101 LA 694, 700 (Pratte, 1993) (reducing discipline for refusal to work overtime from 2-day suspension to written reprimand for first offense).

[52]105 LA 740 (Draznin, 1995).

[53]Id. at 742.

[54]Id. at 744. See also Piedmont Airlines, Inc., 103 LA 751 (Feigenbaum, 1994) (rejecting as insufficient to avoid overtime employee's claim of illness, which did not amount to "emergency").

[55]102 LA 854 (Wilkinson, 1994).

female staff, the arbitrator specifically noted that some of the complaining witnesses did not want him returned to his former location, including at least 2 who said they would attempt to transfer if he were returned to his former location.

D. Off-Duty Conduct

Arbitrators have upheld management's ability to consider the wishes of co-workers when disciplining an employee for off-duty conduct where that conduct leads co-workers not to want to work with that employee. For example, in *North Oakland Medical Centers*,[56] the employee was suspended following being arrested and subsequently convicted of stabbing his former wife's boyfriend while off duty. In upholding the discharge, the arbitrator specifically noted that "[t]he concern expressed by fellow employees to the supervisors regarding his return was definitely a factor [that] the employer was entitled to consider."[57]

In *Federal Aviation Administration*,[58] the employee was arrested for raping and molesting his daughter. Management cancelled its proposed transfer of the employee, an air traffic manager at the time, from his tower position to an administrative position because of secretarial concerns and instead suspended him indefinitely. In overturning the discipline, the arbitrator confirmed that, in order to discipline an employee for off-duty conduct, management "must prove the existence of a nexus, a link between the off-duty misconduct . . . and the efficiency of the service and it must establish the reasonableness of the penalty it has assessed."[59] The arbitrator concluded that no such nexus existed.

---

[56]106 LA 488, 489 (Daniel, 1996).

[57]Id. at 492. See also K & D Indus. Servs., Inc., 112 LA 820 (Allen, 1999) (finding just cause to terminate employee for urinating on co-worker while off duty because act was so disgusting and repulsive).

[58]108 LA 857 (Sergent, 1997).

[59]Id. at 860.

Chapter 6

Substance Abuse

II. Work Rules/Policies Governing Alcohol and Drugs

A. Work Rules

Arbitrators continue to validate the employer's right to implement and enforce drug and alcohol policies.[1] However, there are instances when enforcement is refused. One drug policy was declared invalid because the employer had refused to bargain with the union about the policy.[2] In another case, an employer's policy was held to be unreasonable because it set forth harsher discipline for illegal drug use than for alcohol use.[3] As a general matter, however, the provisions of drug and alcohol policies continue to be allowed. The discharge of an employee who pleaded guilty to possession of a small amount of marijuana was upheld where the policy demanded immediate discharge for a drug possession conviction and was silent as to the minimum amount of drugs required to trigger discipline under the policy.[4] In another case, an employee's discharge was upheld when the drug test was not performed until 3 days after a workplace accident. There the employer's drug policy did not specify that a drug test was required within a certain time after an accident.[5]

Discharge may be upheld when the employer gives the employee an opportunity to rehabilitate and the employee nevertheless subsequently violates the drug and alcohol policy. This is true especially

---

[1]Frito-Lay Inc., 109 LA 850 (Heekin, 1997); Fitzpatrick Co., 108 LA 686 (Briggs, 1997); Pacific Offshore Pipeline Co., 106 LA 690 (Kaufman, 1996); Cajun Elec. Power Coop., 111 LA 769 (O'Grady, 1998).

[2]Lithibar Matik Inc., 109 LA 446 (Hodgson, 1997).

[3]Kelly-Springfield Tire Co., 108 LA 984 (Nicholas, Jr., 1997).

[4]Dunlop Tire Corp., 104 LA 653 (Teple, 1995).

[5]Meijer Inc., 112 LA 668 (Daniel, 1998).

where there is a last-chance agreement with the employee.[6] For example, an employee's discharge for intoxication was upheld because, although he was generally a good employee, the employer had already given him two opportunities at rehabilitation.[7] Another employee's discharge was upheld on a finding that his previous discipline for intoxication was relevant to the decision of whether he should be discharged. There the violation was the same, and the employee had been given an opportunity to correct his behavior.[8]

An arbitrator may reduce the penalty because the employer's drug and alcohol policy does not specifically mandate discharge for a violation of the drug and alcohol policy. One employee was reinstated because the employer's policy prohibiting marijuana on its premises did not specifically mandate discharge.[9] In another case, the discharge for drug possession of a long-term employee with an otherwise excellent work history was overturned where the work rule did not require automatic discharge but stated that a violation could subject an employee to discipline up to and including discharge.[10] A similar result was reached in a case where the employee's violation of the alcohol policy was his first episode of improper behavior in 24 years with the employer.[11]

Discharge may not be appropriate when the employer's past practice for handling violations of its drug or alcohol policy has been lax or inconsistent. In one case, discharge was deemed too harsh for employees who violated the employer's work rule against imbibing alcohol on company premises where the sole previous violator of the rule had received only a verbal warning and a partial shift suspension.[12] Similarly, where the employer had not consistently applied its work rule mandating drug testing of all employees who sustained workplace injuries "requiring outside assistance," the discharge was not sustained.[13] Another employee's discharge for violating the employer's rule against drinking alcohol on the job was not upheld when the employer failed to show that it had ever enforced the work rule before.[14] In fact, where the employer's past practice had been to refer employees to an employee assistance program (EAP) for first-time violations of its alcohol policy, a summary discharge was reversed as inconsistent.[15]

---

[6]Tosco Ref. Co., 112 LA 306 (Bogue, 1999); Eaton Cutler-Hammer Corp., 110 LA 467 (Franckiewicz, 1998); Cajun Elec. Power Coop., 108 LA 641 (Howell, 1997).

[7]Tecumseh Prods. Co., 105 LA 626 (Frockt, 1995).

[8]Georgia-Pac. Corp., 108 LA 43 (Nicholas, Jr., 1997). But see U.S. Steel, 111 LA 385 (St. Antoine, 1998) (discharge too harsh for employee who was alcoholic who previously had sought treatment and who also suffered from domestic abuse).

[9]Georgia-Pac. Corp., 106 LA 470 (Hooper, 1996).

[10]Kimberly-Clark Corp., 107 LA 554 (Byars, 1996).

[11]GAF Bldg. Materials Corp., 112 LA 871 (Marcus, 1999).

[12]Motor Prods., 106 LA 215 (Borland, 1995).

[13]Munster Steel Co., 108 LA 597 (Cerone, 1997).

[14]Coos-Curry Elec. Coop., 111 LA 47 (Calhoun, 1998).

[15]Georgia-Pac. Corp., 108 LA 43 (Nicholas, Jr., 1997).

In addition, the employer must adequately inform the employees and union of the substance abuse policy and its contents.[16] An employee was reinstated where the employer had neither negotiated the new work rule with the union nor adequately informed the employees of the change.[17] In another case, an employee's discharge was overturned (1) where the employer's drug policy was not revealed to the union until the day drugs were found in the employee's vehicle, and (2) where the drug policy had been mailed to, but not received by, employees until 2 days after the drugs were discovered in the employee's vehicle.[18]

B. On-the-Job Use, Possession, or Sale

Comprehensive work rules on substance use and abuse may be upheld even when their reach appears too broad. For instance, a complete smoking ban on all company property, including the parking lot and outside areas of a plant, has been upheld.[19]

1. Use. The work rules must contain a clear prohibition of the action proscribed, and the evidence must support the assertion that such actions occurred.[20] If the employee tests positive for alcohol or drugs, termination may be upheld without evidence of any job impairment.[21]

---

[16]Cajun Elec. Power Coop., 111 LA 769 (O'Grady, 1998) (discharge upheld where employee knew of company's drug policy and of penalties for violation thereof).

[17]Pacific Offshore Pipeline Co., 106 LA 690 (Kaufman, 1996).

[18]Anheuser-Busch Inc., 107 LA 1183 (Weckstein, 1996).

[19]Norris Plumbing Fixtures, 104 LA 174 (Richman, 1995).

[20]Tosco Ref. Co., 112 LA 306 (Bogue, 1999) (employee who tested positive for cocaine where testing was pursuant to policy of unannounced drug tests as condition of postrehabilitation reinstatement properly discharged); Cajun Elec. Power Coop., 111 LA 769 (O'Grady, 1998) (policy allowed postinjury drug testing and employee, who tested positive for marijuana and admitted to its use, not discharged arbitrarily); Argosy Gaming Co., 110 LA 540 (Fowler, 1998) (employer can discharge employee on first drug offense); Bally's Park Place Hotel/Casino, 110 LA 1200 (Herzog, 1998) (discharge upheld based on blood alcohol test and co-employee's testimony that he saw employee drinking on job); Exxon Pipeline Co., 109 LA 951 (Abercrombie, 1997) (just cause found based on positive test for alcohol without consideration of mitigating circumstances because of nature of company's business and danger to public); Cajun Elec. Power Coop., 108 LA 641 (Howell, 1997) (positive alcohol test warrants discharge); Rothe Dev. Inc., 106 LA 97 (Baroni, 1996) (employee who dealt with dangerous machinery discharged properly after positive marijuana test); Dravo Lime Co., 105 LA 54 (Imundo, Jr., 1995) (failed drug screen warranted discharge pursuant to employer's drug and alcohol policy); Burns Aerospace Corp., 104 LA 1210 (Smith, Jr., 1995) (discharge upheld based on positive alcohol test and employee's admission that he came to work intoxicated).

[21]Willow Run Cmty. Schs., 112 LA 115 (Brodsky, 1999) (positive marijuana test provided just cause for termination even though no evidence that employee used drugs at work or was impaired); Frito-Lay Inc., 109 LA 850 (Heekin, 1997) (positive test showing presence of marijuana sufficient for discharge without independent proof of workplace impairment). But see Textron Lycoming, 104 LA 1043 (Duff, 1995) (collective bargaining agreement regulated only conduct at work and positive drug test did not indicate drug was used at work or impaired employee's abilities at work).

Discharge has not been upheld, however, where (1) the employer failed to enforce its policy in the past,[22] (2) there was insufficient proof,[23] (3) there was a failure to fully investigate,[24] or (4) progressive discipline was not properly followed.[25] The employee's service record is often considered in determining whether discharge should be upheld,[26] especially if there is insufficient proof of alcohol or drug use.[27]

The employee's purchase of alcohol during an unpaid lunch hour was insufficient to show just cause for termination without evidence that the employee had consumed the alcohol.[28] The discharge of an employee who tested positive for drugs on the day he went on company property to pick up a workers' compensation check was upheld, however,[29] because the employee was not immune to drug testing—he was on workers' compensation leave and could be tested when he came on company property.

2. Possession. If sound evidence directly links the alcohol or drugs to the employee, there may be just cause for discipline or discharge.[30] Marijuana found in an employee's car in the parking lot

---

[22]Coos-Curry Elec. Coop., 111 LA 47 (Calhoun, 1998) (reinstatement ordered for employee terminated after reporting to work under influence of alcohol because testimony showed employer did not enforce rule prohibiting consumption of alcohol at work); Motor Prods., 106 LA 215 (Borland, 1995) (discharge for alcohol use reduced to suspension because of employer's casual past enforcement of policy).

[23]Greene County Dep't of Human Servs., 109 LA 1160 (Sergent, 1997) (discharge would have been appropriate for intoxication, but employee held discharged unjustly for having alcohol on breath, without more proof).

[24]Pine Ridge Coal Co., 111 LA 568 (Feldman, 1998) (reinstatement without back pay ordered where employer failed to investigate employee with positive alcohol test to determine if resulted from alcohol consumption or cough medicine with alcohol base that employee testified he had taken immediately before the test).

[25]Gary Housing Auth., 110 LA 321 (Belshaw, 1998) (reinstatement ordered for lack of use of progressive discipline as mandated by collective bargaining agreement for first-time drug offenders); Bayer Corp., 108 LA 316 (Zobrak, 1997) (reinstatement ordered without back pay because of employer's failure to follow its own rehabilitation guidelines); Georgia-Pac. Corp., 108 LA 43 (Nicholas, Jr., 1997) (reinstatement ordered because employee not first offered opportunity to participate in established EAP prior to discharge); Kelly-Springfield Tire Co., 108 LA 984 (Nicholas, Jr., 1997) (reinstatement ordered because opportunity to enter EAP offered to other employees should have been offered to grievant).

[26]U.S. Steel, 111 LA 385 (St. Antoine, 1998) (reinstatement ordered for alcoholic employee who had 20 years' service with employer); Vons Cos., Inc., 106 LA 740 (Darrow, 1996) (good 22-year employment history and postdischarge rehabilitation warrant converting discharge for positive alcohol test to suspension without back pay). But see Cajun Elec. Power Coop., 111 LA 769 (O'Grady, 1998) (discharge for positive marijuana test upheld despite 15-year employment record and request for postdischarge rehabilitation assistance).

[27]Pine Ridge Coal Co., 111 LA 568 (Feldman, 1998) (uncontradicted testimony that grievant had taken cough medicine with alcohol base and failure of company to investigate or to consider employee's 18 years of impeccable service merited reinstatement); Hertz Corp., 108 LA 945 (Weckstein, 1997) (employee should be reinstated without back pay although two alcohol tests were positive, because employee contended she had used "Ice Drops" cough medicine and she had good work record); Bruce Hardwood Floors, 108 LA 115 (Allen, Jr., 1997) (reinstatement ordered without back pay for employee with 26-year, problem-free record who testified he accidentally took wife's medication resulting in positive drug test).

[28]City of Albuquerque, 106 LA 1072 (Cohen, 1996).

[29]Solar Turbines Inc., 104 LA 1070 (D'Spain, 1995).

[30]State of Hawaii, 109 LA 289 (Nauyokas, 1997) (upholding discharge of employee who admitted possession of marijuana while on duty).

may not be sufficient for discharge.[31] On the other hand, leaving an unopened beer can in the company refrigerator has been found to be just cause for discharge.[32] An employee's record of service may be considered to determine whether possession of alcohol or drugs warrants discipline or discharge.[33]

In one case it was held that the use of dogs for detection falls within the general authority of the employer to conduct searches and inspections for alcohol or drugs.[34]

3. Sale or Distribution. In one case an arbitrator held that an employer may use undercover investigators to determine whether drugs are being sold or distributed at the workplace.[35] However, strict proof of such activities is required, and the credibility of the undercover investigator is important where there is no other evidence linking the employee to the drugs.

C. On-the-Job Impairment

There is no set formula for determining impairment. In *Lockheed Missiles & Space Co.*,[36] the arbitrator noted that mere "presence in the system" does not mean that the employee is "under the influence." In *Schnuck Markets*,[37] it was held that "under the influence" is a condition that is something less than intoxication but more than mere presence in the system. A positive test, standing alone, does not demonstrate that the employee was "under the influence."

Furthermore, mere observation of an employee's speech and conduct may not prove that the employee was impaired. In *Tenneco Packaging Inc.*,[38] no just cause was found for discharge where the supervisor concluded that the employee was "under the influence" based on the report of a fellow worker and his own observations. There was no drug test given, and no basis was shown to order one.

---

[31]Georgia-Pac. Corp., 106 LA 470 (Hooper, 1996) (plant rule prohibiting use and possession "in the plant" did not include plant parking lot). But see Dunlop Tire Corp., 104 LA 653 (Teple, 1995) (possession of marijuana on company parking lot just cause for discharge).

[32]Alpena Power Co., 112 LA 1008 (Coyne, 1999).

[33]Kimberly-Clark Corp., 107 LA 554 (Byars, 1996) (despite employee's guilty plea to criminal possession of marijuana, the arbitrator found the employer did not have just cause to discharge employee with "immaculate" 26-year record).

[34]Anheuser-Busch Inc., 107 LA 1183 (Weckstein, 1996) (private employers do not have to meet exacting Fourth Amendment standards but must comply with rules of fundamental fairness; use of reputable dog detection enterprise valid even though dogs indicated presence of drugs in 12 cars, but drugs were actually found in only 3).

[35]Briggs & Stratton Corp., 107 LA 1023 (Briggs, 1997) (private investigation firm placed undercover operatives who uncovered drug dealing resulting in termination).

[36]101 LA 804 (Gentile, 1993).

[37]102 LA 1016 (Suardi, 1994).

[38]106 LA 1100 (Felice, 1996).

Where the evidence includes both observation and testing (or a confession), arbitrators are more likely to uphold at least some discipline of the employee.[39]

In *Mansfield Foundry Corp.*,[40] the employer claimed that the grievant had walked right into a forklift, smelled of alcohol, and was having hallucinations. His eyes were red and watery, and, at the hospital, he refused to take the blood-alcohol test (BAT). These suspicious behaviors, taken together, the employer asserted, demonstrated that the employee had been very much under the influence. To the contrary, the arbitrator found that the employee's refusal to take the BAT was not conclusive because it was not required by company policy. Furthermore, he noted that the employer presented no evidence of any suspicious behavior before the accident. Faced with several different accounts of the relevant events, the arbitrator decided that the weight of evidence favored the grievant's version of the accident. The arbitrator thus concluded that, while the employee might very well have been under the influence, the employer simply had failed to prove its case.[41]

Discipline has been reduced or reversed where the employer failed to provide due process,[42] failed to provide proper notice of the rules,[43] or imposed penalties that were deemed unreasonable under the circumstances.[44]

Deference may be given to expert testimony when it comes to interpreting drug test results as long as the decision to discipline is otherwise supported. In *Rothe Development Inc.*,[45] the arbitrator relied, in part, on a medical review officer's testimony that it was reasonable to conclude that the grievant was "under the influence" and "impaired" in his ability to perform skilled work. In *Fitzpatrick Co.*,[46] the arbitrator refused to sustain discipline based on a confirmed reading of the presence of cocaine metabolite, as opposed to actual cocaine, where the expert testified this provided no clue as to when the drug was ingested and was present within the body. In *Independent School District No. 2154*,[47] discipline was reversed where a chemical dependency expert testified that the grievant's admitted two puffs of marijuana 3 days earlier and positive drug test for unspecified amount of

---

[39]Meijer Inc., 112 LA 668 (Daniel, 1998); Bally's Park Place Hotel/Casino, 110 LA 1200 (Herzog, 1998); Cincinnati Metro. Housing Auth., 109 LA 427 (Sergent, 1997); Cajun Elec. Power Coop., 108 LA 641 (Howell, 1997); Hertz Corp., 108 LA 945 (Weckstein, 1997); Tecumseh Prods. Co., 105 LA 626 (Frockt, 1995); United Parcel Serv., 101 LA 589 (Briggs, 1993).

[40]109 LA 593 (Chattman, 1997).

[41]See also Tecumseh Prods. Co., 105 LA 626 (Frockt, 1995); Cajun Elec. Power Coop., 108 LA 641 (Howell, 1997).

[42]Pine Ridge Coal Co., 111 LA 568 (Feldman, 1998).

[43]United Parcel Serv., 101 LA 589 (Briggs, 1993).

[44]Id.; Lockheed Missiles & Space Co., 101 LA 804 (Gentile, 1993).

[45]106 LA 97 (Baroni, 1996).

[46]108 LA 686 (Briggs, 1997).

[47]110 LA 353 (Duly, 1998).

marijuana "particulates" meant the grievant could not have been impaired while at work.

D. Fitness for Duty

Generally, it is held that employees have the duty to report for work psychologically and physiologically prepared to perform their assigned duties and to remain so throughout the workday.[48]

Discharges have been upheld where a drug test, after a driving accident, revealed marijuana in the employee's system;[49] where an employee at work in a hazardous work environment tested positive for marijuana at nearly 8 times the cutoff level;[50] where a drug test showed that an employee had worked while under the influence of cocaine;[51] where an employee was legally drunk when he reported to work;[52] where an employee reported for work under the influence of alcohol and went to sleep on the job to improve his condition;[53] and where an employee's offense of coming to work impaired was compounded by a history of job-related substance abuse problems.[54]

Arbitrators find policy content or wording important. It has resulted in reduction of discipline where (1) an employee was discharged for having alcohol on her breath, but the policy provided for discharge only when an employee was actually "under the influence" or using a prohibited substance while working;[55] and (2) a policy provided discipline for employees "under the influence" during working hours, but the employer had never defined the term "under the influence."[56]

Employer misapplication or misuse of a drug/alcohol policy has resulted in reduction of discipline where (1) an employer charged an employee with violating a rule that had not been communicated;[57] (2) there had been lax rule enforcement;[58] (3) the employer failed to follow a policy or a prior practice of offering rehabilitation assistance before imposing the penalty of discharge;[59] (4) the employer had been inconsistent in assessing the degree of discipline;[60] and (5) the employer

---

[48]Bally's Park Place Hotel/Casino, 110 LA 1200 (Herzog, 1998); Burns Aerospace Corp., 104 LA 1210 (Smith, Jr., 1995); Carson-Mitchell, Inc., 112 LA 25 (Thornell, 1999).

[49]Bi-State Dev. Agency, 105 LA 319 (Bailey, 1995).

[50]Rothe Dev. Inc., 106 LA 97 (Baroni, 1996).

[51]Meijer Inc., 112 LA 668 (Daniel, 1998).

[52]Southern Cal. Edison Co., 90 LA 960 (Draznin, 1988).

[53]Nabisco Brands, Inc., 86 LA 430 (Cox, 1985).

[54]PPG Indus., Inc., 109 LA 399 (Grenig, 1997); Cajun Elec. Power Coop., 108 LA 641 (Howell, 1997).

[55]Greene County Dep't of Human Servs., 109 LA 1160 (Sergent, 1997).

[56]General Dynamics Corp., 91 LA 539 (Marcus, 1988).

[57]Watauga Indus. Inc., 78 LA 697 (Galambos, 1982); Pacific Offshore Pipeline Co., 106 LA 690 (Kaufman, 1996).

[58]MacMillan Bloedel Containers, 92 LA 592 (Nicholas, Jr., 1989).

[59]Georgia-Pac. Corp., 108 LA 43 (Nicholas, Jr., 1997); Bayer Corp., 108 LA 316 (Zobrak, 1997).

[60]Kelly-Springfield Tire Co., 108 LA 984 (Nicholas, Jr., 1997); Motor Prods., 106 LA 215 (Borland, 1995).

did not administer a drug or alcohol test, in accordance with its policy, to confirm its suspicion that an employee was under the influence of alcohol.[61]

Mitigating factors that have been taken into account in reducing penalties include cases where (1) the employee had a long, favorable work record and/or had engaged in rehabilitation efforts;[62] (2) the failed drug test resulted from the employee taking a family member's prescription pill by mistake[63] or from taking alcohol-based cough suppressant;[64] and (3) the employee's violation was otherwise not deemed to be intentional or egregious.[65]

E. Off-Duty Conduct

Under certain circumstances, an employer may have a sufficiently legitimate concern about an employee's off-duty misconduct to justify discipline.

1. Off-Duty Drug Use. In cases where an employee tests positive for use of illicit drugs, discharges may not be sustained in the absence of proof that the employee used drugs on the job.[66] On the other hand, discharges may be upheld in certain situations where there is no proof of on-the-job *use*, but drug tests suggest that there is on-the-job *impairment* due to *recent use*.[67]

2. Off-Duty Alcohol Use. Off-duty use of alcohol can be the basis for discipline where the employee's principal duty is driving and her conduct reflects adversely on the employer's reputation.[68]

3. Criminal Conviction as a Basis for Discipline. Conviction of selling or cultivating illegal drugs may be grounds for discharge even if the employee is off duty when engaging in such conduct.[69]

4. Discipline Assessed While Criminal Charges Pending. Although imposition of discipline on an employee *accused* of violating the

---

[61]Tenneco Packaging Inc., 106 LA 1100 (Felice, 1996).

[62]U.S. Steel, 111 LA 385 (St. Antoine, 1998); Hertz Corp., 108 LA 945 (Weckstein, 1997); Vons Cos., Inc., 106 LA 740 (Darrow, 1996).

[63]Bruce Hardwood Floors, 108 LA 115 (Allen, Jr., 1997).

[64]Pine Ridge Coal Co., 111 LA 568 (Feldman, 1998).

[65]Grand Rapids Area Transit Auth., 107 LA 1132 (Daniel, 1996).

[66]Simmons Co., 112 LA 164 (Riker, 1999); Fitzpatrick Co., 108 LA 686 (Briggs, 1997).

[67]PPG Indus., Inc., 109 LA 399 (Grenig, 1997) (discharge upheld for employee who used drugs 24 hours prior to work because it was likely he was impaired while at work); Frito-Lay Inc., 109 LA 850 (Heekin, 1997) (discharge upheld for employee who tested positive for significant levels of marijuana (72 ng/ml) because levels that high indicate "distinct possibility" that employee had used drugs while on duty and not during previous weeks).

[68]ATC/Vancom of Cal., 111 LA 244 (McKay, 1998).

[69]Kroger Co., 108 LA 229 (Frockt, 1997).

law may be preemptory, termination has been upheld when imposed shortly after the filing of criminal charges.[70]

F. Mitigating and Aggravating Circumstances in Alcohol-Related Discipline

A discharge was reversed when an employee consumed alcohol when off duty but the public sector employer had no rule prohibiting such drinking.[71] Employers must show consistent application of alcohol-related rules.[72]

Reinstatement was granted to an employee who, subsequent to his termination, sought treatment for alcohol abuse.[73] In one case when an employer failed to offer treatment through an EAP in lieu of termination,[74] the grievant was reinstated. In another, a termination of an employee for an alcohol-related offense before completion of an alcohol treatment program was reversed.[75] However, off-duty arrests for alcohol-related offenses plus inconsistent attendance at alcohol rehabilitation sessions may be considered an aggravation that supports upholding subsequent discharge.[76]

If an employee commits infractions in addition to alcohol-related offenses, the combined violations may support just cause for discharge. For example, the termination of a police officer was upheld because, in addition to drinking after hours, he denied the drinking and filed a false report concerning the event.[77] In another case, the discharge of an employee was upheld for violating a work rule prohibiting consuming alcohol on the job where the employee had engaged in additional misconduct, including dishonesty.[78]

---

[70]Avnet Inc., 107 LA 921 (Kadue, 1996).

[71]City of El Paso, 110 LA 411 (Moore, 1998) (reducing discharge of police officer to lesser penalty for involvement in off-duty accident after consuming 4 beers when employer had no rule against off-duty drinking and there was no public complaint regarding grievant's conduct).

[72]Owosso Corp., 96-2 ARB ¶ 6269 (Borland, 1995) (reinstatement granted to employees who admittedly violated alcohol rules because of inconsistent application of such rules).

[73]Vons Cos., Inc., 106 LA 740 (Darrow, 1996) (discharge not warranted when employee contacted EAP during suspension that preceded discharge and completed course of care).

[74]Georgia-Pac. Corp., 108 LA 43 (Nicholas, Jr., 1997) (no just cause existed for discharge when employer failed to follow past practice of allowing employee choice of EAP treatment or discharge).

[75]National Copper Prods., Inc., 97-1 ARB ¶ 3101 (Mackraz, 1996) (discharge not warranted when employee had completed only one session of 30-day treatment program provided for under contract).

[76]Tecumseh Prods. Co., 105 LA 626 (Frockt, 1995); Montgomery County, Ohio, 96-2 ARB ¶ 6346 (Bell, 1996) (discharge upheld for employee who had performed duties under influence of alcohol when substance abuse program not an option).

[77]Paulding County Sheriff's Dep't, 105 LA 1100 (Bittel, 1996).

[78]Norwood Hills Country Club, 108 LA 680 (O'Grady, 1997) (where employer allowed employees to take food from club's lunch buffet, employee abused allowance by taking over 1 pound of turkey and cheese off site in styrofoam container, offense that aggravated alcohol violation).

G. Drug Testing

1. As a Subject of Bargaining. The National Labor Relations Board has ruled that it is a failure to bargain in good faith if an employer unilaterally institutes new drug use policies and unilaterally revises the employee handbook to reflect this.[79] Once implemented, given appropriate notice of opportunity to challenge, a failure to grieve or object to the policy by the union will negate future challenges.[80] A union does not waive its right to bargain over a drug testing policy where it declines to bargain over the policy during contract negotiations and instead suggests that the issue be addressed later.[81] In addition, as with other mandatory subjects of bargaining, if the employer bargains in good faith with the union, it may unilaterally implement the policy upon impasse.[82] An employer may not, however, rely on general contract provisions that allow it to make reasonable rules for safety and health of employees to justify its unilateral implementation of a random drug testing policy.[83]

If the drug testing policy was implemented unlawfully, the employer's discipline decision based on that policy may be reversed.[84] In addition, where a unilaterally implemented drug testing policy contradicts the collectively bargained agreement, the terms in the bargained-for agreement will prevail.[85] Some courts have upheld arbitral awards reinstating employees who tested positive under such

---

[79]Sygma Network Corp., 317 NLRB 411, 149 LRRM 1247 (1995).

[80]Bruce Hardwood Floors, 108 LA 115 (Allen, Jr., 1997) (drug testing policy valid where employer met with union president who voiced no concerns about policy and did not file grievance); Vogel Disposal Co., 108 LA 1121 (Hewitt, 1997) (union could not object to employer's modification of original negotiated drug testing policy because union officers were given copy of new policy and employees were tested under policy without objection); Jefferson Smurfit Corp., 106 LA 306 (Goldstein, 1996).

[81]Lithibar Matik, Inc., 109 LA 446 (Hodgson, 1997).

[82]Atlas Processing Co., 106 LA 172 (Baroni, 1996).

[83]Ohio Star Forge Co., 110 LA 705 (Gibson, 1998).

[84]Tocco, Inc., 323 NLRB 480, 155 LRRM 1138 (1997) (employees discharged under unlawful drug testing policy reinstated with back pay); Ohio Star Forge Co., 110 LA 705 (Gibson, 1998) (employer could not discharge employee for twice testing positive under drug-and-alcohol policy, because it violated contract bar against discipline without proper cause or reasonable suspicion); Lithibar Matik Inc., 109 LA 446 (Hodgson, 1997) (employee reinstated who refused to take drug test because policy unlawful where employer refused to bargain about it on union's request); Kelly-Springfield Tire Co., 108 LA 984 (Nicholas, Jr., 1997) (employee reinstated who tested positive for drug use and wished to undergo rehabilitation again, even though employee had previously undergone rehabilitation, because employer failed to negotiate change to drug policy, which limited access to rehabilitation to one occasion); Pacific Offshore Pipeline Co., 106 LA 690 (Kaufman, 1996) (employee reinstated who tested positive under drug policy despite union's notice of added discharge penalty because employee not notified of policy change).

[85]New Jersey Transit Bus Operations, 111 LA 303 (Gudenberg, 1998) (employer improperly discharged employee for second positive test under unilaterally adopted drug testing policy because employee's first positive test more than 5 years old and collectively bargained agreement's "wipe-out" clause forbade consideration of stale discipline); New Orleans S.S. Ass'n, 105 LA 79 (Nicholas, Jr., 1995) (employer improperly placed employee on permanent suspension for testing positive because reinstatement agreement did not supersede provisions of contract, which did not bar off-duty drug use).

programs and rejected employer arguments that reinstatement violated public policy.[86]

3. Testing Issues. a. When Employer May Test. i. Random Testing. Random drug testing may be warranted where the employee holds a safety-sensitive position.[87]

ii. Reasonable Suspicion Testing. Reasonable suspicion drug testing often occurs after an employee is involved in an accident.[88] However, not every workplace accident provides reasonable suspicion sufficient to warrant a drug test.[89]

Where an anonymous source reported to the union and a state agency that an employee in a safety-sensitive position was working under the influence of drugs, the employer had a reasonable basis to test the employee for drugs.[90] Where an employee exhibits signs of drug use, such as profuse sweating, glassy eyes, slow and incoherent speech, nervousness, and loss of control, the employer has reasonable cause to test the employee under a "reasonable basis" drug testing policy.[91] However, showing of a severe temper on one occasion is not sufficient basis to initiate a drug test.[92]

iii. Other Cause for Testing. An employer may require drug tests of employees as a result of questions raised by earlier tests.[93] A contractual provision that allowed the employer to test when "circumstances or workplace conditions justify it" was found to authorize a test at the employer's discretion, even without reasonable cause.[94]

b. Testing Procedures. The procedures followed by drug testing laboratories often generate challenges regarding the validity of the results. Where the communicated testing procedures were followed,

---

[86]Food & Commercial Workers Local 588 v. Foster Poultry Farms, 74 F.3d 169, 151 LRRM 2013 (9th Cir., 1995) (arbitrator's reinstatement of employees discharged pursuant to unilaterally imposed drug testing program did not violate well-defined and dominant public policy prohibiting employees who test positive for drug use from driving commercial vehicles); Pepsi-Cola Albany Bottling Co. v. Teamsters Local 669, 158 LRRM 2522 (N.D.N.Y., 1998) (arbitrator properly reinstated truck driver discharged for testing positive for drugs under unilaterally modified drug testing policy); First Nat'l Supermkts., Inc. v. Retail, Wholesale & Chain Store Food Employees, 152 LRRM 2963 (E.D.N.Y., 1996). See also the U.S. Supreme Court's discussion of reinstatement after drug policy violations as not being a violation of public policy in Eastern Associated Coal Corp. v. Mine Workers Dist. 17, 531 U.S. 57, 165 LRRM 2865 (2000).

[87]Bayer Corp., 108 LA 316 (Zobrak, 1997).

[88]Jefferson Smurfit Corp., 106 LA 306 (Goldstein, 1996) (policy requiring drug testing upon accident necessitating off-site medical care supported by reasonable cause with reasonable basis to test because employees work with electric machines with rapidly moving parts and policy differentiates between minor and serious accidents).

[89]City of Texas City, 104 LA 534 (Allen, Jr., 1995) (fire department did not have reasonable grounds to order drug test after firefighter involved in minor accident because there were no other variables to suggest that employee was impaired); City of Monmouth, Ill., 105 LA 724 (Wolff, 1995) (city did not have reasonable grounds to require officer to take random drug test after he returned from disability leave caused by on-the-job injury).

[90]BHP Coated Steel Corp., 106 LA 387 (Kaufman, 1996).

[91]Cincinnati Metro. Housing Auth., 109 LA 427 (Sergent, 1997).

[92]Lithibar Matik Inc., 109 LA 446 (Hodgson, 1997).

[93]Textron Aerostructures, 106 LA 936 (Singer, Jr., 1996).

[94]Integrated Metal Tech., 112 LA 676 (Stallworth, 1999).

where no one involved had any personal animus toward the tested employee, and where the questioned procedure at issue would be unlikely to affect the drug test results, discipline based on the test results has been upheld.[95] In addition, where the testing agency maintains the specimen's chain of custody, challenges to the specimen's source have been rejected.[96] An employer's discharge decision has been overturned by one arbitrator where it could not demonstrate the specimen's chain of custody.[97] However, at least one court has held that an arbitrator exceeded his authority in overturning a discharge decision on the basis that the employer could not establish the drug testing laboratory's chain of custody.[98]

The requisite testing procedures also can depend on federal regulation. An employers' disciplinary decisions based on a testing program that violates the federal regulations have been overturned.[99] For instance, in *Coca Cola Bottling Co.*,[100] the employee was reinstated on the condition that he pass a retest because the employer failed to tell him that he had a right to request a second test of his specimen as required by U.S. Department of Transportation regulations. Another decision mitigated discharge of an employee when his blood alcohol level would have warranted discipline less than discharge under federal regulations.[101]

An employer may require an employee to provide the specimen to be tested under the observation of a third party of the same gender where the employer has reasonable cause to suspect that the employee adulterated an earlier drug test.[102] However, in such situations, the employer must follow federal regulations that govern testing under the observation of a third party.[103]

---

[95]Meijer Inc., 112 LA 668 (Daniel, 1998) (drug test that demonstrated employee had cocaine in his system given 3 days after accident sufficient basis for discipline because drug policy did not specify that test had to be given within certain time; test results showed that employee came to work impaired); Rothe Dev. Inc., 106 LA 97 (Baroni, 1996) (drug test results found to be accurate because agency followed well-established testing and sample-handling procedures); Bayer Corp., 108 LA 316 (Zobrak, 1997) (absence of temperature strip from employee's sample did not invalidate test where temperature strip's purpose was to detect employee adulteration of sample); Dravo Lime Co., 105 LA 54 (Imundo, Jr., 1995) (test results accepted as basis for discipline where no one involved in collection and testing of employee's urine specimen bore animus toward him and normal procedures were followed).

[96]State of Del., 104 LA 845 (Gorman, 1993) (employer satisfied chain of custody procedures when it kept sealed-and-signed urine specimen in locked desk drawer for 2 days before submitting it to laboratory).

[97]Eagle Energy, 110 LA 257 (Feldman, 1998).

[98]Logistics Personnel Corp. v. Truck Drivers Local 299, 6 F. Supp. 2d 650, 158 LRRM 2744 (E.D. Mich., 1998).

[99]Textron Aerostructures, 106 LA 936, 941 (Singer, Jr., 1996) (employer could not justify 8-day delay between second drug test and date for which third was scheduled because it violated federal guidelines requiring that "another specimen shall be obtained as soon as possible" if there is "reason to believe that a donor may have altered or substituted the specimen to be provided").

[100]110 LA 8 (Nadelbach, 1998).

[101]Hertz Corp., 108 LA 945 (Weckstein, 1997) (discharge too severe when, under federal regulations, employee's blood alcohol level would have required 24-hour suspension from driving duties but not termination).

[102]Palm Tran, 111 LA 917 (Murphy, 1998).

[103]Weyerhaeuser Forest Prods., 108 LA 26 (Levak, 1997).

Employee tampering with drug test samples or results would merit discipline only if drug test result was negative.[104] Moreover, if an employee immediately offers to produce another sample, an employer may not have just cause to discharge an employee whose first sample was abnormal.[105]

c. Effect of Positive Test. Where a collectively bargained drug policy provides for discharge if an employee fails a drug test, providing that the test was properly done, a positive test result is just cause for the discipline.[106] Additionally, if the industry involved presents overriding safety concerns, the presence of drugs in an employee's system alone may justify termination, especially where the grievant is a short-term employee.[107] If the drug testing policy was implemented with the express purpose of helping employees with a substance abuse problem, mitigating circumstances may be factored into the just cause determination.[108] These factors may include the presence of an EAP and an employee's desire to rehabilitate.[109]

Courts generally uphold arbitral decisions that reinstate an employee who tested positive for drug use, finding that no overriding public policy concerns justify interference with the arbitrator's decision.[110] Prior to the U.S. Supreme Court ruling in *Eastern Associated Coal,*[111] the federal circuits split on the propriety of such a ruling. The Fourth Circuit vacated such a decision on the basis that the arbitrator exceeded his authority under the drug policy.[112] The question of whether the arbitral decision to reinstate an employee who tested positive for drug use violated public policy is fact-specific, as the conflicting decisions of the First, Third, and Fifth Circuits show.[113] The Second and Ninth Circuits have held that an arbitrator's reinstatement of an employee who tested positive for drugs would not

[104]New Jersey Transit, 111 LA 733 (Stiefel, 1998); Textron Aerostructures, 106 LA 936 (Singer, Jr., 1996) (fact that employees emptied pockets before taking drug test and flushed toilet after providing sample did not suggest that he tampered with urine sample).

[105]U.S. Steel, 111 LA 539 (Petersen, 1998).

[106]Cajun Elec. Power Coop., 111 LA 769 (O'Grady, 1998).

[107]Dravo Lime Co., 105 LA 54 (Imundo, 1995).

[108]Simmons Co., 112 LA 164 (Riker, 1999); Bayer Corp., 108 LA 316 (Zobrak, 1997) (on successful completion of rehabilitation program arbitrator reinstated employee discharged after failing second drug test because drug rehabilitation program required optimal level of rehabilitation).

[109]Kelly-Springfield Tire Co., 108 LA 984 (Nicholas, Jr., 1997) (arbitrator overturned discharge based on employee's positive test because employee desired to enter EAP).

[110]Atchison, Topeka & Santa Fe Ry. Co. v. United Transp. Union, 175 F.3d 355, 161 LRRM 2265 (5th Cir., 1999); Tennessee Valley Auth. v. Tennessee Valley Trades & Labor Council, 184 F.3d 510, 161 LRRM 2844 (6th Cir., 1999); Exxon Shipping Co. v. Exxon Seamen's Union, 73 F.3d 1287, 151 LRRM 2161 (3d Cir., 1996); Southern Cal. Gas Co. v. Utility Workers Local 132, 160 LRRM 2488 (C.D. Cal., 1998).

[111]Eastern Associated Coal Corp. v. Mine Workers Dist. 17, 531 U.S. 57, 165 LRRM 2865 (2000).

[112]Mountaineer Gas Co. v. Oil, Chem. & Atomic Workers, 76 F.3d 606, 151 LRRM 2600 (4th Cir., 1996).

[113]Exxon Corp. v. Esso Workers' Union Inc., 118 F.3d 841, 155 LRRM 2782 (1st Cir., 1997); Exxon Corp. v. Teamsters Local 877, 980 F. Supp. 752, 156 LRRM 2832 (D.N.J., 1997), aff'd, 162 F.3d 1150 (3d Cir., 1998); Exxon Corp. v. Baton Rouge Oil & Chem. Workers, 77 F.3d 850, 151 LRRM 2737 (5th Cir., 1996).

violate public policy if the employee was required to complete a rehabilitation program.[114] Whether the Supreme Court's 2000 ruling has resolved these divergent approaches has yet to be seen.

d. Refusing a Drug Test Order. An employee risks discharge if he refuses a drug test permitted by the applicable labor agreement.[115] Similarly, if an employee delays in providing a testing specimen, discharge may be warranted.[116] However, where no employee had been discharged previously for refusing to take a drug test or the drug testing program was unlawfully instituted, the discharge may not be sustained.[117]

Where discharge is not an appropriate remedy for an employee's refusal to take a drug test, a court may be unwilling to interfere with that decision.[118]

H. Employee Assistance Programs

When a negotiated alcohol and drug policy mandates discharge upon testing positive on the first occasion, the discharge decision may be upheld because the proper disciplinary remedy was written into the policy by the parties.[119] This exception has been held not to apply, however, when there is a past practice of providing employees with an opportunity to enter an EAP upon their first positive test result, regardless of the language used in the policy.[120]

Discharge for the first violation of an alcohol and drug policy may be sustained when an employee is unwilling to participate in a rehabilitation program.[121]

---

[114]Electrical Workers (IBEW) Local 97 v. Niagara Mohawk Power Corp., 143 F.3d 704, 158 LRRM 2198 (2d Cir., 1998); United Transp. Union v. Union Pac. R.R. Co., 116 F.3d 430, 155 LRRM 2700 (9th Cir., 1997). See also Pepsi-Cola Albany Bottling Co. v. Teamsters Local 669, 158 LRRM 2522 (N.D.N.Y., 1998).

[115]Cincinnati Metro. Housing Auth., 109 LA 427 (Sergent, 1997) (employee reinstated where he had good record and did not show signs of drug use); Integrated Distrib. Sys., 108 LA 737 (Neas, 1997).

[116]Bandag, Inc. v. Steelworkers Local 922, 157 LRRM 2673 (E.D.N.C., 1996).

[117]Lithibar Matik Inc., 109 LA 446 (Hodgson, 1997); Munster Steel Co., 108 LA 597 (Cerone, 1997) (discharge unwarranted where employer did not consistently require all employees with workplace injuries to be tested).

[118]Teamsters Local 238 v. Cargill, Inc., 66 F.3d 988, 150 LRRM 2469 (8th Cir., 1995); Trinity Indus., Inc. v. Steelworkers, 891 F. Supp. 342, 149 LRRM 3050 (N.D. Tex., 1995). But see Gulf Coast Indus. Workers Union v. Exxon Co. USA, 70 F.3d 847, 151 LRRM 2017 (5th Cir., 1995).

[119]Cajun Elec. Power Coop., 111 LA 769 (O'Grady, 1998) (negotiated drug policy including provision that discharge will follow all positive test results bars arbitrator from considering lesser penalties or credible mitigating circumstances).

[120]Simmons Co., 112 LA 164 (Riker, 1999) (overturning discharge despite past practice to terminate employees testing positive for drugs because policy, read and considered in its entirety, based on principle not to punish but to assist employees to be productive workers); Georgia-Pac. Corp., 108 LA 43, 46–47 (Nicholas, Jr., 1997) (employee reinstated because he should have been offered EAP and wasn't).

[121]U.S. Steel, 109 LA 1025, 1026 (Vernon, 1997) (upholding discharge on the basis of a positive drug test result where employee previously had refused rehabilitation when disciplined for refusal to be drug tested, having convinced employer and union that his refusal to be tested was based on principle and not drug problem); Raytheon Aircraft Co., 105 LA 1081 (Thornell, 1996) (discharge of employee upheld because he refused mandatory referral to EAP for depression and alcohol dependence, both of which were affecting his work).

1. Discipline of Employee Enrolled in an EAP. Discipline of an employee enrolled in an EAP continues to depend on the frequency and severity of the employee's noncompliance with the rehabilitation program.[122] If an employee who is participating in a mandatory drug rehabilitation program does not follow a program that requires her to remain drug free, the employee may be subject to discharge if she subsequently fails a drug test.[123]

3. The Effect of Postdischarge Rehabilitation. Some arbitrators do not give weight to a request for postdischarge rehabilitation by the employee.[124] One arbitrator said that the employer has discretion when deciding whether a former employee should be rehired based on postdischarge rehabilitation.[125]

If the employee does not have a substance abuse problem, such as alcoholism, then there is no purpose in mandating rehabilitation.[126] If an employee has sought rehabilitation, even if it is *after* discharge, the request itself may be grounds for reinstatement,[127] because the fact that an employee was successfully rehabilitated may be said to have removed the cause for termination.[128]

4. Effectiveness of EAPs [New Topic]. Employees generally have been unsuccessful at challenging the effectiveness of the EAPs they are referred to as a reason for mitigating the discipline imposed; however, it has become an increasingly popular argument by grievants. These grievants tend to rely on the language in the drug and

---

[122]Rexam Metallising, 105 LA 939 (Nolan, 1995) (discharge upheld of employee who tested positive for marijuana pursuant to random drug test expressly authorized by drug policy for 12 months for any employee who returns to work following rehabilitation program as condition of continued employment); Tecumseh Prods. Co., 105 LA 626, 630 (Frockt, 1995) (discharge upheld of employee who, despite 17 years of service, failed to prove commitment to rehabilitation in that he was arrested twice for public intoxication, admitted continual consumption, and admitted not attending rehabilitation program as prescribed).

[123]Rothe Dev. Inc., 106 LA 97, 101 (Baroni, 1996) (upholding discharge of employee with positive result in test administered pursuant to rehabilitation program); BHP Coated Steel Corp., 106 LA 387 (Kaufman, 1996).

[124]Willow Run Cmty. Schs., 112 LA 115, 120 (Brodsky, 1999) (employer's failure to offer EAP irrelevant because grievant did not request assistance until after discharge); Cajun Elec. Power Coop., 108 LA 641, 648 (Howell, 1997) (employer would be placed in untenable position whenever employee is discharged for intoxication if employee's discharge for serious act could be reversed by request for rehabilitation after incident); Baltimore Sun Co., 107 LA 892, 896 (Liebowitz, 1996) (postdischarge rehabilitation does not mitigate employer's right to discharge employee for misconduct).

[125]Associated Third Party Adm'rs, 109 LA 1047, 1050 (Kaplan, 1997) (employer's discretion whether it wants to rehire grievant based on postdischarge rehabilitation).

[126]Ocean Spray Cranberries Inc., 105 LA 148, 151 (Dichter, 1995); Willow Run Cmty. Schs., 112 LA 115, 120 (Brodsky, 1999) (company's failure to offer EAP irrelevant because employee acknowledged that he did not have drug addiction but used marijuana to curb side effects of prescription medication).

[127]Tecumseh Prods. Co., 105 LA 626, 630 (Frockt, 1995) (arbitrator upheld discharge decision but noted that he would have reinstated employer under strict terms and conditions if employee had sought rehabilitation during period between discharge and arbitration hearing).

[128]Vons Cos., Inc., 106 LA 740 (Darrow, 1996) (discharge reduced to disciplinary suspension without back pay because grievant had contacted rehabilitation center, had been evaluated, had completed recommended course of treatment, and had made excellent progress).

alcohol policy regarding its intention not to punish but to strive for rehabilitation through effective use of an EAP.

It has been argued that discipline based on an insufficient EAP is without just cause because it could not have resulted in the employee's rehabilitation. In response, in *Rexam Metallising* the arbitrator opined:

> Non-professionals are in no position to judge which form of rehabilitation is appropriate for a particular employee. That is the job of experts retained by any EAP provider. Those expert counselors can be wrong, of course, but so long as the Company relies on their advice it has satisfied its contractual obligation.[129]

I. Last-Chance Agreements

1. Purpose and Elements. The last-chance agreement continues to serve as "a legitimate and very often useful form of corrective action to get employees to make permanent, positive changes in their behavior."[130] Such an agreement, as described by one arbitrator,

> has been viewed as a valuable device because it serves to benefit all parties concerned and is supported by consideration. The employee obtains the opportunity for continued employment, while in return the employer can impose particular terms which normally are more stringent than those which applied to the employee previously and which continue to apply to other bargaining unit employees under the just cause provisions of the collective bargaining agreement.[131]

Last-chance agreements, which generally are entered into as an alternative to discharge,[132] are frequently used to "deal with some of the grave problems that result from workers performing poorly because of abuse of alcohol or use of illicit drugs."[133]

Although the terms of last-chance agreements vary according to the particular circumstances involved, in drug and alcohol cases common elements include:

(1) The employee agrees to remain drug and alcohol free;
(2) The employee agrees to participate in and to complete an EAP or rehabilitation program and to comply with the program requirements;

---

[129]105 LA 939, 942 (1995). But see Bayer Corp., 108 LA 316, 320 (Zobrak, 1997) (3 hours of therapy insufficient for successful rehabilitation based on grievant's known history of drug use).

[130]Devro-Teepak, Inc., 98-2 ARB ¶ 5220 at 6277 (Goldstein, 1997).

[131]Id. See also Philip Morris U.S.A., 104 LA 948, 951 (Florman, 1995). See Chapter 12 for a general discussion of last-chance agreements.

[132]Eaton Cutler-Hammer Corp., 110 LA 467, 470 (Franckiewicz, 1998).

[133]International Paper Co., 109 LA 472, 476 (Terrill, 1997).

(3) The employee agrees to submit to further drug and alcohol screening, either randomly or under specified circumstances (failure to cooperate with such screening or a positive test result constitutes a violation of the last-chance agreement);
(4) The employee agrees to maintain specified performance and attendance levels, typically agreeing that any further violation of the rules that resulted from the abuse will result in termination; and
(5) The employee acknowledges that violation of any of the terms of the last-chance agreement will result in immediate discharge.[134]

2. Role of Arbitrator and Validity of Last-Chance Agreements. As a general rule, where the agreement specifies both the conduct prohibited and the penalty, the arbitrator's role is limited to determining whether the grievant has violated the terms of the agreement:

> In an arbitration proceeding pursuant to a last chance agreement, the arbitrator's first task is normally to examine whether the misconduct alleged is covered by the last chance agreement. If the last chance agreement provides that the employer may discharge an employee for the type of conduct of which the grievant is accused, the arbitrator's function is usually limited to determining whether in fact the employee engaged in the misconduct alleged.[135]

Last-chance agreements have been found not to strip an employee of her right to grieve, even if the agreement contains a waiver of this right.[136] On this issue, one arbitrator commented that last-chance "agreement[s] should not cause an employee to relinquish basic contractual rights, particularly the right to grieve and be confronted with the evidence against him and the opportunity to challenge that evidence and to present a defense."[137]

In some cases, last-chance agreements that are signed by the employer and the grievant, but not the union, have been held to be

---

[134]For examples of last-chance agreements, see generally, Eaton Cutler-Hammer Corp., 110 LA 467; U.S. Steel, 109 LA 1025 (Vernon, 1997); U.S. Steel, 108 LA 897 (Petersen, 1997); City of Detroit, 106 LA 1131 (Brown, 1996).

[135]Eaton Cutler-Hammer Corp., 110 LA 467, 470-1 (Franckiewicz, 1998). See also Michigan Dep't of Military & Veteran Affairs, 98-2 ARB ¶ 5174 at 6042 (Allen, 1998) ("All that must be proven is the employee committed the specific misconduct."); Lenzing Fibers Corp., 105 LA 423, 428 (Sergent, 1995) ("The sole question to be decided is whether the grievant violated the last chance agreement."). Compare International Paper Co., 109 LA 472, 476 (Terrill, 1997) (arbitrator concluded that published awards indicate arbitrators reject contention that their role is simply to determine whether grievant violated terms of last-chance agreement).

[136]Cross Oil Ref. Co., 111 LA 1013, 1023 (Bumpass, 1999); GTE of Fla. Inc., 108 LA 1115, 1119 (Cohen, 1997); GenCorp Auto., 104 LA 113 (Malin, 1995) (arbitrator declared issue is whether conditions triggering discharge without recourse occurred, unless it is clear from language that parties intended total reliance on management's good faith evaluation of employee's conduct); Gaylord Container Corp., 97 LA 382 (Goodman, 1991).

[137]Lenzing Fibers Corp., 105 LA 423, 428 (Sergent, 1995).

valid.[138] This precedent has been extended in one holding that a last-chance agreement that had not been signed by either the grievant or the union was nevertheless valid and binding because all parties were aware of the agreement, had fully participated in its drafting, and the grievant had orally indicated his assent.[139] Similarly, in another case, it was held that although an agreement that was not signed by the employee did not constitute a formal last-chance agreement, it could be likened to such an agreement or, at least, a final warning.[140]

Although most arbitrators concur that last-chance agreements must have reasonable time limits,[141] in at least one instance a last-chance agreement that was expressly *unlimited* in duration was upheld. In another case, the arbitrator found that "the permanent nature of [the grievant's third last-chance agreement] was knowingly inserted with the clear understanding and approval of both the Union and Grievant who were trying to emphasize that it was truly his last, last, last chance."[142]

3. Majority View. In substance abuse cases, one arbitrator explained that the discharge would be sustained as long as the employer could prove that the grievant violated a term of the last-chance agreement:

> As a definition of just cause in the context of the particular employee, a last-chance agreement is binding on an arbitrator no less than on the parties. The typical last-chance agreement removes from the arbitrator two aspects of judgment which arbitrators normally exercise under the just cause standard: proportionality and evenhandedness. Thus under the usual last-chance agreement, the arbitrator no longer has the discretion to consider whether the discipline imposed is too harsh for the offense involved. Likewise, the arbitrator may not consider whether the discipline imposed on the grievant is in keeping with that administered to other employees.[143]

At the employee's first positive drug test following such an agreement, discharge for violating the employer's substance abuse policy was upheld. The arbitrator rejected the union's argument that the schedule of penalties contained in the substance abuse policy incorporated the random testing provision, thus making discharge inappropriate.

---

[138]Columbia Gas of Pa., 102 LA 513 (Duff, 1994); Exxon Co., U.S.A., 101 LA 997 (Sergent, 1993). See also Tosco Ref. Co., 112 LA 306 (Bogue, 1999) (arbitrator rejected union contention that postrehabilitation, return-to-work agreement signed by employer and employee was "side deal" that could not meet definition of just cause where employee had been offered but rejected union representation when he met with company concerning return to work).

[139]Western Textile Prods., 107 LA 539 (Cohen, 1996). But see Appalachian Reg'l Healthcare, 112 LA 884 (Murphy, 1999) (in non-substance abuse setting, unsigned statement reduced to writing by employer did not constitute valid last-chance agreement because oral discussion of terms by employer, union, and grievant did not constitute assent by either union or grievant).

[140]BHP Coated Steel Corp., 106 LA 387, 390 (Kaufman, 1996).

[141]International Paper Co., 109 LA 472, 477 (Terrill, 1997).

[142]A. Schulman Inc., 105 LA 1076, 1080 (Duda, Jr., 1996).

[143]Eaton Cutler-Hammer Corp., 110 LA 467, 470–71 (Franckiewicz, 1998).

"The whole point of a last-chance agreement is normally to dispense with the usual requirement of progressive discipline, and permit the employer the discretion to discharge for even minor offenses."[144]

Last-chance agreements have been held to mean discharge when the employee fails a drug or alcohol test,[145] fails to take a drug or alcohol test,[146] fails to comply with a rehabilitation program,[147] reports to work under the influence,[148] violates work rules normally associated with substance abuse (failure to report),[149] or is arrested for illegal drug possession or use.[150]

4. Exceptions to Majority View. Strict adherence to and application of the last-chance agreement is often required.[151] Thus, discharges have been overturned where the employer failed to prove that the grievant violated the terms of the last-chance agreement, either because the conduct alleged was not covered by the agreement[152] or because the employer did not establish that the grievant committed the alleged conduct.[153] Similar grievances have been sustained where the grievant's due process rights were violated as a result of the employer's conduct;[154] where the agreement was invalid or improperly

---

[144]Id. at 471. See also City of Detroit, 106 LA 1131 (Brown, 1996) (off-duty alcohol consumption in violation of last-chance agreement).

[145]Tosco Ref. Co., 112 LA 306 (Bogue, 1999) (postaccident drug test); Eaton Cutler-Hammer Corp., 110 LA 467 (Franckiewicz, 1998) (alcohol test); U.S. Steel, 109 LA 1025 (Vernon, 1997) (periodic drug test); Memphis Light, Gas & Water Div., 98-1 ARB ¶ 5105 (Nolan, 1997) (positive result received after execution of last-chance agreement on sample collected before signing); BHP Coated Steel Corp., 106 LA 387 (Kaufman, 1996) (off-work, random drug screen).

[146]U.S. Steel, 99-1 ARB ¶ 5601 (Vernon, 1999) (employee refused to submit to second test after providing abnormal first test).

[147]Union Carbide Corp., 97 LA 1079 (Bittel, 1991) (failure to follow prescribed course of treatment); Diesel Recon Co., 96 LA 1193 (Odom, 1991) (drug use while in rehabilitation program).

[148]U.S. Steel, 96-1 ARB ¶ 6181 (Neyland, 1995); Ohio Dep't of Highway Safety, 96 LA 71 (Dworkin, 1990).

[149]A. Schulman Inc., 105 LA 1076, 1080 (Duda, Jr., 1996).

[150]Avnet Inc., 107 LA 921 (Kadue, 1996).

[151]Michigan Dep't of Military & Veteran Affairs, 98-2 ARB ¶ 5174 at 6042 (Allen, 1998) ("A Last Chance Agreement must be applied strictly."); Devro-Teepak, Inc., 98-2 ARB ¶ 5220 at 6277 (Goldstein, 1997) ("Arbitrators have recognized the validity of last chance agreements as a restriction on their authority to modify an employer's decision *if* the facts substantiate that the grievant has violated its terms. The burden still rests with the Employer to prove that the violation occurred").

[152]Michigan Dep't of Military & Veteran Affairs, 98-2 ARB ¶ 5174 (Allen, 1998) (employer's unilateral decision that grievant failed to comply with treatment program did not support discharge because agreement provided that failure to comply would be "determined by the health care professional and the Personnel Director jointly.").

[153]U.S. Steel, 111 LA 539 (Petersen, 1998) (grievant did not fail to comply with testing procedures in violation of agreement where, after employer was given suspicious and unacceptable sample, grievant had thrice offered to provide another sample); U.S. Steel, 108 LA 897, 897 (Petersen, 1997) (grievant did not violate provision of last-chance agreement that mandated immediate discharge for "failure to strictly adhere to report off procedures, absence without just cause, tardiness, early quit, and conduct which triggered his [last-chance agreement]").

[154]Devro-Teepak, Inc., 98-2 ARB ¶ 5220 (Goldstein, 1997) (grievant reinstated despite positive test result and lack of evidence to conclude contamination of specimen, because failure to advise grievant that he could have portion of sample retested violated due process and reflected management's failure to fulfill duty to fully and fairly investigate offense that led to discharge). Compare Avnet Inc., 107 LA 921 (Kadue, 1996) (supervisor's comment to employee that he was "starting on a clean slate" did not invalidate employee's last-chance agreement).

communicated to the employee;[155] and where, by its failure to act on previous violations, the employer waived its right to immediate discharge.[156]

5. Miscellaneous. Where last-chance agreements are silent as to their precedential effect, an employer must enter into such agreements with other employees who subsequently engage in similar offenses to establish a precedent.[157] However, it has also been held that last-chance agreements are non-precedent setting by their own terms and are therefore "irrelevant" in subsequent arbitrations concerning similar offenses.[158]

J. Termination of the Employer's Duty to Accommodate

When an employee requests assistance from an employer for a substance abuse problem or makes progress in rehabilitation, an employer may be required to accommodate that employee.[159] However, postincident behavior, including an employee's request for assistance *after the fact*, may not carry much weight.[160]

Safety of other co-workers and the danger associated with an employee's job,[161] length of service,[162] and work record[163] are all factors that may be considered in determining whether an employer has a duty to accommodate an employee with a substance abuse problem. In addition, distinctions among the types of drugs, whether legal or

---

[155]City of Chicago, 95-2 ARB ¶ 5196 (Wolff, 1995) (settlement and EAP agreements did not place employee on notice that he would not be entitled to rehabilitation as alternative to discipline in future). See also Cross Oil Ref. Co., 111 LA 1013 (Bumpass, 1999) (language "if any further incidents occur" in non-substance abuse last-chance agreement left question as to what specific rules of conduct were prohibited).

[156]Standard Prods. Co., 112 LA 76, 83 (Brodsky, 1999) ("The [last-chance agreement] itself gives notice of what circumstances will result in discharge under its terms. If the employee who is subject to the [agreement] violates [it] and is consequently terminated, she had proper warning. If the employee violates [it] and nothing happens, the notice provisions of the [agreement] are diluted and the employee must again be put on notice that additional violations will subject her to termination").

[157]TRW, Inc., 90 LA 31 (Graham, 1987); Navistar Int'l Corp., 88 LA 179 (Archer, 1986).

[158]Avance Circuits Inc., 106 LA 353 (Daly, 1996) (case involving workplace violence).

[159]Vons Cos., Inc., 106 LA 740 (Darrow, 1996) (alcoholic driver to be given second chance where he had excellent work record, contacted EAP during suspension preceding discharge, and made excellent progress in rehabilitation).

[160]Cajun Elec. Power Coop., 108 LA 641, 648 (Howell, 1997). See also Associated Third Party Adm'rs, 109 LA 1047 (Kaplan, 1997) (fact that grievant enrolled in drug rehabilitation program after discharge irrelevant to determining just cause for discharge); Avnet Inc., 107 LA 921 (Kadue, 1996) (under California law, because, in part, claimant never at any time before termination asked to enroll in drug rehabilitation, employer does not have to accommodate subsequent request for enrollment); Ocean Spray Cranberries Inc., 105 LA 148 (Dichter, 1995).

[161]Rothe Dev. Inc., 106 LA 97 (Baroni, 1996) (employee's use of marijuana at work is serious offense meriting discharge, especially where work deals with operating hazardous machinery, including cutting and drilling tools, whether or not any actual injury occurred).

[162]Simmons Co., 112 LA 164 (Riker, 1999) (32 years of quality service by employee was factor in arbitrator's determination that employer interpreted drug policy too rigidly).

[163]Anne Arundel County, 96-2 ARB ¶ 6402 (Wahl, 1996) (although employee violated substance abuse policy, termination too harsh a punishment because of employee's exemplary work record and voluntary submission to drug treatment).

illegal,[164] and the level of an employee's substance abuse have been considered by arbitrators before determining the necessity for an accommodation. The less serious the problem, the more likely an accommodation will be deemed appropriate.[165]

The kind of charge against the employee for which she is disciplined makes a difference, be it a drug or alcohol policy or a violation of another work rule caused by a substance abuse problem.[166] Where an employee violates an attendance rule because of an addiction to drugs, if circumstances are egregious an obligation to accommodate is less likely to be required.[167]

The responsibility to "properly" rehabilitate an employee as an accommodation may be deemed to belong to the rehabilitation program and not the employer.[168] However, where language in the collective bargaining agreement details a specific level of rehabilitation, an employer may be faced with a responsibility to the employee that he receives proper care and treatment.[169]

---

[164]Willow Run Cmty. Schs., 112 LA 115 (Brodsky, 1999) (marijuana and other drug-related offenses may be treated differently from alcohol-related offenses). Contra Kelly-Springfield Tire Co., 108 LA 984 (Nicholas, Jr., 1997) (even though sale of alcohol is legal, there should be no distinction between discipline for use of marijuana and alcohol).

[165]Montgomery County Gov't, 109 LA 513 (Hockenberry, 1997) (despite zero-tolerance policy, employer did not have just cause to discharge driver/warehouse worker who tested positive for marijuana where EAP representative indicated that there was little evidence that grievant had drug problem and work record was good).

[166]Andex Indus., 111 LA 615, 619 (Allen, 1998) (employer has just cause to discharge employee who consumed too much alcohol to come to work where he had received written warnings for unexcused absences).

[167]King County Metro Transit, 111 LA 198 (Beck, 1998) (under collective bargaining agreement and Washington state law, employer has no obligation to accommodate individual discharged for attendance problems because of addiction to crack cocaine where employer was unaware of drug problem at time of termination).

[168]Rexam Metallising, 105 LA 939 (Nolan, 1995) (1-day meeting with EAP counselor enough to constitute rehabilitation under collective bargaining agreement; EAP's responsibility to determine if grievant is properly rehabilitated, not company's).

[169]Bayer Corp., 108 LA 316 (Zobrak, 1997) (term "optimum level of rehabilitation" in collective bargaining agreement resulted in reinstatement of employee after second failed drug test for marijuana following return from "successful" rehabilitation; 3 hours of rehabilitation not sufficient to meet collective bargaining requirement of "optimum level").

Chapter 7

Dishonesty and Disloyalty

II. Theft

A. *Elements of Theft*

The common law definition of "theft" requires that there be some intentional wrongdoing. Thus, for example, an arbitrator upheld the termination of an employee who had been observed removing a vacuum plate from a machine before leaving the plant to participate in a strike.[1] The employee removed the plate from his pants when confronted by a foreman and gave it to the supervisor before leaving the plant. The union argued that theft had not been shown because the plate never left the plant. The arbitrator disagreed, characterizing the action as a special kind of theft: "There is recognized in the law, a form of theft known as 'asportation'. This means the appropriation by a person of an article in such a way as to clearly demonstrate an intent to remove it from the owners premises. . . . "[2]

A similar conclusion was reached by another arbitrator in *GTE Florida.*[3] In that case the employer discharged an employee for taking 86 quarters from a vending machine and placing them in a supply box. The coins were never removed from the plant, but this did not prevent the termination. The employee, in the arbitrator's opinion, had exercised enough control over the coins by taking them out of the machine and placing them in the box to be found to be stealing. The arbitrator opined that the company need not have allowed destructive conduct to reach full potential before acting.

Failure to submit to a lunch box inspection was considered the equivalent of stealing by another arbitrator.[4] The employee was terminated after refusing to allow a security guard to inspect the lunch

---

[1]Contempo Colors, 112 LA 356 (Daniel, 1998).
[2]Id. at 360.
[3]112 LA 950 (Sergent, 1999).
[4]Cleveland-Cliffs Iron Co., 110 LA 314 (Vonhof, 1997).

box to determine if he had stolen anything. The discharge was upheld even though the grievant was a long service employee with no previous record of discipline. The arbitrator commented:

> The Grievant refused to obey a reasonable order to open his lunch box for search, and the Board already has ruled that the Company's rule permitting discharge for this offense is reasonable. It is not unreasonable for the Company to treat such refusal, under the present facts, as an offense equivalent to theft.[5]

In another case, the termination was set aside and the employee was reinstated without back pay where the arbitrator concluded that he did not steal company property as claimed.[6] Some discipline was deemed proper, however, because the employee impeded the investigation, effectively covering up the theft, and was insubordinate. These acts were in themselves dischargeable offenses, but because the termination notice specified "theft," and the arbitrator held that the company had failed to prove the charge, the termination was converted into a disciplinary suspension. The arbitrator noted: "Had the Employer taken the time to fulfill its contractual requirements by making sure that there was a direct correlation between what it said and what it did, the discharge would have been upheld."[7]

Other arbitrators have found other kinds of takings to be tantamount to theft and have ruled they may be treated as such. In *Goodmark Foods*,[8] it was held that time card fraud for punching another's time card after that individual left early to clean up before going home was a form of theft for which discharge was appropriate. Similarly, a termination of an employee who continued to bowl while on disability leave was upheld in *Southwestern Bell Telephone Co.*[9] on the finding that the employee's fraudulent claim of total disability amounted to a theft of disability benefits under the circumstances.

An employer's lack of thorough investigation or appropriate notice may be sufficient to merit reinstatement, however. For example, an employee's discharge for theft was set aside in *United Parcel Service*[10] on the basis of the employee's lack of interest in and insufficient proof of theft by the employee. The grievant had taken two speakers that were outside a customer's house under the mistaken belief that the customer's housekeeper had given him permission to do so. The employer had not interviewed the housekeeper, and it was possible that a misunderstanding had occurred because of the

---

[5]Id. at 320.

[6]Nelson Tree Serv., 111 LA 1143 (Draznin, 1998).

[7]Id. at 1147.

[8]112 LA 1191 (Nolan, 1999).

[9]109 LA 274 (Nolan, 1997). See also Duke Univ., 112 LA 365 (Nolan, 1999) (upholding termination of supervisor for giving university property to contractor without permission); Associated Third Party Adm'rs, 109 LA 1047 (Kaplan, 1997) (upholding termination of employee who left premises during workday to take drugs and lied about her whereabouts).

[10]111 LA 392 (Draznin, 1998).

housekeeper's limited English skills. Moreover, the employee had not intended to be dishonest and returned the speakers upon learning of the misunderstanding.[11]

III. Falsification

B. Types of Records Falsified

1. Time Records. Time-record falsification continues to be difficult to defend. In *Heritage Cable Vision of San Jose California,*[12] the employee was terminated for, among other things, entering erroneous starting times on her time sheet, leaving work early without permission, and failing to complete her time sheet while on vacation. The grievant claimed that she wrote the correct time for the start of her day whenever she was late and followed appropriate procedures when leaving early. The employer failed to provide evidence or documentation to refute the grievant's testimony. Evidence established that others also left early without permission and that supervisors routinely completed time sheets for employees who were absent or on leave. The arbitrator concluded that the employer had not established just cause for termination but refused to reinstate the employee because of an incident that warranted termination that had occurred between the time discharge was decided on and the time it was implemented. (The grievant had failed to complete 69 tasks and lied about it, thereby causing other dispatchers to work overtime.) Back pay was awarded for the 3 weeks it would have taken to implement the decision to fire the grievant.

2. Business and Production Records. Mitigating circumstances can make falsification an insufficient basis to support a discharge. In *Trailmobile Trailer,*[13] the grievant answered "no" in response to the question on the employment application if he had ever been convicted of a felony. The form included a printed warning that false statements would be grounds for discharge. The grievant was reinstated without back pay, however, because the arbitrator concluded that discharge was too severe. The grievant had worked for approximately 1½ years without incident, except for a workers' compensation injury. The felony had occurred when he was 18 or 19 years old. At the time of the discharge, the grievant was 27, married, and an expectant father. The arbitrator commented: "Society is coming to

---

[11]See also Lane County, 111 LA 481 (Downing, 1998) (employee who yelled at co-workers about equipment maintenance problems did not commit offense of dishonesty); Army & Air Force Exch. Serv., 111 LA 545 (Monat, 1998) (setting aside discharge for theft where company offered little evidence of conspiracy other than fact that grievants were Filipinos).

[12]112 LA 316 (Feller, 1998).

[13]112 LA 1108 (Cohen, 1999).

realize that if convicted felons are not given employment and a second chance, they will have no recourse but to resort to lawlessness."[14]

Dishonesty was also the issue in *Sonoco Flexible Packaging*,[15] a challenge to a discharge of an employee who took sick leave for spastic colitis and went to Las Vegas after submitting a doctor's slip declaring she was under his care. The arbitrator reversed the discharge because the employee believed she obtained a legitimate medical excuse to cover her period of illness. The grievant had visited the doctor's office and picked up medication on the date she also obtained the excuse and plainly believed she was under his care for spastic colitis. The arbitrator found that the grievant had not been dishonest:

> "It is in fact common practice for physicians in general to provide employees with medical excuses covering days before the doctors, or their office nurses or other persons, have contact with the patient. The Grievant's submission of [her doctor's] representation that she was under his care on dates he never saw her may not have been enough to insulate her from incurring points under the Company's absenteeism program, but it was not a dishonest act meriting discharge."[16]

On the other hand, where circumstances do not raise questions about alleged falsification or otherwise support mitigation, discharge has been upheld.[17] In *King Soopers, Inc.*,[18] the termination of a pharmacy technician who falsified her prescription for Prozac and illegally continued to refill it was upheld.

3. Medical and Insurance Records. Falsification of medical records for the purpose of obtaining some benefit to which the employee is not entitled is generally considered theft. Thus, in *Aurora Casket Co.*,[19] the discharge was upheld where an employee hunted deer while on workers' compensation leave that included medical restrictions that prevented her from prolonged standing, sitting, stooping, bending, and lifting or carrying more than 20 pounds. Similarly, the termination of an employee who abused sick leave by using part of a sick day to work on a private job for a homeowner was upheld in *Portland Water District.*[20] The employee spent part of the day digging a hole for the private job, and the arbitrator reasoned that if he was well

---

[14]Id. at 1110.

[15]109 LA 824 (Duff, 1997).

[16]Id. at 828.

[17]See also Mine Workers (UMW) Dist. 6, 110 LA 84 (Ruben, 1997) (bookkeeper's falsifying daily reports noting that she performed work she had not in fact done warranted discharge but penalty mitigated by grievant's chronic depression); Empire Dist. Elec. Co., 110 LA 348 (Murphy, 1997) (recording of old meter readings by grievant warranted only 7-month suspension rather than discharge); City of Tampa, 109 LA 453 (Soll, 1997) (termination for submitting false statements concerning time and location of cocaine seizure incident to an arrest reduced to disciplinary suspension because lieutenant investigating matter told grievant she would reduce charge if he honestly described what happened and he did).

[18]110 LA 242 (Snider, 1998).

[19]111 LA 205 (Donnelly, 1998).

[20]111 LA 673 (Sheiber, 1998).

enough to hand-dig a hole, he was well enough to report for work and install meters.[21]

C. Factors Considered in Falsification Cases

8. Mitigating Circumstances [New Topic]. Penalties may be reduced in cases where the grievant's conduct is found not to be deliberate, willful, or intended to deceive. In *County of San Benito*,[22] a correctional officer with 13 years of service with average or above-average performance ratings and no history of discipline was discharged for gambling with inmates and smuggling cigarettes to an inmate. The employer's rules of conduct provided that disciplinary actions were corrective rather than punitive and were to be commensurate with the seriousness of the offense and enforcement of the rule had been lax. Consequently, the termination was converted to a 3-week suspension without pay.

Severe depression over the death of the grievant's father and her mother's Parkinson's disease were used to reduce a discharge penalty imposed in *Mine Workers (UMW) District 6*,[23] where the grievant was a long service employee with a good record. The arbitrator acknowledged that the grievant's performance would otherwise have warranted termination.

Lack of procedural due process also continued to be a mitigating factor in cases involving dishonesty and disloyalty. In *Gerstenslager Co.*,[24] an employee who was discharged for allegedly leaving her work station early to go to lunch was reinstated because management denied her request for a union steward at the time she was handed her termination notice and failed to give her a predisciplinary hearing at which she could have given an explanation of her conduct.

V. The Duty of Loyalty: Disparaging the Employer

A number of recent cases have considered the duty of loyalty owed an employer by its employees. In *City of Milwaukee*,[25] a sergeant was suspended for dishonesty after agreeing to post a notice concerning the settlement of baby-food litigation. When the settlement turned out to be a hoax, causing the employer embarrassment, the employer

---

[21]See also ATC/Vancom, Inc., 111 LA 429 (Prayzich, 1998) (termination of employee sustained in part because she falsely stated she was denied right to visit company's medical facility and denied right to file workers' compensation claim after being injured); Southwestern Bell Tel. Co., 109 LA 274 (Nolan, 1997) (discharge upheld because employee continued bowling while on disability leave with herniated disk).

[22]113 LA 231 (Pool, 1999).

[23]110 LA 84 (Ruben, 1997).

[24]111 LA 238 (Lalka, 1998).

[25]112 LA 682 (Dicter, 1999).

accused the grievant of lying or engaging in behavior that displayed a reckless disregard for the truth. The discipline was overturned on a finding that the grievant had neither lied nor acted in reckless disregard of the truth. In *Indianapolis Public Schools*,[26] however, the discharge of a custodian who made false charges against two supervisors that they had threatened him with a knife was upheld. But a termination for malicious gossip and aggressive behavior was set aside in *Brockway Standard, Inc.*,[27] where the grievant orally asserted to management, and reiterated in a letter to employees, that a corrupt relationship existed between the company and union. Reducing the discharge to a 4½-day suspension, the arbitrator concluded that the grievant's conduct was protected free speech rather than an attempt to bring disrepute to the company's name. Similarly, in *University of Illinois, Chicago*,[28] a discharge was set aside where an employee brought false criminal charges against a manager accusing him of assault. The arbitrator concluded that the grievant had not been blatantly dishonest, although he had probably exaggerated the nature of the discussion with his manager. The discharge was converted to a 30-day suspension. Nor did just cause for discharge exist in *Comair, Inc.*,[29] where an airline pilot told a co-worker at another job that the chief executive officer had been airlifted off his yacht as a result of a cocaine overdose. The arbitrator said that the comment was inappropriate and irresponsible, but it was not an admission; the grievant was reinstated without back pay.

In *Ralphs Grocery Co.*,[30] the grievant was terminated for violating a rule that prohibited unauthorized possession of company property when she was found to be collecting, copying, and taking company documents to support her claim that her job was misclassified. Reinstating the grievant without back pay, the arbitrator discussed the meaning of dishonesty and disloyalty:

> "Dishonesty" is a word easy to define, but elusive to establish and prove in the context of administering discipline in the workplace. Its ordinary and customary meaning is a "lack of truth, trustworthiness and integrity" with a "disposition to lie and be deceptive." Interwoven in the fabric of what constitutes "dishonesty" and an integral component as well is the employee's intent. The difficult inquiry is at what point is the established and proved conduct simply an errare humanus es or an inadvertent act made in good faith, but not in accord with the rules, or a knowing and willful act to deceive and be untruthful.[31]

---

[26]112 LA 858 (Dean, 1999).

[27]111 LA 1153 (Nathan, 1998).

[28]110 LA 50 (Doerias, 1998).

[29]110 LA 59 (Sergent, 1998). See also Metro Wash. Airports Auth., 111 LA 712 (Simmelkjaer, 1998) (off-duty conduct private unless it harms employer's business).

[30]110 LA 33 (Gentile, 1998).

[31]Id. at 36.

In *Associated Wholesale Grocers*,[32] the grievant was discharged for supposedly writing a statement on a memo that violated the company's antiharassment policy. The grievant was found to have lied during the investigation and at the initial investigatory hearing when he denied writing the memo in question. Furthermore, the grievant's dishonesty impaired the investigation. Although his original conduct did not warrant discharge, the grievant's dishonesty did justify the denial of back pay. Similarly, the arbitrator reversed the terminations of two employees who were accused of putting a brick on weighing scales so as to look as if they produced more than they actually did in *Lancaster Electro-Plating*.[33] In that case, management failed to prove which employee actually put the brick on the scale. Because just cause for termination was not established, both employees were reinstated, but without back pay.

VI. The Burden of Proof [New Topic]

There are conflicting opinions about the appropriate burden of proof that employers must carry when imposing discipline for dishonesty. In *King Soopers, Inc.*,[34] the arbitrator discussed various theories concerning the burden of proof:

> When an offense involves a crime or an act of moral turpitude, many arbitrators require an employer to prove its case on the basis of the criminal law standard of proof beyond a reasonable doubt. * * * However, other arbitrators in such cases have applied lesser quantums of proof, such as clear and convincing evidence or even a preponderance of the evidence. * * *
>
> Some arbitrators have concluded that rules applicable to criminal cases or fine technical distinctions in burdens of proof should not necessarily be imposed upon just cause determinations in labor arbitration. * * * The Arbitrator agrees that the application of strict rules regarding proof is not necessary to a proper analysis. Rather, in determining whether good and sufficient cause exists to terminate an employee for an infraction as serious as the one in this case, the realities of the employee's situation must be recognized. * * * The circumstances relied upon to terminate an employee in such cases should be consistent with a theory of guilt and inconsistent with any reasonable theory of innocence.[35]

In *ATC/Vancom, Inc.*,[36] speaking on the burden of proof, the arbitrator said: "Arbitrator[s] will seek only to determine whether

[32]112 LA 1212 (Murphy, 1999).
[33]110 LA 210 (Beckjord, 1998).
[34]110 LA 242 (Snider, 1998).
[35]Id. at 247–48 (citations omitted).
[36]111 LA 429 (Prayzich, 1998).

the Employer's evidence is sufficient to warrant a finding of just cause to sustain the Grievant's discharge."[37]

Both of these arbitrators appear to be adopting a standard that is analogous to proof by a preponderance of the evidence.

[37]Id. at 433.

Chapter 8

Workplace Misconduct

III. Accidents

Under the concept of discipline for chargeable accidents, it was held to be appropriate for an employer to consider discipline at the occurrence of a second accident regardless of whether the employee was at fault.[1]

IV. Sleeping on the Job

A. Workplace Rules and Enforcement

Sleeping on the job is considered a violation of the basic "pay for work" bargain inherent in all collective bargaining agreements. Where the rule is clear and the discipline for violation is announced and made known to all, the employer is well within its right to terminate employees caught sleeping when they should have been working, no matter how long their previous employment or how many previous disciplinary actions had been taken against them.[2] This is particularly important in the health care industry.[3]

B. Proving an Employee Is Actually Asleep

With sleeping on the job, the problem is usually not so much the wording of the rule as it is a question of fact: What is sleep, and was

---

[1]Pepsi Cola, 113 LA 523 (O'Grady, 1999).

[2]Manley Bros. of Ind. Inc., 106 LA 442 (Cohen, 1996).

[3]VOCA Corp., 105 LA 368 (Rybolt, 1995) (employee at residential facility for disabled persons discharged for sleeping on the job without regard to longevity or lack of previous offenses because, in part, of need for vigilant employees in health care industry).

the individual really sleeping? Proof that an employee was sleeping on the job thus depends on the circumstances. For example, in *PPG Industries, Inc.*,[4] an arbitrator agreed that a work rule against sleeping on the job was violated when a team leader found an employee in a position that had the appearance of sleep and the employee did not move or get up when the pump he was next to was turned off; the conclusion was that he was sleeping on the job when he should have been working. In *Phelps Dodge-Hidalgo Smelter*,[5] sleeping on the job was found to have occurred when the supervisor, who was standing 2 feet from the window of the cab of a truck, saw an employee sitting with back against a wall, arms folded across chest, head leaned over to one side, with hard hat resting against the glass and a foot on the control panel. In *Art of Illinois, Captain Mine*,[6] sleeping on the job was found to occur where light shone on the closed eyelids of employee viewed by managers through the glass of the cab did not rouse him. In another matter, discharge was upheld of an employee on light-duty assignment who, while watching a safety film, was found lying down on the floor and dozing off.[7]

C. *Aggravating and Mitigating Circumstances*

Because circumstantial and situational proof must be used, disparate treatment is frequently raised as a defense.[8] Distinction has been made between sleeping while on break and sleeping during paid time while one is supposed to be working.[9]

D. *Safety*

A rule against "inattentiveness" has been used to cover instances of nodding off or sleeping on the job where constant surveillance has safety implications. The discharge of a reactor operator for repeated instances of uncontrollable urges to nap under the heading of "inattentiveness" was upheld despite a postdischarge diagnosis of sleep apnea.[10] The importance of vigilance as a matter of safety in the industry was stressed. The fact that the employee, although warned,

---

[4]110 LA 372 (Suntrup, 1998).

[5]107 LA 175 (Brisco, 1996) (discharge reduced to suspension because of disparate treatment, not because of lack of proof of sleeping on the job).

[6]107 LA 178 (Feldman, 1995) (arbitrator emphasized finding that sleeping on the job had occurred although discharge reversed on basis of 20-year exemplary record of employee).

[7]Trane Co. Lexington Mfg. Plant, 106 LA 1018 (Kindig, 1996).

[8]Phelps Dodge-Hidalgo Smelter, 107 LA 175 (Brisco, 1996) (reinstatement ordered because, although employee violated clear company rule, others who committed same offense not discharged).

[9]See the discussion of distinction between sleeping on breaks and on paid time in PPG Indus., Inc., 110 LA 372 (Suntrup, 1998).

[10]Texas Utils. Elec. Co. Prod. Div., 103 LA 152 (Shearer, 1994).

did not seek medical attention to diagnose and deal with the problem until after he was discharged was held against him.

V. Fighting and Threats

In evaluating the appropriateness of the penalty for fighting, the question of disparate treatment may be at issue. Where the employer had discharged two employees for fighting, its subsequent action 4 months later allowing one of them to return to work with no back pay and 1 year of probation was held to have violated the rights of the other discharged employee.[11]

A disparate treatment problem may not be created where last-chance agreements are used, however. Thus, discharge was upheld for an employee who threatened to kill a supervisor and himself under a no violence in the workplace rule where other employees in similar circumstances were given last-chance agreements and were allowed to continue working.[12]

A. Fighting

Discharge was held appropriate for employees who were fighting on the job even though it was a first-time offense, where both were involved in provoking the incident and both were short-term employees.[13]

The provocation of name-calling or use of profanity does not justify a physically violent reaction. The person who takes the physical action is considered responsible for her own conduct. Thus, discharge was upheld when an employee pushed a co-worker who had called her a bitch.[14] Similarly, it was held that the employer had just cause to discharge a female employee who slapped a male employee after he cursed at her and used abusive language. The arbitrator held that words do not give provocation to justify battery.[15] In another case, just cause for discharge was found where an employee punched a co-worker even though he claimed it was in self-defense. The arbitrator found that the other person was bigger and had time to hit the grievant but did not do so. Therefore, he concluded that there was no real provocation to justify the violent reaction.[16] Similarly, a supervisor's

---

[11]Geauga County, 106 LA 220 (DiLeone, 1996).

[12]Advance Circuits Inc., 106 LA 353 (Daly, 1996) (additional circumstances factored in assessing appropriateness of discharge, including fact that human resources director was required to call police to have employee removed from premises).

[13]Tecumseh Prods. Co., Sumerset Compressor Div., 107 LA 371 (Keenan, 1996).

[14]Champion Internat'l Corp., 111 LA 100 (Duda, Jr., 1998).

[15]Robertshaw Controls Co., 110 LA 801 (Duff, 1998).

[16]Westvaco Corp., 111 LA 887 (Nicholas, 1998).

conduct, including profanity with a raised voice and finger pointing at employees in a disrespectful manner, did not constitute sufficient provocation for the grievant to physically bump the supervisor's chest where choices other than hitting the supervisor existed.[17]

On the other hand, where the provocateur actually made the initial contact, the provocation may be sufficient to mitigate the severity of the punishment of the responding employee. In *Martin-Bower Co.*,[18] where a supervisor started a fight with an employee in the company parking lot, there was no just cause found for discharge of the employee.

In addition, the physical action itself must be sufficiently serious and within the work rules to be deemed appropriate for disciplinary action. When a union steward poked a supervisor in the chest with his finger to make his point, it was found not to constitute violence within the terms of the work rule or to merit a discipline of discharge.[19]

Mental instability or the illness of grievants involved in fighting has not been found to be an absolute defense against termination. For example, just cause for discharge was found where the grievant hit a fellow employee, violating a work rule that specifically prohibited fighting, even though the grievant had a record of 18 years of unblemished service and was admittedly paranoid.[20] Similarly, it was held that an employer had just cause to discharge an employee who had bipolar disorder and who believed fellow employees thought he was a management spy where the employee had violated the work rule against fighting 3 times and had signed a last-chance agreement acknowledging that he would be fired if he were involved in such conduct again.[21]

B. Threats of Violence

Direct threats of violence are considered tantamount to the violent act itself in some situations. An employee was held to be discharged for just cause for violent action where he pointed his finger at another employee, saying "you are about to get your ass whipped," and swung at him with a clenched fist, even though he did not actually hit the other employee.[22]

Racial epithets used as means to provoke a fight can also be considered tantamount to the physical violence itself. In *Mason & Hanger Corp.*,[23] there was just cause found to discharge an employee

---

[17]Welch Foods, 112 LA 69 (Block, 1999).

[18]111 LA 929 (Felice, 1998).

[19]United States Graphite, 113 LA 208 (Ellman, 1999).

[20]Aladdin Indus., 111 LA 361 (Jewett, 1998).

[21]Beckett Paper Co., 106 LA 1135 (Goggin, 1996).

[22]American Olean Tile Co., 107 LA 338 (Welch, 1996).

[23]111 LA 469 (Baroni, 1998).

who tried to provoke a fight with an African-American co-worker by calling him a "chicken eater." The provocation was held to have violated the employer's equal employment opportunity and zero tolerance policies. The fact that previous similar incidents had not merited similar discipline was held not to be dispositive.

It may be more a question of intent than anything else. For example, in *Horizon Technology Group*,[24] no just cause for discharge was found for an employee who defied a supervisor's order and was written up for abusive behavior toward a supervisor. The supervisor claimed that the grievant had intimidated him by coming very close to his face and being very angry. However, the arbitrator found that the employee's ire was general, not personal, that the grievant did not direct profane or abusive language toward the supervisor personally, and that no physical contact was threatened or occurred. In another matter, *Samaritan Hospital*,[25] the arbitrator held no just cause for discharge for violence existed where the only threat made was to file a grievance and get even.

However, the setting and circumstances may make a difference. The response time and responsive reaction may reflect the perception of severity or reality of the threat and thereby affect whether there is just cause for subsequent punitive action. In *Ryder / ATE (Los Angeles, Cal.)*,[26] no just cause for discharge for a threat to kill a supervisor was found even where the employer had a policy of zero tolerance for violence. In that case, the supervisor, who heard the threat, took no immediate disciplinary action against the employee and did not inform anyone who could take action about the threat, including the police, the company's general manager, and the employee's immediate supervisor, against whom the employee was directing his vituperation. The arbitrator concluded that the lack of perception of seriousness of the threat should have been reflected in the discipline meted out against the employee.

On the other hand, it may be a problem of proof rather than situational facts. In one case, no just cause for discharge was found where the employee allegedly threatened a supervisor but the supervisor did not see the grievant making the threat and the grievant denied having made it.[27]

In another matter, the failure of the employer to interview a coworker who had witnessed the incident where an employee allegedly threatened to kill a supervisor was one of the factors that was cited in finding no just cause to discharge the employee.[28] Similarly, an arbitrator found no just cause for discharge for fighting where the

---

[24]111 LA 1027 (Ellman, 1998).

[25]112 LA 18 (Monat, 1999).

[26]111 LA 1038 (Prayzich, 1999).

[27]Van De Kamps, Inc., 111 LA 180 (DiLauro, 1998).

[28]Milbank Mfg. Co., 112 LA 464 (Crider, 1999).

evidence presented supporting the allegation was hearsay and was contradicted by the live testimony of the only witness of the event presented at the hearing, the grievant.[29]

VI. Abusive, Profane, or Other Inappropriate Language

Generally, the use of profanity, when provoked, is common and not considered in itself an act of violence that would support discharge.[30] Where the employee used profanity in the course of a meeting called to discuss his refusal to immediately come to work when called in, his language was found not to be directed personally at his supervisors but was general in tone and was merely emphatic relating to the extent of the disagreement between the union steward and the company position.[31] The arbitrator found that in this case there was no just cause for discharge.

Language includes actions intended to communicate in lieu of words. For example, discharge was held appropriate for an employee who rolled his eyes and threw something down on a counter where the employee was subject to a last-chance agreement that barred "tantrums" and "visual displays of disgust."[32] Discharge was also upheld despite the lack of progressive discipline for an employee who kissed a female co-worker.[33] A written warning was found to be appropriate for spitting in trash receptacles where the employee previously had been counseled informally about inappropriate confrontational misconduct and had not stopped.[34] In addition, it was found that the employee tended to yell in response to complaints against his actions. In another case, just cause was found for the discharge of employees who engaged in a car chase, even though no one was injured or killed, where the work rule included hostile and abusive actions in its prohibition of violent acts and language.[35]

On the other hand, there was no just cause found for a 3-day suspension of an employee who kicked and damaged a vending machine that had not given him product after he deposited money in it.[36] The arbitrator found that he did not try to hide what he had done and had offered to pay for any damage done. In another matter, no just cause was found for discharge because of lack of progressive discipline where the employee had taken a bus on a joyride and lied

---

[29]IBP, Inc., 112 LA 981 (Lumbley, 1999).

[30]Square D Co., 112 LA 342 (Goodman, 1999).

[31]Bunge Corp., 111 LA 1201 (Hilgert, 1998).

[32]Hugo Bosca Co., 109 LA 533 (Franckiewicz, 1997).

[33]Ralphs Grocery Co., 112 LA 120 (Prayzich, 1999).

[34]Wards Bldg. Maint., 111 LA 1088 (Bogue, 1998).

[35]National Castings, Inc., 109 LA 974 (Gordinier, 1997).

[36]Mid-Cent./Sysco Food Servs. Inc., 109 LA 124 (Bailey, 1997).

to the company president about what he was doing. No criminal charges had been filed and no one thought he was stealing the bus.[37]

Communication of offensive language may make the difference in the severity of the penalty imposed. Although the words "sucks donkey" could have been considered shop talk, when written on the side of a forklift driven around the plant it became more public than comments made to a co-worker; as such, the words were considered susceptible to a broader interpretation and therefore were held to be grounds for discharge.[38] Similarly, an arbitrator declared, a union steward who used the phrase "m–f" in the presence of other employees and residents of a health care facility within the hearing range of the supervisor may be discharged with just cause.[39] In *King Soopers, Inc.*,[40] suspension was upheld where the direct testimony showed that the employee told the supervisor over the telephone "you and the rest of management are prejudiced mother fuckers."[41]

A. *Type of Statement*

Fighting words can be the basis for discipline in and of themselves. Just cause for discipline was found against an employee of a federal agency who used the phrase "going postal" where there was a rule against the use of fighting words.[42]

Where the language in question amounts to sexual harassment, additional criteria, such as the intent of the statement, may apply. The discharge of a lead man for sexually harassing female employees was upheld even though he was a 23-year employee.[43] He was charged with making obscene and vulgar comments and placing the women in fear for their jobs should they complain. It was also held that shop talk does not include sexual harassment profanity that is not directed at one person but was intended to intimidate and denigrate female employees. However, without the requisite intent, discharge has been held too severe a penalty. In *Fleming Cos.*,[44] the arbitrator found that the comment "when you do that your ass shakes" made to a female worker did not in itself justify discharge.[45] Similarly, a male employee who committed sexual harassment through various offensive comments was reinstated and his termination reduced to a suspension

[37]SBS Transit Corp., 108 LA 1134 (Skulina, 1997).
[38]Beta Steel Corp., 112 LA 877 (Brookins, 1998).
[39]Sheridan Health Care Ctr., 106 LA 1125 (Draznin, 1996).
[40]112 LA 491 (Watkins, 1998).
[41]Id. at 492.
[42]Internal Revenue Serv., 113 LA 523 (Abrams, 1999).
[43]International Extrusion Corp., 106 LA 371 (Brisco, 1996).
[44]112 LA 257 (Duff, 1999).
[45]Id. at 258.

with a last-chance agreement where he recognized the seriousness of the offense and appeared to be rehabilitated.[46]

Racial epithets have been treated similarly. However, the extent of the direct proof that the employee actually made the statement is important. The use of a graphologist to determine the origin and author of a racially offensive statement was acceptable as supporting proof of just cause in *Associated Wholesale Grocers.*[47] In another matter, an inadequate investigation was held to defeat just cause for discharge where the employee was charged with making racially offensive remarks, despite the assertion that the charge was not based on the claims of an ex-employee with whom the grievant had fought and other black employees had stepped forward to support the assertion that the grievant had made the insensitive remarks with which he was charged.[48] In *Ohio Power Co.*,[49] the arbitrator found that the use of the term "nigger" was a basis for discipline, but not for suspension, where the employee had no history of being racist and the remark was generally attributed to ignorance and stupidity. However, just cause was found where the employee had a history of using racial epithets in the workplace as well as a history of insubordination, rudeness, and poor attitude.[50]

B. Setting

In some stressful situations, more leeway is given for what otherwise could be considered punishable language. For example, no just cause was found for the discharge of an employee who, upon leaving the nurses' office, called to the nurse that she had better call someone because she was going to need to "take my foot out of your ass."[51] The arbitrator concluded that this was not a real threat, and other employees were not discharged for conduct that could be considered of similar import. In another case, remarks made by an employee at the end of a heated discussion with the human resources director about a planned reduction in force were considered inappropriate bases for discharge.[52] The arbitrator held that the statements were too general, did not threaten any follow-up action or conditions, and did not include any timetable for any perceived threat. The grievant was returned to the status quo, which included the right to grieve over the reduction in force. Similarly, where a union steward used profanity after a dispute with management over failure to implement

[46]Safeway, Inc., 109 LA 768 (DiFalco, 1997).
[47]112 LA 1212 (Murphy, 1999).
[48]Coca Cola, USA, 112 LA 193 (Rezler, 1999).
[49]111 LA 158 (Hewitt, 1998).
[50]Schnuck Mkts. Inc., 111 LA 288 (Hilgert, 1998).
[51]South Bend Metal Stamping, 111 LA 995, 997 (Goldstein, 1998).
[52]Children's Hosp., 110 LA 471 (Feigenbaum, 1998).

salary increases, there was no just cause to discharge, even though the employee had been previously disciplined, including a suspension, for outbursts of profanity.[53] The arbitrator took the setting and context of the outburst into consideration and determined that a lesser discipline was merited because the employee had recognized his misconduct and apologized.

However, the setting can also make inappropriate discipline based on language that could be jokes in other situations. For example, discharge was upheld for an employee who refused to produce a badge for a security guard and asked if the guard would like to see his gun, frightening the guard, during the month in which the plant had received bomb threats of which the employee was aware.[54]

C. Defenses

Failure to take criminal action against an employee accused of threatening management does not alter the finding of just cause for discharge where the contract allows discharge for addressing threatening language.[55]

A last-chance agreement is a basis for discharge for use of profane, threatening, and abusive language when an employee lost his temper and threatened co-workers, even though the employee had not been given prior notice, because the rule that was violated said that discharge was a possible penalty for the offense.[56]

D. Legally Protected Speech

Discharge was upheld as an appropriate penalty for distribution of pamphlets in the workplace that included unsubstantiated assertions of criminal conduct by fellow employees.[57] The arbitrator found that this was not First Amendment–protected free speech. Similarly, it was held that an employer had just cause to suspend an employee for distributing a document entitled "Oakland Ebonics Quiz" in the workplace, even though the employer did not follow progressive discipline.[58] The arbitrator found that it was not protected speech and that the distribution violated the employer's policies barring racial and sexual bias and harassment, and agreed with the employer that the penalty must impress on the employee the seriousness of the offense.

---

[53]Will-son Corp., 108 LA 920 (Nadelback, 1997).

[54]Pioneer Flour Mills, 109 LA 1016 (Crider, 1998).

[55]Troy City (Ohio) Sch. Dist. Bd. of Educ., 107 LA 981 (Heekin, 1996).

[56]Western Textile Prods. Greensteak, 107 LA 539 (Cohen, 1996).

[57]City of Wooster, 111 LA 1167 (Richard, 1999).

[58]Pepsi Cola Co., 110 LA 803 (Bernhardt, 1998).

VII. Firearms or Weapons in the Workplace

B. Using or Threatening to Use a Weapon

Discharge was upheld for an employee who violated a work rule against discharging a gun while on the premises, even though he only fired blanks.[59] Discharge was also upheld in a case where a loaded gun was found in the grievant's locker at work, because possession was considered sufficient to imply an intent to use it in some way.[60]

C. Level of Discipline

The level of discipline may depend on the wording of the work rule itself. An employee who brought a gun to work and fired accidentally was given a 12-month suspension but was not terminated because the rule did not specify termination as a possible discipline for its violation.[61] In another matter, discharge was reduced to a 21-month suspension without pay for a teacher in a defense department school who had brought a gun to school when there was no intent to cause a problem and there was a question of whether the teacher understood the nature of the offense.[62]

VIII. Horseplay

In *In re Pratt and Whitney,*[63] the arbitrator added to the concept of horseplay by including uncivility, impoliteness, and the potential for violence to the definition of the word.

A. Intentional or Accidental Conduct

Lack of requisite intent to injure was the basis for the reduction of the penalty from discharge to a suspension in *Trailmobile, Inc.*[64] The arbitrator found that, although the grievant threw the sledgehammer and injured a co-worker, his aim was to stop objects from being thrown at him, and the injury of the co-worker was deemed inadvertent.

---

[59]Sandusky Cabinets, 112 LA 373 (Morgan, 1999).

[60]San Diego Trolley, 112 LA 323 (Prayzich, 1999) (arbitrator found that gun possession was separately actionable from agreement relating to promised test for fitness for duty that had not yet occurred where subject of gun had not been raised or discussed and issue was not part of agreement).

[61]Johnstown Wire Techs., 111 LA 216 (Franckiewicz, 1998).

[62]Fort Knox Cmty. Schs., 112 LA 1073 (Cantor, 1999).

[63]112 LA 461 (Chandler, 1999).

[64]113 LA 182 (Fowler, 1999).

B. Risk of Injury or Damage

An example of lack of injury or damage being a factor in the assessment of the appropriate penalty can be seen in *Eaton Corp.*,[65] where the arbitrator found the employee's actions, taking pictures of her bare breasts on company equipment, to be analogous to intentional horseplay. Because no one was injured and there was no malicious intent, discharge was held to be too harsh.

C. Defenses

Where horseplay was "a way of life in the plant," discharge for unintentionally causing an injury when participating in such activities was deemed too harsh a remedy. Expressions of remorse afterward by the grievant were considered evidence that the employee did not intend to cause the injury.[66] In another case, suspension but not discharge was considered appropriate for male employees who lured another male employee into a room, turned off the lights, and accosted him physically and verbally, where the assault was not carried to the level of a sexual act nor was intended to cause physical harm. The suspension was based in part on the fact that the victim's fear was real.[67]

IX. Failure to Meet Grooming or Appearance Standards

A. Arbitral Principles

Reasonable grooming and appearance standards must be appropriately promulgated and be clear and specific to be enforceable. In one instance, it was held that a newly instituted dress code was unenforceable and was a violation of the contract because it was not bargained about.[68] In another, the arbitrator found inappropriate an oral reprimand based on a rule requiring that teachers "dress in a professional manner that conforms with their positions as leaders and role models of the student population."[69] To be enforceable, the rule itself needed to be very specific and only applicable to unquestionably inappropriate attire, and the proof of violation needed to be clear and specific as well, neither of which was true in this case.

---

[65]112 LA 705 (Gregory, 1999).

[66]Trailmobile, Inc., 113 LA 182 (Fowler, 1999).

[67]Coca Cola Bottling Co. of N. Ohio, 106 LA 776 (Borland, 1996).

[68]Macy's & Retail, Wholesale & Dep't Store Union, Local 1, 108 LA 489 (Gregory, 1997).

[69]Board of Educ. of Bethlehem Ctr. Sch. Dist., 105 LA 285, 285 (Talarico, 1995).

Another arbitrator opined that a rule against indecent clothing could reasonably apply to prohibit a female employee from wearing a t-shirt from the Hooters Restaurant that read "More Than A Mouthful" where the rule was intended to eliminate crude and vulgar pictures and slogans on clothing in the workplace.[70] Similarly, an arbitrator upheld the enforceability of a rule requiring that employees "maintain good grooming and dress in a manner consistent with the nature of the work to be performed."[71]

C. *Civil Rights Statutes*

A federal district court in Pennsylvania asserted that case law grants an employer "a certain amount of latitude to adopt employee grooming standards that are not entirely gender neutral."[72] A prohibition on wearing nose jewelry was upheld despite a claim that a prohibition interfered with the employee's expression of her cultural heritage.[73] The arbitrator found that Title VII of the 1964 Civil Rights Act does not protect employees' ability to express their cultural heritage in this way in the workplace.[74]

In another case, a court found that there was no Title VII violation where the supervisor repeatedly criticized a receptionist for wearing an inappropriately provocative dress.[75] Although the criticisms were unwelcome, the court said that they were the opposite of the sexual conduct Title VII was intended to prohibit.

Title VII was also held not to bar uniformly enforced different grooming standards based on gender that were not in and of themselves evidence of disparate treatment, particularly where the rule preserved the employer's image with customers.[76] Similarly, nonpro-

---

[70]Clarion Sintered Metals Inc., 110 LA 770 (Cohen, 1998) (discipline reversed because of inordinate delay in enforcement and disparate enforcement where male employees not disciplined for tool box pictures that included explicit sexual content and references).

[71]Park Mansions Inc., 105 LA 849, 850 (Duff, 1995) (discharge reduced to suspension without back pay for 7-year employee with average work record provided employee cut his hair and comply with grooming requirement).

[72]Kleinsorge v. Eyeland Corp., 81 FEP Cases 1601, 1602, 2000 U.S. Dist. LEXIS 812 (E.D. Pa., 2000) (favorably citing Doe v. City of Belleville, 119 F.3d 563, 74 FEP Cases 625 (7th Cir., 1995)).

[73]Motion Picture & Television Fund, 103 LA 988 (Gentile, 1994) (manager's repeated inquiry into basis for employee's claim of interference with cultural heritage held not to violate contractual provisions calling for employees to be courteous and work for "harmonious working environment" where inquiry was reasonable in view of employee's stated reasons for wearing jewelry).

[74]But see Liberty Med. Ctr. Inc., 109 LA 609 (Harkless, 1997) (Muslim employee not insubordinate in telling supervisor that dress code requiring employees to tuck in shirts did not apply to him where supervisor unreasonably ordered grievant to comply until he could provide religious documentation rather than giving him time to present documentation).

[75]Schmitz v. ING Secs., Futures & Options, Inc., 10 F. Supp. 2d 982, 77 FEP Cases 481 (N.D. Ill., 1998).

[76]Southwest Airlines, 107 LA 270 (Jennings, 1996). See also USCP-Wesco, Inc., 109 LA 225 (Grabuskie, 1997) (insubordination charge upheld against Hispanic employee who refused to remove African print scarf but penalty reduced to apology to black co-workers and supervisor and requirement to attend sensitivity training).

vocative decorations such as t-shirts or "girlie" posters have been held not to create a hostile work environment per se.[77]

However, rules that impose a greater burden on one sex than the other may be found to be discriminatory and therein unenforceable. In *Frank v. United Airlines*,[78] separate weight requirements for male and female flight attendants were held to violate Title VII and the Age Discrimination in Employment Act because women were required to follow weight maximums for medium body frames while men were required to follow weight maximums for large body frames.

X. Conduct and Speech Toward Third Parties

There was just cause to discharge a union steward for saying "m-f" in the presence of other employees and residents of a health care facility where he had been counseled and previously disciplined for committing similar offenses.[79] The communication factor may be the key. In another case, no just cause was found for termination where the grievant had referred to the employee of an outside service as "queer" and "homo" when speaking with his own manager but the remarks were not made to anyone else. The arbitrator held that, although the comments were tasteless and sexually offensive, the lack of communication made them have no negative effect.[80]

A. Obligations Toward Those in the Employee's Care

There was just cause for discharge of an employee at a home for mentally retarded persons where the employee prodded and intimidated the patients with a hairbrush when she loaded them onto the bus.[81] Patient care was considered paramount even where there was provocation, and the work rules specifically provided for termination for such actions. In another case, a nursing home was found to be justified in terminating an employee who was cursing and swearing at a resident she was force-feeding even though she acted out of frustration, not anger, where the work rule provided termination as the only specified discipline.[82]

---

[77]McKeown v. Dartmouth Bookstore Inc., 975 F. Supp. 403 (D.N.H., 1997).

[78]216 F.3d 845, 83 FEP Cases 1 (9th Cir., 2000). Note that this case also raises the question of whether weight requirements qualify as bona fide occupational qualifications.

[79]Sheridan Health Care Ctr., 106 LA 1125 (Draznin, 1996).

[80]ABC Rail Prods. Corp., Anderson Ind. Plant, 110 LA 574 (Kenis, 1998) (grievant reinstated without back pay because he threatened to get even with management at a meeting discussing the incident).

[81]Gateway to Better Living, 108 LA 210 (Hewitt, 1996).

[82]Manor West Health Care & Retirement Ctr., 106 LA 344 (Oberdank, 1996).

B. Obligations Toward Customers and Third Parties

Suspension for discourteous treatment of the public was held to be arbitrable because the conduct was covered by the collective bargaining agreement, even though the specific rules of behavior were school board rules that were not contract-dependent.[83]

A driver operating under a continuing services contract of a package delivery service who acted unprofessionally in carrying out his delivery duties, thereby generating customer complaints, was justifiably terminated for inappropriate actions toward the customers.[84]

There was just cause for discharge for an employee who persisted in calling the female cashier of a customer "honey," "sweetie," and "babe," where use of the terms made the cashier uncomfortable and the employee had been given a warning for similar harassing behavior with other customers' employees in the past.[85]

---

[83]Sandusky County Educ. Serv. Ctr. Governing Bd., 114 LA 33 (Skulina, 2000).

[84]Roadway Package Sys., 112 LA 540 (Richard, 1999).

[85]Pepsi Cola Bottling Co. of St. Louis, Inc., 108 LA 993 (Thornell, 1997).

Chapter 9

Off-Duty Conduct

II. The "Workplace Nexus" Standard: Relevance and Notoriety

B. Harm to the Employer's Business

Realizing that the employer would lose public confidence if it continued to employ the grievant, an agency's discharge of a driver who failed a drug test was held to be with just cause, even though the employer did not provide him with union representation when it was requested.[1] The arbitrator reasoned that even if the grievant had had representation and was told not to take the test, he could have been terminated for insubordination. However, accepting the union's argument that the agency should be penalized for not providing union representation, the arbitrator awarded the grievant 1 month's back pay even though he upheld the termination.

The line between actual and speculative harm to the employer is difficult to draw. In *City of Joliet*,[2] it was held that the city did not have just cause to discharge a laboratory technician in a wastewater treatment plant who had been convicted of arson and conspiracy and whose conviction was widely reported in local newspapers. The grievant had 21 years of excellent, discipline-free service, the newspaper had not disclosed his city employment or the nature of his work, and he had cooperated with the government. The arbitrator found that there was not a sufficient nexus between his employment and the misconduct to support the termination.

---

[1]Bi-State Dev. Agency, 105 LA 319 (Bailey, 1995).

[2]108 LA 7 (Cox, 1996).

C. An Employee Unable to Work

Arbitrators continue to uphold discipline and discharge issued against employees who are unable to work because of incarceration.[3]

There can be mitigating circumstances surrounding an employee's absence from work that justify reinstatement.[4] In *Smith Fiberglass Products*,[5] the employee's fear of a husband who had threatened her and who had even come to the plant looking for her was sufficiently mitigating to overturn her discharge for an 8-day absence from work without notice. In *U.S. Steel Fairfield Works*,[6] the employee was incarcerated for 15 days. He called the company on a daily basis until he was informed that he no longer needed to call. When he called immediately upon his release from jail to inform the company of his availability for work, he was fired. The arbitrator reinstated him even though he was working under his second last-chance agreement.[7]

Employees also have been reinstated after it was determined that their procedural due process rights were violated. In *Facility Management of Louisiana*,[8] an employee was reinstated with full back pay because the employer failed to conduct a thorough investigation and failed to provide adequate notice to the employee and the union, as required by the collective bargaining agreement. The arbitrator also found that the no-fault attendance policy had been improperly applied and that the employee's absence for incarceration did not require discharge under that policy.

Past practice has been used to evaluate the appropriateness of discipline because of absence from work due to incarceration. In *Appleton Papers, Inc.*,[9] the arbitrator cited a past practice that all discipline would be held in abeyance until after an employee's criminal

[3]U.S. Steel, 107 LA 581 (Petersen, 1996) (discharge upheld of employee incarcerated for 7 months for conviction of conspiracy to distribute marijuana even though employee had 20 years' seniority and good work record); Dunlop Tire Corp., 106 LA 84 (Teple, 1995) (discharge upheld of employee incarcerated for 14 months for possession and intent to distribute marijuana, noting that employee's activities also violated work rule against drug possession and sale); Mosinee Paper Corp., 104 LA 281 (Lundberg, 1995) (termination upheld of employee after 14 days of continuous absence, noting that cause of absences was that employee was in jail because of probation violation).

[4]Orpack-Stone Corp., 102 LA 545 (Hilgert, 1994) (just cause to suspend but not discharge existed for employee whose arrest caused him to be absent for 1 day, in spite of fact that employee had previously signed last-chance agreement on attendance; employee was ultimately cleared of the charges and the arbitrator reasoned that, in spite of last-chance agreement, incarceration was beyond employee's control).

[5]108 LA 225 (Allen, Jr., 1997).

[6]102 LA 652 (Dybeck, 1993). See also Metropolitan Transit Auth., 98 LA 793 (Allen, Jr., 1992) (9-year bus driver with no record of excessive absence who was incarcerated for 2½ weeks, reported to work immediately upon release, and spoke honestly about his incarceration presented sufficient mitigating circumstances to justify reinstatement without back pay).

[7]See also Sammons & Sons, 96 LA 216 (Darrow, 1990) (reinstating employee who missed over 3 consecutive workdays because of incarceration because employee's wife notified employer of her husband's absence and employer failed to give employee 2 written warnings, as required by contract).

[8]106 LA 879 (O'Grady, 1996).

[9]109 LA 413 (Duff, 1997).

case was completed. As a result, the employee's incarceration prior to conviction or acquittal could not be used against him.

In cases where an employee's absence was for a reason other than incarceration and the incarceration was found to be a coincidence, the grievance may be sustained.[10]

D. Refusal of Other Employees to Work With the Grievant

If the employer can show a nexus between the nature of the crime and the work environment, employees may not be reinstated, mitigating circumstances notwithstanding. This rationale requires an examination of the nature of the work performed and the effect of reinstatement on the grievant's co-workers. In *North Oakland Medical Centers*,[11] the discharge of an employee convicted of stabbing his former wife's boyfriend was upheld. The employee was a food service aide who had a history of angry confrontations with his co-workers, and the co-workers expressed concern about his return. Their fear was compounded because he worked in the kitchen, giving him ready access to knives.

III. "Workplace Nexus" in the Public Sector: Public Trust

Public employees may be held to a higher standard, implying a public trust to be upheld. Even in such instances, however, a nexus between the workplace and the off-duty conduct must be established. The nexus distinction can be seen in two separate cases involving Ohio state troopers. Both cases were decided by the same arbitrator. Both grievants were suffering financial difficulties and were disciplined because of the resulting repercussions.

In the first case, the officer, a 16-year employee, had undergone a divorce and then filed for bankruptcy.[12] Calls were made to the highway patrol about late payments; as a result, the officer was given a 10-day suspension for bringing discredit on the service. The arbitrator

---

[10]City of Albuquerque, 106 LA 577 (White, 1996) (reinstating employee after he took Family and Medical Leave Act (FMLA) leave to care for his mother while also serving 9-month sentence on home detention because reason for FMLA leave was valid; fact that employee ended up serving limited time in jail simultaneously did not change result, because employee was unaware that he would be serving jail time at time he requested FMLA leave); Indianapolis Water Co., 102 LA 316 (Duff, 1994) (ordering reinstatement after employee called in sick while also incarcerated for intoxication; arbitrator reasoned that, even if employee was not incarcerated, he was too sick from drinking to be at work next day). But see Hospital Cent. Servs., 109 LA 785 (D'Eletto, 1997) (employee's job preserved only during period of incarceration, which coincided with workers' compensation leave; once legitimate leave expired, if employee was still in jail, he could be found to have abandoned job).

[11]106 LA 488 (Daniel, 1996).

[12]State of Ohio, 105 LA 110 (Feldman, 1995).

found the activities that triggered the calls from creditors were clearly off-duty events, there was no reflection on the service, and there was no nexus with the officer's employment to merit any discipline. In the second case, a different trooper took a vehicle home because he was required to be available for emergency recall.[13] The fact that his phone had been cut off affected his ability to be on call. His 5-day suspension was reduced to a 2-day suspension because there was a nexus between the employment and the financial problems due to the policy allowing troopers to take vehicles home while remaining on call.

Similarly, a nexus has been found to exist when a law enforcement officer conducts herself in a manner that violates the oath to serve as an example to the public at all times.[14] In *Township of East Lampeter*,[15] a demotion from corporal to patrol officer on administrative duty was upheld for an officer who violated a protection from abuse order obtained against him by his wife.[16]

However, the nexus to employment is not automatic, despite publicity about a conviction of an employee. In *City of Joliet*,[17] there was no just cause found to discharge a laboratory technician in the wastewater treatment plant where the conviction for arson and conspiracy was widely reported in the local news without reference to the identity of the employer and where the individual cooperated with the government in an ongoing investigation.

In *Central Arkansas Transit Authority*,[18] the discharge of a bus driver for just cause was upheld because she had an off-duty driving while intoxicated conviction and therefore was uninsurable through the authority's insurance.[19]

---

[13]State of Ohio, 105 LA 361 (Feldman, 1995).

[14]City of Las Vegas, 105 LA 398, 404 (Robinson, 1995) (24-year firefighters' discharge upheld for shoplifting while off-duty where "the theft was a serious and repeated infraction of the law" that brought discredit on department); City of Rogers City, 110 LA 92 (Daniel, 1997) (discharge upheld of police officer convicted of misdemeanor of providing alcoholic beverages to minor, despite minor being officer's fiancée); Orange County, 108 LA 216 (Throttle, 1997) (discipline of bus driver for careless driving citation while off duty has nexus to job because driving record is pertinent and relevant to job of transporting children); City of Saginaw, 109 LA 188 (Daniel, 1997) (discharge upheld of building inspector convicted of larceny for taking copper pipe from vacant house in course of performance of official duties).

[15]105 LA 133 (DiLauro, 1995).

[16]But see City of Mansfield, 105 LA 935 (Shanker, 1995) (suspension for 20 days reduced to 7 days for domestic violence because of off-duty status of incident and question of which spouse provoked incident); City of El Paso, 110 LA 411 (Moore, 1998) (reinstated police officer discharged for off-duty drunk driving where intoxication not established at arbitration hearing and department had no rule about consuming alcoholic beverages while off duty); Veterans Admin. Med. Ctr., 107 LA 965 (Tharp, 1997) (demotion for security officer at medical center where off-duty driving under influence charges would be dropped after participation in rehabilitation program and no publicity arose from incident changed to 1-year suspension with reinstatement thereafter to previous police officer position).

[17]108 LA 7 (Cox, 1996).

[18]107 LA 219 (Allen, 1996).

[19]See also North Oakland Med. Ctrs., 106 LA 488 (Daniel, 1996) (fact that food service aide had been convicted of off-duty stabbing found to have nexus to workplace because of history of angry confrontations with other employees and fact that other employees were concerned about his return to kitchen position where potential weapons were present).

Procedural contractual violations may be grounds for requiring public employers to reinstate employees even though a clear nexus to the employment relationship can be found. In *City of Newark*,[20] reinstatement was ordered of an equipment operator who was discharged for immoral conduct after being convicted of off-duty sexual battery of his 11-year-old niece. The arbitrator found that the employer violated the contractual requirement that a predisciplinary conference be scheduled within 10 working days after acquiring knowledge of the violation.

In *County of Napa*,[21] there was no just cause found to discipline a county corrections officer for failing to notify management of her plan to marry a state prison inmate where the officer was not marrying a county inmate incarcerated at a facility where she served.

IV. The Nexus Requirement in Federal Sector Cases

Generally, adverse actions may be taken against federal government employees "only for such cause as will promote the efficiency of the service."[22] Thus, a nexus must be found between the misconduct and efficiency of the service. This applies to both off-duty and on-duty conduct.[23]

In *United States Marine Corps*,[24] the arbitrator explained that the standard of review for a letter of reprimand and letter of caution was just cause. Under the master labor agreement between the Marine Corps and the American Federation of Government Employees, disciplinary actions were letters of reprimand and suspension of 14 days or less, while adverse actions were removals. The standard for disciplinary actions and letters of reprimand under the agreement was just cause.[25] On this basis, the arbitrator upheld the disciplinary written warning.

[20] 107 LA 775 (Kindig, 1996).
[21] 102 LA 590 (Knowlton, 1994).
[22] U.S.C. § 7513(a).
[23] Novo Nordisk of N. Am. v. Genentech, Inc., 77 F.3d 1364 (Fed. Cir., 1996).
[24] 110 LA 955 (Cornelius, 1998).
[25] Id. at 957–58.

Chapter 10

Union Activities

I. Participation in Unlawful Concerted Activities

Encouraging fellow employees to engage in a work slowdown remains a basis for the imposition of discipline,[1] as do quasi-secondary boycott actions.[2] Where the evidence is insufficient to establish that a work stoppage was intended, though, discipline will not be sustained.[3] Likewise, discipline will be rescinded if the employer cannot establish that the disciplined employee took part in the job action.[4]

The proof necessary to sustain a discharge may come from another award. Where one arbitrator had concluded that a sickout had occurred, another arbitrator subsequently held a different group of employees to be collaterally estopped from disputing that they engaged in the illegal activity and then sustained their terminations.[5]

---

[1]Power Flame, Inc., 107 LA 904 (Hilgert, 1996) (employee intended to cause slowdown by inviting colleagues to leave work to attend party during workday).

[2]Merck-Medco RX Servs. of Tex., 110 LA 782 (Baroni, 1998) (shop steward falsified sick leave requests in order to participate in picketing on behalf of shop steward's union against unrelated employee).

[3]Champlain Cable Corp., 108 LA 449 (Sweeney, 1997); New Boston Coke Corp., 107 LA 325 (Kilroy, 1996) (equipment stoppage could not be blamed on relief leader because agreement, practice, and job description did not require him to step into shoes of leader in latter's absence); Army & Air Force Exch. Serv., 106 LA 1103 (Dale, 1996) (union did not have to post notice admitting guilt when advice by union representative to employee not intended to allow her to leave job without permission); Q.C., Inc., 106 LA 987 (McGuryn, 1996) (insufficient evidence that steward encouraged job action where there were 3 versions of a 2-minute conversation and claimed interference with work was, at most, remote, ineffectual, and involved discussion about incidental aspects of employee's job).

[4]Lockheed Martin, 108 LA 482 (Gentile, 1997) (reinstatement appropriate because shop steward neither initiated nor led sickout, but no back pay awarded because steward failed to affirmatively attempt to postpone or stop job action).

[5]Washington Hosp. Ctr., 112 LA 495 (Liebowitz, 1999).

III. Refusals to Cross Picket Lines

A. *Contractual Rights and Obligations*

Discipline resulting from a refusal to cross a picket line may be modified if in imposing it the employer violated a contract's no-strike no-lockout provision.[6]

B. *Other Factors*

In addition to factors such as fear of harm, notice of discipline, or disparate treatment, a grievant's own conduct may be considered in determining whether to sustain or overturn disciplinary action.[7] Discipline imposed for similar offenses that is more severe for the group of employees who refused to cross a picket line than for others has been overturned.[8]

IV. Discipline of Stewards and Other Union Officials

A. *Discipline of Union Officials for Activity Undertaken on Behalf of the Union or Its Members*

3. Insubordination and Self-Help. Where management's order is reasonable and not unlawful, it must be obeyed. For example, in *Stone Container Corp.*,[9] the discharge of a union steward was upheld based in part on his refusal to follow management's directive not to go through unit members' time cards. Self-help defenses are not encouraged.[10]

A union representative's refusal to comply with a direct order based on concerns of an imminent threat to safety must be explicit and in good faith.[11]

---

[6]Hugo Neu-Proler Co., 109 LA 880, 886 (Richman, 1997) (when employees returned to work following 1-day lockout, they refused to cross picket line; however, because their regular work remained available to them, arbitrator limited back pay to the 1 day they were ordered home, indicating that under these circumstances employees "had a contractual right to refuse to cross the picket line, but not at the expense of the employer").

[7]Merck-Medco RX Servs. of Tex., 110 LA 782 (Baroni, 1998).

[8]National Maint. Corp., 107 LA 601 (Nicholas, 1996) (grievant foreman was only one of 85–90 employees discharged; others received only written warning).

[9]106 LA 475, 480 (Gentile, 1996) ("If the grievant felt this [directive] was an infringement on his stewardship responsibilities, the [appropriate] response was to pursue this in the grievance procedure or into the legal forum.").

[10]Transco Ry. Prods., 106 LA 103 (Coyne, 1996) (upholding discharge of union leader where he engaged in self-help after attending management meeting by shouting obscenities at management and leaving work early with 3 other employees to go fishing).

[11]Georgia-Pac. Corp., 106 LA 28 (Kahn, 1995) (just cause existed to suspend union steward who was member of union safety committee where steward did not specify safety reason for refusal to carry 2 bunks on his forklift truck).

5. Absences to Engage in Union Activities. In *Nature's Best*,[12] the discharge of a union steward was upheld in part because he left his work area to report an altercation between 2 employees without first obtaining his supervisor's permission, where the collective bargaining agreement required notification and the steward previously had been warned to get permission from the supervisor before leaving work to investigate, present, and process grievances and problems.

B. Disciplinary Immunity for Behavior Engaged in on Behalf of the Union

When distinguishing protected from unprotected activity, cases continue to rely on location, provocation (or the absence thereof), and the relation of the alleged insubordination to the matter at hand.

Repeatedly interrupting a company president during an informational crew meeting warranted a shop steward's discharge.[13] Likewise, a 5-day suspension was appropriate where activity undertaken under the guise of union representation interfered with an employer's legitimate interest in examining an employee for suspected alcohol intoxication.[14]

Discipline imposed on union representatives who engage in inflammatory conduct, including use of obscene or threatening language where the conduct is not itself egregious, has not been sustained.[15]

---

[12]110 LA 365 (Gentile, 1998).

[13]Converters Paperboard Co., 108 LA 149, 156 (Brodsky, 1997) ("The grievant stepped over the boundary [between protected and nonprotected activity] by letting his own personality (and not his 'union personality') take over his action.").

[14]Corpus Christi Army Depot, 108 LA 1006 (Halter, 1997) (grievant, a union representative, gave gum to suspected inebriate to mask odor of alcohol and then physically restrained employee from being examined by company physician).

[15]Army & Air Force Exch. Serv., 105 LA 332 (Shieber, 1995) (reducing to long-term suspension discharge of local union president who had directed profanity against and gestured wildly at manager and then grabbed security manager on shoulder and attempted to push him out of union office; mitigating factors included impulsive and unpremeditated nature of behavior by individual with no known propensity for violence); EWI, Inc., 108 LA 50 (Brookins, 1997) (vacating discharge of shop steward who muttered "one of these days" during dispute with supervisor after having previously expressed concern to same supervisor about safety hazard in floor); Tennesco Corp., 107 LA 689 (Nicholas, 1996) (vacating discharge of shop steward who called company manager "a bare faced liar" during grievance meeting where grievant was representing another employee at meeting, thus engaging in protected activity; while use of "liar" might have been "bad choice of words," conduct was neither egregious nor malicious).

Chapter 11

Evidentiary and Procedural Considerations

I. Application of Legal Rules of Evidence

Although arbitration proceedings are more informal than judicial proceedings, objections sometimes are raised when the failure to follow procedural rules that govern court actions appears to make a difference in the outcome. For example, in *ABC Rail Products Corp.*,[1] an employer was held not to have met its burden of proving just cause to discharge the grievant for threatening the employee of an outside service where the outside employee gave a written statement but did not appear as a witness. The arbitrator held that the matters contained in the statement were too important to deprive the union of the right to cross-examination.

Hearsay evidence has been held not sufficient to establish just cause to discharge an employee for inadequate production.[2] However, hearsay has been admitted and used as corroboration of firsthand evidence.[3]

Although hearsay evidence usually is admitted subject to argument regarding the weight to be given to it, evidence regarding settlement discussions usually will not be received at all. As one arbitrator explained,

> [E]vidence of settlement offers is normally excluded because of the importance of encouraging full and open settlement discussions. If the parties expected that such discussions could be utilized in later arbitration proceedings, they might be either inhibited in offering settlement

[1]110 LA 574 (Kenis, 1998). Similarly, in IBP Inc., 112 LA 981 (Lumbley, 1999), in setting aside a discharge for fighting, it was held that contradictory hearsay evidence could not outweigh the apparently credible live testimony of the grievant, who was the only witness at the hearing.

[2]Albertson's Inc., 105 LA 913 (Kaufman, 1995).

[3]See PPG Indus., Inc., 109 LA 399 (Grenig, 1997); Kroger Co., 107 LA 801 (Howell, 1996).

> proposals, or else tempted to speak more for the record . . . than in a genuine effort to settle the matter at hand.[4]

Unlike settlement discussions, actual settlements of prior grievances, unless made on a nonprecedential basis, are admissible and may be relied on as evidence of past practice and of the parties' interpretations and understanding of the collective bargaining agreement.[5]

II. Procedural Issues

A. Quantum of Proof

The spectrum of standards for the quantum of proof in discipline and discharge cases remains preponderance of the evidence, clear and convincing evidence, and beyond a reasonable doubt, in ascending order of the amount of proof required. The preponderance of evidence standard is commonly used where no allegations of criminal activity or moral turpitude are involved.[6] The clear and convincing standard is still commonly used in cases involving allegations of criminal activity or moral turpitude.[7] The beyond a reasonable doubt standard, however, may be applied in discharge cases where the alleged criminal activity itself involves moral turpitude.[8]

C. Improperly Procured Evidence

The question of the admissibility of a recording made without the consent of the parties was a serious concern in an improper conduct case. Management in a hotel installed a hidden video camera in the ceiling to effect 24-hour surveillance because it suspected theft was occurring in its banquet office. Instead of obtaining proof of theft, however, the hotel discovered a sexual liaison between a banquet

---

[4]Lithonia Hi Tek-Vermillion, 109 LA 775, 780 (Franckiewicz, 1997). See Fed. R. Evid. 408 ("Evidence of conduct of statements made in compromise negotiations is . . . not admissible."). In Gerstenslager Co., 111 LA 238, 243 (Lalka, 1998), statements of the union steward quoting the grievant were held not admissible both because they were made during settlement discussions and because they were hearsay.

[5]Lithonia Hi Tek-Vermillion, 109 LA 775 (Franckiewicz, 1997).

[6]"I see no reason to depart from the 'preponderance of the evidence' rule. The grievance procedure is a means of effecting dispute resolution. Adopting a more stringent standard would make that end more onerous on both parties." Fermco Envtl. Restoration Mgmt. Co., 104 LA 596, 598 (Cocalis, 1995). In the federal sector, by statute, the evidentiary standard in removal cases is a preponderance of the evidence, regardless of the cause for removal. 5 C.F.R. § 1201.56; 5 U.S.C. § 7701(c)(1)(B). See Naval Weapons Station Earle, 100 LA 1097, 1100 (Robinson, 1993).

[7]Vista Chem. Co., 104 LA 818 (Nicholas, 1995) (discharge for sexual harassment); Yellow Freight Sys., Inc., 106 LA 1062 (Briggs, 1996) (discharge for dishonesty in accepting pay for days not worked); Grand Rapids Area Transit Auth., 107 LA 1132 (Daniel, 1996) (discharge for supplying false information for reports).

[8]Yellow Freight Sys., Inc., 103 LA 731 (Stix, 1994) (discharge for theft); City of Cleveland, 108 LA 912 (Skulina, 1997) (dismissal of police officer convicted of criminal assault for striking child of woman he was living with).

cashier and her supervisor. Both were fired. The arbitrator held the surveillance videotape was admissible even though the sexual acts took place in a locked office. The arbitrator found that the grievant had consented to at least a limited invasion of her privacy by voluntarily engaging in sex on company premises in a room to which at least a dozen other employees had keys and could have abruptly entered.[9]

D. Missing Witnesses

The failure of a party to call an available witness has been held to give rise to the presumption that the witness' testimony would be adverse to that party. One arbitrator opined that the failure to call the key management witness to testify to the events for which the grievant was discharged "seriously weakens the credibility of significant pieces of evidence the company has introduced."[10] The employer had relied only on the absent supervisor's written and oral reports regarding the events leading to the discharge.

III. Validity of Work Rules

Where a collective bargaining agreement referenced the employer's drug and alcohol policy but did not quote it verbatim in the collective bargaining agreement, the plain language of the policy requiring termination of employees who refused to take an alcohol test was held to be secondary to the just cause provision of the contract.[11] Upholding the arbitrator's reinstatement of the grievant, the Eighth Circuit held that because the policy was not written verbatim into the agreement, the arbitrator's determination based on the just cause provision of the contract was appropriate.

The specificity of a work rule in conjunction with the way it is implemented can also affect its enforceability. In one case, an employer had a work rule against "use of intoxicants or illegal substances during working hours."[12] An employee failed a random drug test and

---

[9]Wyndham Franklin Plaza Hotel, 105 LA 186 (Duff, 1995).

[10]Cal-Compact Foods, 105 LA 865, 868 (Oestreich, 1995).

[11]Teamsters Local 238 v. Cargill, Inc., 66 F.3d 988, 150 LRRM 2469 (8th Cir., 1995). While it was found that the grievant had consumed alcohol on the job and had refused to be tested, the arbitrator held that the grievant's many years of good service mitigated against there being just cause for termination. The appellate court reversed the district court's action vacating the arbitration award, affirming the precedence of the collective bargaining agreement. The district court had held that, in ignoring the plain language of the drug and alcohol policy, the award did not draw its essence from the collective bargaining agreement.

[12]Textron Lycoming, 104 LA 1043, 1046 (Duff, 1995). The arbitrator explained, "The parties' explicit prohibitions of the use of illegal substances 'in the work place,' 'while performing work,' and 'during working hours' clearly imply that there is no undertaking to regulate employees' conduct away from work." Id. at 1048. But see Frito-Lay, Inc., 109 LA 850, 851 (Heekin, 1997) (drug testing policy stated, "if the test results return positive, termination will result"; arbitrator upheld dismissal).

was fired. The arbitrator held that because the failed test did not prove that the grievant had used or possessed drugs or alcohol during working hours and because there was no specific rule covering failure of a test, there was no just cause to terminate the grievant. The employer also attempted to support the discipline using an alternative theory based on a general rule requiring employees "to maintain proper standards of conduct." This argument was rejected on the ground that the specific rule superseded the general provision.

X. Res Judicata and Collateral Estoppel Effect of Other Proceedings

A. General Principles

A concept related to res judicata and collateral estoppel is the "law of the case," a term one arbitrator equated to the existence of a binding past practice such as might be recognized in an earlier arbitration award.[13]

B. Res Judicata

The doctrine of res judicata does not automatically apply in arbitration. One arbitrator opined that it applies only if "the forum from which the prior judgment emanated, no matter how competent its jurisdiction, [is] one in which the burdens and standards of proof imposed were essentially the same as would be imposed by the arbitrator before whom the assertion is made."[14] An analysis of the identities of the parties also remains essential to application of the doctrine. In a grievance submitted on behalf of an entire bargaining unit, the arbitrator gave res judicata effect to a prior arbitration decision involving the same contractual provisions and fact patterns, despite the fact that the earlier decision had been filed on behalf of a single grievant. The arbitrator held that there was complete identity of the parties, the union and the employer, and rejected the contention that the prior arbitration's broader scope precluded it from being afforded binding effect.[15]

D. Effect of Determinations of Administrative Tribunals

Administrative tribunal rulings may not govern in all instances. Despite a finding of the Federal Railroad Administration Locomotive

---

[13]United Techs. Automotive, 108 LA 769, 773–74 (Richard, 1997).

[14]City of Hialeah, 110 LA 481, 485 (Richard, 1998).

[15]Arch of Ill., 105 LA 445 (Feldman, 1995). See also West Licking Joint Fire Dist., 1999 WL 638089 (Franckiewicz, 1999) (prior arbitration regarding relative seniority of 2 employees binding even though grievant in second arbitration did not participate in first matter; same union and employer were parties in both arbitrations).

Engineer Review Board that an employee who had failed a drug test was required to attend drug rehabilitation counseling before reinstatement of his federal license,[16] an arbitrator in a subsequent proceeding found that the drug test was flawed and had ordered the employcc rcinstated with back pay.[17] The license was a prerequisite to holding the position. The union sought enforcement of the arbitration award in district court. The court remanded the case to the arbitrator for clarification. The arbitrator clarified that the employee, who by now had had his license reinstated, was to be reinstated to his position but that he would not receive back pay for the period of time during which his license was suspended.[18]

XI. New Evidence

A. *After-Acquired Evidence*

In autumn 1995, the U.S. Supreme Court held that after-acquired evidence could be used to limit recovery in an age discrimination action but could not be used to defeat the claim.[19] Since then, courts have applied the doctrine in employment cases in a variety of contexts. The vast majority of these cases follow the lead of *McKennon*, although it has been distinguished by some courts.[20] Many of the suits involve résumé fraud;[21] some involve job misconduct.[22] Courts have emphasized that after-acquired evidence is an affirmative defense that must be specifically pleaded and proved by the employer.[23]

---

[16]National R.R. Adjustment Bd., First Div. Award No. 24682 (1996).

[17]Id.

[18]Id., interpretation 1 (1999).

[19]McKennon v. Nashville Banner Publ'g Co., 513 U.S. 352 (1995).

[20]See, e.g., Schiavello v. Delmarva Sys. Corp., 61 F. Supp. 2d 110 (D. Del., 1999) (after-acquired evidence of fraud can be complete defense to employment claim); Cedeno v. Montclair State Univ., 725 A.2d 38, 79 FEP Cases 364 (N.J. Super. Ct. App. Div., 1999) (discrimination plaintiff who was statutorily barred from obtaining public employment because of previous criminal conviction held not able to maintain claim for wrongful discharge from position he could not lawfully hold in first place, while noting that in general after-acquired evidence will not defeat claim but merely limit damages); Lewis v. Fisher Serv. Co., 495 S.E.2d 440, 13 IER Cases 1043 (S.C., 1998) (no recovery for plaintiff fired for tape-recording conversations with supervisor in light of "serious offense" language in handbook and after-acquired evidence of similar misconduct in previous positions).

[21]Trico Tech. Corp. v. Montiel, 949 S.W.2d 308, 13 IER Cases 35 (Tex., 1997) (after-acquired evidence of material misrepresentations on job application held not to affect punitive damage workers' compensation retaliation action award, but back pay limited to period from date of unlawful discharge to date employer discovered evidence of employee's misconduct); Crawford Rehab. Servs. v. Weissman, 938 P.2d 540, 12 IER Cases 1071 (Colo., 1997) (following McKennon, claim allowed but no damages awarded to plaintiff who failed to disclose previous termination and misrepresented previous experience).

[22]O'Day v. McDonnell Douglas Helicopter Co., 959 P.2d 792, 13 IER Cases 1868 (Ariz., 1998) (workplace theft limited recovery in tortious wrongful discharge claim but served as complete bar to recovery in contract claim); Castle v. Rubin, 78 F.3d 654 (D.C. Cir., 1996) (limited back pay awarded to plaintiff fired for poor performance where employer later found employee had plagiarized work product).

[23]Sheehan v. Donlen Corp., 173 F.3d 1039 (7th Cir., 1999) (using after-acquired evidence as affirmative defense requires showing that, if information had been found earlier, it would

After-acquired evidence may be considered in arbitration proceedings when it relates directly to the offense that is the stated basis of the discipline.[24] For example, one arbitrator considered evidence of 11 additional incidences of error discovered after the grievant was discharged in finding that an employer had just cause for terminating the grievant; those "subsequent occurrences are so closely related to the event or events leading to the discharge, in substantial effect, to constitute an extension or continuation or integral part" of what led to the discharge.[25] Another arbitrator considered after-acquired videotape evidence of a grievant at a race track because the videotape supported the discipline of the grievant, who had claimed he was ill, for culpable conduct relating to absences.[26]

While after-acquired evidence may not be adequate to deny a grievance, it may, in accordance with *McKennon*, limit the remedy. For example, one arbitrator found there was no just cause to discharge a grievant based on a videotape of an incident of alleged theft, despite after-acquired evidence proving another incident of identical misconduct. However, while sustaining the grievance, the arbitrator denied any remedy, including refusing to reinstate the grievant, based on the after-acquired evidence.[27]

B. Postdischarge Conduct

Generally, a grievant's posttermination conduct is irrelevant to the issue of just cause, because the conduct did not factor into the discharge decision.[28] Postdischarge conduct, like after-acquired evidence, can be relevant to the remedy, however. In one case, it was

have been grounds for discipline or discharge); Jones v. Board of Trustees of Cmty. College Dist. No. 508, 75 F. Supp. 2d 885 (N.D. Ill., 1999) (employer waived affirmative defense of after-acquired evidence by not raising it in pleadings); Red Deer v. Cherokee County, 183 F.R.D. 642, 78 FEP Cases 1463 (N.D. Iowa, 1999) (employer must plead and prove after-acquired evidence as affirmative defense).

[24]C & D Techs., Inc., No. 97-048, 1998 WL 1057710 (Goldstein, 1998) (considering after-acquired evidence of infractions relating to incident giving rise to 3-day suspension); Franklin County Sheriff, 1998 WL 1048298 (Briggs, 1998) (considering after-acquired evidence of misrepresentation in addition to evidence related to reason for discharge given at time of termination, because employer discovered after-acquired evidence during investigation of events related to discharge and immediately informed grievant of additional basis for termination). But see Kaiser Sand & Gravel Co., 1999 WL 269723 (Oestreich, 1999) (refusing to consider after-acquired evidence of fraud directly related to reason for discharge because its existence only underscored insufficiency of employer's investigation before discharge).

[25]Bell Fed. Credit Union, 1999 WL 705017, at p. 38 (Neas, 1999).

[26]Retail Mkts. Co., 1999 WL 752113 (Duff, 1999).

[27]Bowater, Inc., FMCS No. 97-13213, 1997 WL 878268, at p. 17 (Nolan, 1997) (because previous "theft would itself justify his discharge, [grievant] is not entitled to reinstatement or to back pay, despite the Company's erroneous discharge" for subsequent incident).

[28]Osram Sylvania, Inc. v. Teamsters Local 528, 87 F.3d 1261, 1265, 152 LRRM 2808 (11th Cir., 1996) (reversing district court's decision vacating arbitration award, noting that posttermination conduct of employee "had no bearing on whether the employee's conduct constituted just cause for firing"); Tecumseh Prods. Co., 1999 WL 638194 (Frockt, 1999) (posttermination arrest not considered in assessing whether discharge was for just cause). But see Reliance Steel Co., 113 LA 816 (Gentile, 1999) (posttermination verbal abuse during telephone call considered in determining grievant's attitude about his unacceptable behavior; grievance denied).

found that misconduct that occurred after the decision to discharge but before implementation of the termination was posttermination conduct that would not be considered in determining whether there was just cause for the discharge, but it would be considered on the issue of reinstatement.[29]

C. Reopening the Record to Accept New Evidence

There must be a compelling reason to reopen the record after completion of a hearing but before a decision has been issued.[30] For example, an employer's request to reopen a discharge hearing to admit evidence that the grievant had engaged in fraudulent conduct that could preclude recovery was denied because there was a failure of due process in the original disciplinary process that the new evidence, which was unrelated to the due process issue, would not have cured.[31]

Similarly, in response to a request to submit new evidence on a grievance of a 5-day suspension, the arbitrator declined to reopen the hearing because new data that went to the degree of discipline could not be useful to a decision based on the necessity of imposing any discipline.[32]

---

[29]Heritage Cable Vision of San Jose, 112 LA 1 (Feller, 1999) (sustaining grievance but denying reinstatement based on posttermination conduct).

[30]Glendale Aluminum Co., FMCS No. 98-01359, 1998 WL 1041396 (Monat, 1998) (refusing to consider evidence submitted after hearing when evidence had been available earlier).

[31]Chicago Transit Auth., 1999 WL 908648 (Wolff, 1999); Southern Foodservice Mgmt., Inc., FMCS No. 980929-17147 (Lalka, 1999) (record reopened on limited issue of proper implementation of arbitration award).

[32]Delaware County Sheriff's Office, 113 LA 851 (Brodsky, 1999).

Chapter 12

Remedies for Inappropriate Discipline

I. General Considerations

Remedies must draw their "essence" from the collective bargaining agreement.[1]

A. Make Whole

Make whole is often ordered where the employer fails to provide procedural due process or follow agreed-upon progressive discipline, although the seriousness of the conduct of the employer and the grievant are factors in the determination of what is appropriate.[2]

B. Partial Relief

Mitigating factors frequently cause arbitrators to grant only partial relief.[3] An employee terminated for absenteeism was reinstated

---

[1]Marrowbone Dev. Co. v. District 17, 147 F.3d 296, 158 LRRM 2449 (4th Cir., 1998).

[2]Wyndham Franklin Plaza Hotel, 105 LA 186 (Duff, 1995) (failure to provide union representation during investigation of misconduct); Mount Sinai Hosp., 105 LA 1047 (Duff, 1995) (failure to follow progressive discipline procedures contained in published 3-step process warranted); Southern Frozen Foods, 107 LA 1030 (Giblin, 1996) (discharged employee denied industrial due process when employer failed to investigate his version of events); Kroger Co., 108 LA 417 (Baroni, 1997) (failure of employer to conduct predischarge hearing and proper investigation).

[3]Lenzing Fibers Corp., 105 LA 423 (Sergent, 1995) (grievant discharged under last-chance agreement for leaving early reinstated because he was denied representation but without back pay because he attempted to take advantage of faulty clock); Champion Internat'l Corp., 108 LA 218 (Barron, 1997) (grievant discharged for leaving post reinstated without back pay because of other discipline in his file and placed at second step of progressive discipline); Mason & Hanger Corp., 109 LA 957 (Jennings, 1998) (grievant discharged for fighting reinstated without

in *Penske Truck Leasing*[4] because he was not given proper notice. However, back pay was not awarded, because the employee did not have a good excuse for missing work on the day in question.[5] In *Webster Industries*,[6] the grievant was discharged for overstaying a break. The arbitrator, finding the employer should have employed progressive discipline, sustained the grievance in part and reinstated the employee without back pay, justifying the remedy under the totality of the circumstances, which included numerous counselings for performance as well as other issues.

Unemployment benefits may be deducted from a back pay award.[7] However, this move is controversial. On the one hand, because the obligation to repay lies with the individual, union advocates argue that there is no reason to give the employer credit and deduct the amount of unemployment benefits from the back pay award. On the other hand, the concept of "make whole" does not recognize a windfall to the individual, which no deduction would effect.

In *General Mills*,[8] the grievant was reinstated after being discharged for absenteeism under a point system. The arbitrator concluded that "[t]he Union has demonstrated that mitigating circumstances existed, including the Grievant's long and good work record and the exceptional and extraordinary occurrences which tainted and mitigated the absences . . . such that . . . discharge was not warranted in this case."[9]

In *Norshipco*,[10] the arbitrator considered mitigating factors in reinstating without back pay a grievant who was involved in an

---

back pay because grievant had unblemished record, no punches were thrown, other employee not injured, employer's psychologist found no evidence of psychopathology, and offense not directly related to employer's product); Arch of Ill., 107 LA 178 (Feldman, 1995) (employee discharged for sleeping on job reinstated without back pay based on long service and fact that previous sleeping incident occurred 13 years earlier); Bethlehem Structural Prods. Corp., 106 LA 452 (Witt, 1995) (employee discharged for physically assaulting crew leader reinstated based on employee's diagnosed depression and other factors, but without back pay because grievant disabled by depression and unable to work); Valuerx Pharmacy Program, 111 LA 1063 (Allen, 1999) (grievant discharged for failure to return from medical leave reinstated but without back pay because she was lax in keeping employer informed of situation); Vons Cos., Inc., 106 LA 740 (Darrow, 1996) (employee discharged for testing positive for alcohol reinstated without back pay based on grievant's unblemished previous record, entering employee assistance program during suspension and before discharge actually occurred, and having made excellent progress in rehabilitation).

[4]110 LA 833 (Bumpass, 1998).

[5]See also Harmon House Convalescent Ctr., 109 LA 477, 480 (Felice, 1977) (employee discharged under "no fault" attendance policy without benefit of representation reinstated but without back pay because overall attendance record "not laudable"); Missouri Gas Energy, 110 LA 164 (Madden, 1998) (employee discharged for absenteeism reinstated because denied due process but without back pay because she had missed approximately 40% of available work time in preceding 3 years); Unibus, Inc., 110 LA 597 (Skulina, 1998) (employee discharged for absenteeism reinstated because last absence in question approved by employer; however, back pay denied because it was clear grievant had missed too much work time).

[6]107 LA 147 (Statham, 1996).

[7]Ralphs Grocery Co., 108 LA 718 (Prayzich, 1997) (unemployment benefits received to be deducted from back pay award).

[8]112 LA 152 (Bailey, 1998).

[9]Id. at 158.

[10]105 LA 529 (Hockenberry, 1995).

altercation with a knife-wielding employee. The principal mitigating factor was provocation of the grievant during the altercation.

II. Components of a Make Whole Remedy

Back pay and reinstatement are the most common elements of a make whole remedy.[11] However, arbitrators often exercise their authority to fashion equitable remedies.[12]

A. Traditional Components

Reinstatement may be conditioned on the grievant's fitness for duty.[13] Additionally, the grievant's effort to mitigate back pay losses may also be taken into account.[14] If a grievant conceals interim earnings, back pay may be forfeited for the periods of concealment.[15]

B. Other Possible Components

In addition to reinstatement and back pay, arbitrators may award other relief to the grievant, including restoring seniority,[16] vacation, holiday and leave credits, and unreimbursed medical expenses.[17]

---

[11]See Pegasus Broadcasting v. NLRB, 82 F.3d 511, 152 LRRM 2065 (1st Cir., 1996).

[12]Teamsters Local 878 v. Commercial Warehouse Co., 84 F.3d 299, 152 LRRM 2347 (8th Cir., 1996) (arbitrator did not exceed authority when he awarded employee 3 months' back pay for procedural irregularities where employer failed to provide union chain of custody information and precise basis for discharge until day of arbitration); Yukon Mfg., Inc., 105 LA 339 (Brown, 1995) (employer that refused to discharge employees who had paid no union dues ordered to comply in future with contractual union security clause); San Benito Health Found., 105 LA 263 (Levy, 1995) (grievant awarded vacation and sick leave accrual, out-of-pocket medical expenses incurred and paid, and interest at 10% if back pay not paid within 12 working days).

[13]Peoples Natural Gas, 105 LA 37 (Murphy, 1995) (employee discharged for poor performance reinstated to 12-week probationary period during which he was to be given additional training and have progress monitored); New Orleans S.S. Ass'n, 105 LA 79, 85 (Nicholas, Jr., 1995) (grievant discharged for testing positive for off-duty drug use reinstated conditioned on certification by "a recognized physician as being fully capable and drug free"); Arvin Indus., 109 LA 539 (Keenan, 1997) (employee discharged for fighting reinstated but required to successfully complete a program for rage control); Owens-Brockway Plastic Prods., Inc., 109 LA 655 (Bailey, 1997) (grievant discharged for making threatening remarks reinstated after being found mentally ill and absence converted to medical leave with provision that grievant be permitted to return to work on release by company approved psychiatrist); Safeway, Inc., 109 LA 768 (DiFalco, 1997) (employee discharged for sexually harassing comments reinstated to different working environment conditioned on his attending sensitivity training); Mine Workers (UMW) Dist. 6, 110 LA 84 (Ruben, 1997) (bookkeeper discharged for insubordination, absenteeism, and poor performance found to be suffering from depression and reinstated on submission of appropriate medical evidence of present fitness and ability to work); Cross Oil Ref. Co., 111 LA 1013 (Bumpass, 1999) (emotionally disturbed grievant discharged after customer complaint reinstated conditioned on proof of mental and emotional fitness submitted by psychologist or psychiatrist selected jointly by union and employer).

[14]Ralphs Grocery Co., 108 LA 718 (Prayzich, 1997).

[15]Lithibar Matik, 112 LA 957 (Sugerman, 1999) (grievant must forfeit back pay for each month in which he concealed and did not report interim earnings).

[16]District of Columbia Pub. Schs., 105 LA 1037 (Johnson, 1995); Facility Mgmt. of La., 106 LA 879 (O'Grady, 1996); Plymouth Tube Co., 108 LA 1016 (Heekin, 1997).

[17]San Benito Health Found., 105 LA 263 (Levy, 1995); King Soopers, Inc., 112 LA 585 (Watkins 1999) (in supplemental proceeding, grievant awarded pay for Sunday work as part of back pay because grievant had worked most Sundays during base period).

The increased tax bite caused by taking a substantial amount of back pay in 1 tax year is an example of an expense incurred by the grievant related to the back pay orders. The payment to the employee in a lump sum frequently moves the recipient to a higher tax bracket. These increased tax payments could be requested as part of the remedy to a grievant. Thus, reimbursement could be claimed for the additional income tax liability incurred because of lump sum back pay awards.

C. *Remedies Not Generally Included*

Arbitrators usually do not award damages that go beyond making the grievant whole.[18] Punitive damages will ordinarily only be awarded if provided for in the collective bargaining agreement.[19] Interest on back pay owed by the employer is sometimes awarded,[20] but usually is not.[21] Nor will arbitrators normally award a party its expenses for the arbitration[22] or for attorneys' fees.[23]

D. *Reinstatement With Back-Pay Computation*

Arbitrators continue to confirm that a full back pay award is intended to put an aggrieved employee in the same financial position as if the improper suspension or discharge had never occurred.[24] Back pay is usually equal to wages lost as a result of the improper discipline.[25]

---

[18]See Hill & Sinicropi, Remedies in Arbitration, 2d ed., 436–38 (BNA Books, 1991).

[19]Ralphs Grocery Co., 108 LA 718 (Prayzich, 1997) (union's request for award of punitive damages rejected because nothing in contract supported it and there was no showing of bad faith on part of employer).

[20]Champlain Cable Corp., 108 LA 449, 453 (Sweeney, 1997) ("interest is a natural and consequential result from a breach of contract"); Laidlaw Transit Inc., 109 LA 647 (Landau, 1997) (interest awarded because of employer's dilatory and bad faith conduct).

[21]Machinists, 109 LA 339 (Bernhardt, 1997).

[22]Safeway Stores, Inc., 107 LA 448 (Snider, 1996) (expenses not allowed under contract provision awarding costs to winner because neither party was sole, clear winner); Okonite Co., 112 LA 501 (Frockt, 1999) (where agreement is silent, parties must share $30 fee for arbitrator panel).

[23]See Champlain Cable Corp., 108 LA 718 (Prayzich, 1997) (no award of attorneys' fees to union in absence of bad faith on part of employer); Schnuck Mkts., Inc., 111 LA 288 (Hilgert, 1998) (attorneys' fees not allowed either employer or union); H. Meyer Dairy Co., 105 LA 583 (Sugerman, 1995) (union's request for its attorneys' fees as part of "costs" of arbitration to be awarded under contract provision when position of either party is unreasonable not allowed).

[24]Laidlaw Transit, Inc., 109 LA 647, 649–50 (Landau, 1997) (appropriate remedy for unjustly suspended bus driver was back pay sufficient to make employee whole for any losses suffered); Plymouth Tube Co., 108 LA 1016, 1019–20 (Heekin, 1997); Ralphs Grocery Co., 108 LA 718, 721 (Prayzich, 1997) (back pay not intended to penalize employer but to make grievant whole by placing him in same financial position that he would have been in had employer not acted wrongfully); Kroger Co., 108 LA 417, 421–22 (Baroni, 1997).

[25]University of Cincinnati, 105 LA 946, 949 (Katz, 1996) (discharged employee ordered reinstated with full back pay); Rexam Graphics, 111 LA 1176, 1186 (Gangle, 1998) (even though employee not reinstated, arbitrator awarded grievant back pay for period between discharge and date of hearing).

1. Time Period. Where the reasonableness of the length of the actual suspension is excessive or unreasonable, back pay may be awarded.[26] The back pay award may also be limited to the period during which the employee was physically able to work.[27]

2. Rate. The back pay rates are measured by the wages the employee would have earned but for the unjust suspension or discharge.[28]

The "average earnings" formula is appropriate where the nature of the grievant's job, the level of earnings, and the employer's business have all remained relatively constant during the predischarge and back pay periods.[29] The "average hours of work" formula calculates the average number of hours worked by the grievant per pay period during a representative period before discharge.[30] It is used where the grievant has established a regular work pattern and the employer's business is not seasonal or where the employer's wage rates have not changed during the back pay period.[31]

Arbitrators also have used other employees' work records as guidance to calculate the back pay period if the wage rate, work, working conditions, and terms of employment are similar to the grievant's.[32] This formula is most useful in cases where there are long back pay periods involving multiple pay periods and pay changes.[33] However, if the grievant was replaced after discharge, a "replacement employee" formula, taking the actual earnings of the replacement employee as

---

[26]Laidlaw Transit, 109 LA 647, 649–50 (Landau, 1997) (unjustly disciplined employee entitled to back pay for 2 days beyond end of suspension after unemployment compensation ended, but not entitled to back pay for period where he received unemployment compensation); Weyerhaeuser Forest Prods., 108 LA 26, 32 (Levak, 1997) (employee improperly discharged for refusing to submit to drug tests but only entitled to back pay for part of suspension period because he should have submitted to tests and grieved later).

[27]Exxon Co., 110 LA 534, 539–40 (Allen, 1998) (disabled employee terminated for job-related stress condition caused by problems with co-workers awarded partial back pay where employer refused to transfer her to another team); Owens-Brockway Plastic Prods., Inc., 109 LA 655, 658 (Bailey, 1997) (mentally ill employee unjustly discharged reinstated and placed on 1-year medical leave, but without back pay); Price Indus., Inc., 109 LA 1, 4 (Gordinier, 1997) (pregnant employee improperly discharged for absenteeism reinstated but without back pay because she should have been granted Family and Medical Leave Act leave).

[28]USAir Shuttle, 108 LA 496, 499 (Hockenberry, 1997) (back pay award equal to wages employee would have earned during suspension); Champlain Cable Corp., 108 LA 449, 453–54 (Sweeney, 1997) (award of back pay includes gross earnings that grievant lost in addition to reimbursement for all medical expenses incurred because of loss of medical insurance); United States Steel Mining Co., 105 LA 524, 528 (Roberts, 1995) (back pay held appropriate remedy for employee wrongfully deprived of work opportunity).

[29]Newport Steel Corp., 100 LA 1007 (Gibson, 1993); Niemand Indus., 94 LA 669, 670 (Nolan, 1990) (one method of estimating gross pay is to make a projection of average earnings based on grievant's experience before discharge).

[30]Safelite Glass Corp., 1997 WL 753723 (Hooper, 1997) (back pay computed at straight time for average number of hours worked per week in last 3 months before termination).

[31]Newport Steel Corp., 100 LA 1007, 1010 (Gibson, 1993).

[32]Washington Hosp., 110 LA 1055 (Franckiewicz, 1998); Fingerhut, 105 LA 1146, 1152 (Lundberg, 1995) (laid-off employees denied work because temporary employees hired before they were recalled entitled to back pay based on hours worked by temporary employees).

[33]Newport Steel Corp., 100 LA 1007, 1010 (Gibson, 1993) ("representative employee" formula most useful in cases where there are long back pay periods involving different jobs and pay changes).

a reasonable measure of what the grievant would have earned, may be used.[34]

The "representative employee" and "replacement employee" methods continue to be favored because they make adjustments for additional overtime that may have been available to the grievant during the time of suspension or discharge as well as wage increases that may have come into effect during that time.[35] However, the "average earnings" and "average hours" formulas are useful where the grievant's past work record shows chronic absenteeism, refusal of overtime opportunities, or other circumstances indicating that the grievant's weekly income would have been significantly different from that of the replacement or representative employee.[36]

3. Amount. Benefits provided for in the collective bargaining agreement are included with back pay,[37] including vacation pay,[38] unless the employee had received unused vacation at the time of discharge.[39] Likewise, paid holidays are generally included in a back pay award.[40]

Appropriate reductions may be made in back pay awards where necessary in order to reflect the grievant's historical employment problems, such as chronic absenteeism,[41] or reflect the percentage of time that the grievant would likely have been absent from work during the back pay period.[42]

Arbitrators may modify back pay awards to apportion fault as between the employee and the employer.[43] For example, where a

[34]Vision-Ease, 102 LA 1106 (Mathews, 1994) (lost overtime award based on actual overtime pay replacement employee received); Niemand Indus., 94 LA 669, 670 (Nolan, 1990) (back pay for wrongfully discharged grievant based on replacement's earnings where replacement's seniority and job experience virtually duplicated grievant's); National Metal & Steel Corp., 86 LA 217, 219 (Rothschild, 1985) (improperly demoted employee who lost opportunity for overtime pay awarded same overtime pay as earned by replacement).

[35]Niemand Indus., 94 LA 669, 670 (Nolan, 1990) (using replacement or peer employee as reference point preferred because it automatically includes overtime pay and wage raises).

[36]Nevada Power, 110 LA 949, 955 (Ross, 1998) (back pay did not include overtime because employee had been reluctant to work overtime in past).

[37]Plymouth Tube Co., 108 LA 1016, 1020 (Heekin, 1997) (reinstatement award included all back pay, benefits, and seniority lost); Champlain Cable Corp., 108 LA 449 (Sweeney, 1997); Kroger Co., 108 LA 417, 422 (Baroni, 1997) (back pay award included full seniority, back pay, and other benefits that had been discontinued as result of termination).

[38]Park 'n Fly, Inc., 108 LA 611, 612 (Marino, 1997) (discharged employee entitled to back pay for period she was on vacation despite fact that she was simultaneously working second job, because vacation time belongs to grievant); San Benito Health Found., 105 LA 263, 264 (Levy, 1995) (employer that improperly discharged employee ordered to pay for 2 weeks of vacation and to put 3 weeks in grievant's vacation account).

[39]MRS Transp. Co., 95 LA 514, 518 (Massey, 1995) (if employee had not been improperly discharged and vacation had been taken during that period of time as required by contract, employee's earning capacity would have been reduced by equivalent of vacation time; therefore, offset against back pay award for amounts already paid as unused vacation was proper).

[40]King Soopers, Inc., 112 LA 585 (Watkins, 1999) (grievant awarded holiday pay).

[41]Missouri Gas Energy, 110 LA 164, 169 (Madden, 1998) (reinstatement but no back pay awarded where employee had been absent 40% of time in past 3 years).

[42]United States Can Co., 104 LA 863, 870 (Briggs, 1995) (improperly discharged employee only entitled to 35% of what her full-time earnings would have been had she remained in company's employ because she had been absent about 65% of time in past 3 years).

[43]Penske Truck Leasing, 110 LA 833, 837 (Bumpass, 1998) (employee unjustly discharged for prior absenteeism reinstated without back pay where he had no excuse for his absence

grievant and an employer are equally at fault, it is possible for an award to halve the back pay that otherwise would have been due.[44] In a situation where the arbitrator might normally award no back pay, where the employer acted to unreasonably delay bringing the case to arbitration, thereby unreasonably extending the unemployment period, some amount of back pay may be awarded.[45]

4. Duty to Mitigate / Interim Earnings. Back pay may be wholly or partially denied to employees who fail to make reasonable efforts to mitigate their losses.[46] The burden of proving that the employee did not make a good faith effort to mitigate is on the employer.[47]

The mitigation duty may require a grievant to accept a position similar in duties, wages, hours, and location to the former position.[48] The due diligence standard by which the mitigation effort is evaluated does not require the employee to succeed in finding alternative employment.[49]

Voluntarily leaving any interim position (even a dissimilar one) without good cause may constitute a breach of the employee's mitigation duty.[50] Where a grievant voluntarily leaves an interim position without good cause, an arbitrator may reduce the back pay award by the amount that the employee would have earned had he retained

---

when employer decided to discharge him); Union Carbide Corp., 110 LA 667, 673 (Caraway, 1998) (discharge too severe where employee responsible for equipment malfunction but recovery limited to back pay because of his negligence); Marriott Servs. Corp., 109 LA 689, 692–93 (Kaufman, 1997) (sales associate improperly discharged because investigation was improperly conducted reinstated without back pay because erred giving discount to customer); Smith Fiberglass Prods., 108 LA 225, 229 (Allen, Jr., 1997) (employee who was hiding from husband who had threatened her unjustly discharged for absenteeism but only awarded back pay for 6 weeks of 9 months she was absent because she should have made certain that she had authorized personal leave).

[44]Washington Hosp., 110 LA 158, 163–64 (Franckiewicz, 1998) (employee unjustly discharged for absenteeism reinstated but with 50% back pay on grounds that he never would have reached discharge stage of discipline procedure but for his abysmal attendance record); Means Indus., Inc., 108 LA 831, 832 (Ellmann, 1997) (manic-depressive employee improperly discharged for absenteeism reinstated with only 50% back pay where management showed effort to seek accommodation).

[45]Laidlaw Transit, Inc., 109 LA 647, 651 (Landau, 1997) (grievant entitled to back pay where company acted in bad faith by paying little attention to repeated requests to resume arbitration).

[46]J.L. Clark, 108 LA 1012, 1015 (Gordinier, 1997) (wrongfully discharged employee not entitled to back pay where she made no attempt to mitigate losses); Ralphs Grocery Co., 108 LA 718, 722 (Prayzich, 1997) (employee's failure to exercise reasonable diligence to mitigate losses precluded recovery of back pay); Ogden Support Servs., Inc., 104 LA 432, 434 (Weisheit, 1995) (grievant must mitigate lost employment as part of determination of back pay recovery).

[47]Wayne State Univ., 111 LA 906, 908–09 (Daniel, 1998) (employer had burden of proving grievant's failure to mitigate damages); Sammons Communications, Inc., 1995 WL 862383 (Levak, 1995) (burden of proving lack of good faith in mitigating damages is on employer).

[48]Spann Bldg. Maint., 1996 WL 807557 (Hilgert, 1996) (arbitrator refused to award back pay to employee who failed to mitigate damages: he could have accepted job at $3 an hour less than regular rate of pay and continued with grievance).

[49]Sammons Communications, 1995 WL 862383 (Levak, 1995) (determination of whether employee used reasonable effort to mitigate damages does not hinge on whether individual was successful in actually finding employment); Wilen Mfg. Co., 1997 WL 753721 (Hooper, 1997) (grievant's efforts to find other employment must be made in view of all circumstances); Sammons Communications, supra (employee has the duty to seek substantially equivalent employment, taking into account individual's qualifications and relevant job market).

[50]Cone Mills Corp., 106 LA 23, 25 (Nolan, 1995) (although wrongfully discharged employee not obligated to accept work not substantially equivalent to that from which he was fired, once grievant accepts lesser work he may not quit without affecting back pay award).

the interim position.[51] However, where an employee voluntarily leaves an interim position in anticipation of impending reinstatement, the duty to mitigate damages may be deemed fulfilled, and the back pay award remains unaffected.[52]

Generally, consistent with the theory behind make whole relief, back pay awards are often reduced by interim earnings in order to prevent grievants from profiting as a result of their discharge.[53] For purposes of back pay calculations, interim earnings may reflect reductions for interim vacation and holiday pay,[54] interim retirement benefits,[55] and, in many cases, interim unemployment compensation.[56] However, some arbitrators adopt the National Labor Relations Board approach to unemployment insurance, holding that it is a nondeductible collateral benefit rather than an alternative source of income.[57] It has also been held that state employment compensation payments should not be deducted from back pay awards where the payments were made from state funds derived from taxation.[58]

In response to a ruling that interim earnings are going to be deducted from the back pay award, the grievant has a duty to disclose information regarding those earnings.[59] However, back pay awards and deductions are discretionary. An arbitrator's silence as to whether

---

[51]Wayne State Univ., 111 LA 906, 909 (Daniel, 1998) (wrongfully discharged employee entitled to back pay offset by interim earnings he would have received from temporary job had he not quit before being reinstated).

[52]Glover Bottled Gas Corp./Synergy Gas Corp., 91 LA 77, 92–93 (Simons, 1987) (grievant's departure from interim employment in reasonable reliance on union agent's report that his grievance had been sustained and his reinstatement had been ordered did not constitute breach of duty to mitigate damages).

[53]Milbank Mfg. Co., 112 LA 464 (Crider, 1999) (arbitrator awarded grievant back pay offset by any interim earnings he received during period of discharge); City of Okla. City, 1999 WL 269114 (Bankstown, 1999) (status quo restored when back pay award offset by interim earnings); Mansfield Foundry Corp., 105 LA 353, 356 (Coyne, 1995) (reinstatement with full back pay reduced by income from other employment, not including income from private business grievant had both before and after discharge).

[54]Stark County Sanitary Eng'r, 1997 WL 753736 (Ruben, 1997) (back pay will not include compensation for any paid holiday or vacation periods); Toledo Edison, 104 LA 933, 940 (Shanker, 1995) (back pay need not be awarded during time period where employee has taken vacation).

[55]City of Okla. City, 1998 WL 1048331 (Goodman, 1998) (reinstatement with back pay less any retirement benefits employee could have earned).

[56]Mid-Am. Packaging, 111 LA 129 (Bankston, 1998); Washington Hosp., 110 LA 218 (Franckiewicz, 1998); Quaker Oats Co., 110 LA 204, 205–06 (Moreland, 1998) (unemployment compensation to be considered earnings and will offset back pay award); Morrison Constr. Co., 1999 WL 454667 (Brunner, 1999); Howmedica, Inc., 112 LA 587 (Liebowitz, 1999); Ryder Student Transp. Servs., Inc., 108 LA 1124 (Franckiewicz, 1997); Ormet Aluminum Mill Prods., 1997 WL 1068757 (Nelson, 1997); Ralphs Grocery Co., 108 LA 718 (Prayzich, 1997).

[57]Celebrity Ford, 1998 WL 1048300 (Briggs, 1998); Teter Tool & Die, Inc., 1998 WL 409551 (Cohen, 1998); Ryder Student Transp. Servs., Inc., 108 LA 1124 (Franckiewicz, 1997); Fitzpatrick Co., 108 LA 686 (Briggs, 1997); Food & Commercial Workers, 1997 WL 218748 (Marino, 1997).

[58]San Benito Health Found., 105 LA 263, 264 (Levy, 1995) (unemployment compensation paid to grievant by state not deductible from back pay due employee).

[59]ITT Hancock Automotive, 1995 WL 852259 (Daniel, 1995) (grievant ordered to provide employer with necessary information for offsetting back pay award by interim earnings); Nabisco Foods, Inc., 1995 WL 707560 (Briggs, 1995) (grievant required to provide employer with necessary information for calculating deductions of interim earnings and unemployment compensation benefits from back pay award).

certain deductions should be made may be construed as a purposeful omission. It may be argued that no deductions can be made from back pay awards unless specified by the arbitrator.[60]

5. Lost Opportunities. Compensation for lost overtime pay as well as other lost opportunities to which the grievant may be entitled under the terms of the collective bargaining agreement may be included in the computation of back pay in the absence of a contract provision to the contrary.[61] Such additional relief may need to be specifically requested in the grievance.[62]

a. Overtime. Where overtime is speculative or discretionary, it will not be included in the back pay calculation.[63] Whether the overtime is optional or mandatory is important in determining whether damages for lost overtime would be speculative.[64] Lost overtime pay may still be denied even where a grievant had worked significant overtime in the past if it would require the arbitrator to speculate that the grievant would have accepted the overtime offered.[65]

b. Other Lost Opportunities. Other lost opportunities, including promotional possibilities, may be included in the award where they are not speculative.[66]

E. Reinstatement Without Back Pay

Reinstatement may be ordered without back pay. Factors used to determine whether back pay should be omitted or limited include,

---

[60]Operating Eng'rs Local 841 v. Murphy Co., 82 F.3d 185, 189, 152 LRRM 2315 (7th Cir., 1996) (arbitrator silence with regard to offsets in back pay means that no offsets are to be made); Automobile Mechanics' Local No. 701, 1996 WL 556961 (N.D. Ill., 1996), aff'd, 171 F.3d 432, 160 LRRM 2656 (7th Cir., 1999) (arbitrator's failure to exclude certain benefits from arbitration award to be understood to mean that no exclusion exists).

[61]Schwebel Baking Co., 1997 WL 753734 (Ruben, 1997) (incorporation of overtime component into back pay award appropriate when it appears with reasonable certainty that employee would have earned overtime had his employment not been improperly terminated).

[62]International Paper Co., 108 LA 758, 765 (Nicholas, 1997) (grievant not entitled to consequential damages because union did not request them as part of grievance); San Benito Health Found., 105 LA 263, 264 (Levy, 1995) (arbitrator refused to award interest on back pay where union did not request it).

[63]King Soopers, Inc., 112 LA 585 (Watkins, 1999) (back pay awards commonly include vacation and holiday allotments but not discretionary overtime because former can be presumed earned but latter cannot be presumed taken); Morrison Constr. Co., 112 LA 276 (Brunner, 1999) (rejecting overtime request as speculative because grievant failed to provide evidence of specific amount of overtime lost or average weekly overtime amount for worker in grievant's classification); Nevada Power, 110 LA 949 (Ross, 1998) (denying overtime award in light of evidence that grievant had some choice of working overtime and that he was reluctant to work overtime before discharge).

[64]Schwebel Baking Co., 1997 WL 753734 (Ruben, 1997) (overtime back pay awarded where employee generally had to work overtime to complete his normal job responsibilities); Ormet Aluminum Mill Prods., 1997 WL 1068757 (Nelson, 1997) (when it is clear that employee was entitled to and would have worked overtime if not wrongfully discharged, overtime should be included in back pay calculation).

[65]Shell Oil Co., 87 LA 473 (Nicholas, 1986).

[66]U.S. Dep't of Housing, 1996 WL 901992 (Bankston, 1996); Mid-Am. Packaging, 111 LA 129 (Bankston, 1998) (awarding grievant pay raise he would have received had he not been improperly discharged); Board of Dirs., Little Rock Sch. Dist., 110 LA 1114 (Bankston, 1998); Vision-Ease, 102 LA 1106 (Mathews, 1994) (awarding lost attendance bonus).

but are not limited to, the severity of the grievant's conduct,[67] whether the employer used progressive discipline,[68] and whether the employer treated the grievant disparately from other employees found or accused of engaging in the same conduct.[69] Reinstatement without back pay has been ordered in a wide variety of situations, including insubordination,[70] theft of company property,[71] fighting at work,[72] violating work safety rules,[73] overstaying scheduled breaks,[74] engaging in immature acts,[75] testing positive for drug use[76] or alcohol consumption,[77] walking off the job,[78] threatening others with physical harm,[79] and submitting a false employment application.[80]

---

[67]Appleton Papers, Inc., 106 LA 11 (Duff, 1995) (reinstating grievant without back pay because employer resorted to "disciplinary overkill" when it discharged grievant for hitting co-worker over head with cooler lid); Ralphs Grocery Co., 101 LA 634 (Ross, 1993) (reinstating employee without back pay because his refusal to write out and sign statement regarding his knowledge of damage to company fence did not amount to gross insubordination).

[68]SBS Transit Corp., 108 LA 1134 (Skulina, 1997) (reinstating grievant without back pay because employer failed to follow principles of progressive discipline as outlined in collective bargaining agreement); Webster Indus., 107 LA 147 (Statham, 1996).

[69]Packaging Corp., 105 LA 898 (Weisheit, 1995) (employee who walked off job reinstated without back pay because employer-imposed discipline for such activity in past was less severe).

[70]Houston Grinding & Mfg. Co., 106 LA 875 (Shieber, 1996) (reinstating employee who tore up time sheet and held up middle finger while looking directly at acting supervisor); Ralphs Grocery Co., 101 LA 634 (Ross, 1993) (reinstating employee who refused to comply with management order).

[71]Cummings, Inc., 104 LA 1012 (Hart, 1995) (reinstating employee discharged for stealing air freshener dispenser from company's storage area because employer could not prove that grievant removed air freshener from company premises and item taken had minimal value).

[72]Nevada Power, 110 LA 949 (Ross, 1998) (reinstating employee involved in workplace fight); Appleton Papers, Inc., 106 LA 11 (Duff, 1995) (reinstating employee who used excessive retaliatory force in physical altercation).

[73]Interstate Brands Corp., 104 LA 993 (Gentile, 1995) (reinstating employee terminated for violating work rule prohibiting possession of firearms on company property where employee brought unloaded gun to work to sell to another employee).

[74]Century Tel., Inc., 110 LA 528 (Murphy, 1998) (reinstating grievant who either improperly extended breaks or did not properly record time); Webster Indus., 107 LA 147 (Statham, 1996) (reinstating employee who overstayed breaks on 6 separate occasions).

[75]Trailmobile, Inc., 113 LA 182 (Fowler, 1999) (reinstating employee discharged for throwing 6-pound sledgehammer that ricocheted off tub and inadvertently hit co-worker where offense was employee's first and employer-operated plant had excessive horseplay); SBS Transit Corp., 108 LA 1134 (Skulina, 1997) (reinstating employee discharged for taking company bus for joyride through company property, misusing company hotline for childish prank, and lying to company president about his actions).

[76]Montgomery County Gov't, 109 LA 513 (Hockenberry, 1997) (reinstating grievant who tested positive for marijuana use but who claimed he was unwittingly exposed to drug in spaghetti sauce served at party, where grievant had good work record including awards for efficient performance).

[77]Vons Cos., Inc., 106 LA 740 (Darrow, 1996) (reinstating grievant driver who tested positive for alcohol consumption where grievant had unblemished work record and made postdischarge efforts at rehabilitation).

[78]Packaging Corp., 105 LA 898 (Weisheit, 1995) (reinstating employee who walked off job following oral admonishment concerning unsatisfactory work performance); Stone Container Corp., 105 LA 385 (Berquist, 1995) (reinstating employee who walked off job because he felt threatened by fellow employee).

[79]Kuhlman Elec. Corp., 112 LA 691 (Goldberg, 1999) (reinstating grievant who told female co-worker he intended to cut gas line to supervisor's motorcycle as act of revenge for perceived mistreatment by supervisor where grievant did not have propensity for violence and was attempting to impress female employee with bravado); B.F. Goodrich Aerospace, 105 LA 1053 (Strasshofer, 1995) (reinstating employee who threatened company nurse).

[80]Trailmobile Trailer, 112 LA 1108 (Cohen, 1999) (reinstating grievant who falsely responded on employment application that he had ever been convicted of felony where grievant worked for nearly 1 ½ years without incident, appeared rehabilitated, and had previously been refused jobs when he revealed his background); Freightliner Corp., 103 LA 123 (Galambos, 1994)

F. Other Components of the Make Whole Remedy

1. Accrued Leaves. Reinstated grievants often are entitled to receive compensation for lost vacation[81] and holiday time.[82] In addition, back pay remedies frequently include credit for annual and sick leave.[83]

2. Contributions to Retirement. Reinstated grievants may also be entitled to contributions to health, welfare, and pension plans in accordance with the terms of the collective bargaining agreement.[84] Moreover, arbitrators normally award reinstated employees reimbursement for out-of-pocket losses for any medical expenses that would have been covered by the employer's medical plan had the employee not been improperly discharged.[85]

III. Reduction In Penalty

A. Authority

The authority to designate the appropriate remedy as stipulated in the issue includes the authority to make the penalty appropriate to the facts and contractual requirements.[86]

B. Factors Considered

2. Due Process Violations. a. Procedural. Arbitrators may refuse to uphold disciplinary action where contractual requirements have not been met.[87]

(reinstating grievant who allegedly gave false "no" response to criminal conviction question on employment application because grievant reasonably believed his prior conviction had been expunged).

[81]Fry's Food & Drug, 101 LA 1179 (Oberstein, 1993) (ordering employer to credit reinstated employees with vacation benefits they would have accrued).

[82]King Soopers, Inc., 112 LA 585 (Watkins, 1999) (awarding improperly discharged employee holiday pay); James Hardie Gypsum, 111 LA 210 (Olson, 1998) (including payment for paid holidays in back pay award).

[83]Mid-Am. Packaging, 111 LA 129 (Bankston, 1998) (ordering employer to credit reinstated employee with annual and sick leave he would have accrued); Board of Dirs., Little Rock Sch. Dist., 110 LA 1114 (Bankston, 1998).

[84]James Hardie Gypsum, 111 LA 210 (Olson, 1998) (ordering employer to credit reinstated employee with appropriate health, welfare, and pension contribution he would have accrued); West Co., 103 LA 452 (Murphy, 1994) (awarding reinstated grievant pension plan credits for period of time he was off work as result of improper suspension).

[85]Square D Co., 112 LA 125 (Goggin, 1998) (ordering employer to reimburse improperly discharged employee for medical costs he otherwise would not have incurred); Champlain Cable Corp., 108 LA 449 (Sweeney, 1997); University of Cincinnati, 105 LA 946 (Katz, 1996).

[86]ABC Rail Prods. Corp., 110 LA 574, 581 (Kenis, 1998) (where discharge penalty was improper, arbitrator has authority to fashion lesser penalty or direct make-whole remedy as facts require).

[87]Kroger Co., 107 LA 801, 807 (Howell, 1996) (reinstatement ordered where employer did not provide required written notice of discharge to union); Facility Mgmt. of La., 106 LA 879, 881 (O'Grady, 1996) (employer failed to adhere to contractual requirement of suspending

b. Rules. Penalties for rules that employees were unaware of may not be upheld.[88]

ii. Lax Enforcement of Rules. Unequal discipline will result in a reduction in some penalties, as will lack of consistent enforcement of rules.[89]

4. Management Also at Fault. Managerial fault in connection with a particular incident mitigates against harsher penalties.[90]

6. Employment History. An employee's employment record, including the quality of the performance evaluations, the disciplinary record, and the length of service, should be considered in assessing appropriate discipline.[91] A clean record continues to be viewed in the employee's favor.[92]

---

grievant pending investigation prior to discharge); Penske Truck Leasing, 110 LA 833, 837 (Bumpass, 1998) (reinstatement without back pay ordered when employer failed to give employee contractually required written notice of complaint before taking disciplinary action); Ken Meyer Meats, 107 LA 1017 (Sergent, 1996) (reinstatement ordered because penalty for emotional confrontation with company president not based on rational determination of facts); Tenneco Packaging Corp., 106 LA 606 (Franckiewicz, 1996) (discharge of insubordinate employee overruled where employer had not disciplined employee when he previously had engaged in similar acts of insubordination).

[88]International Paper Co., 106 LA 464 (Odom, 1996) (reinstatement ordered where employer had not made employee aware that leaving work site without permission carried discharge penalty).

[89]Unibus, Inc., 110 LA 597, 600 (Skulina, 1998) (employee's discharge unwarranted in light of employer mistakes and because employees involved in two other similar cases of mistaken calculations not terminated); Exxon Co., 110 LA 534, 539 (Allen, 1998) (employee who was "disability terminated" for job-related stress conditions awarded 10 weeks' back pay where employer refused to transfer employee to another team although it had made such transfers for many other employees in past); Kelly-Springfield Tire Co., 108 LA 984, 992 (Nicholas, Jr., 1997) (grievant reinstated where evidence showed that company not consistent in punishment of employees for violating drug and alcohol policy); Metropolitan Med. Ctr., 108 LA 974, 982 (Franckiewicz, 1997) (no just cause to discharge security guard where other employees who committed similar offenses not discharged); Kasle Steel Corp., 107 LA 1006, 1010 (Kerner, 1996) (reinstatement ordered of employee discharged for absenteeism because he was treated differently from 4 other employees with similar absenteeism records); Mead Chilpaco Mill, 106 LA 1066, 1068 (Feldman, 1996) (employee's termination rescinded where employer's rule against theft not applied evenhandedly); Tenneco Packaging Corp., 106 LA 606 (Franckiewicz, 1996) (reinstatement ordered of insubordinate employee where employee's past insubordination had not incurred discipline).

[90]Welch Foods, 112 LA 69 (Block, 1998) (supervisor's conduct, including use of profanity, pointing his fingers at employees in disrespectful manner, and raising his voice, considered as mitigation that justified changing discipline from discharge to reinstatement without back pay); Union Carbide Corp., 110 LA 667 (Caraway, 1998) (discharge overturned where employer partially responsible for negligence by failing to install safety device that would have avoided incident causing discipline); Unibus, Inc., 110 LA 597 (Skulina, 1998) (employee reinstated where employer misinformed employee he could take day off without incurring discipline beyond suspension but then discharged him after recalculating his attendance record).

[91]Pine Ridge Coal Co., 111 LA 568, 571 (Feldman, 1998) (employee's 18 years of service supported imposing lesser penalty); Hawaiian Airlines, Inc., 110 LA 631, 634 (Najita, 1998) (employee's 12-year record of faithful and efficient performance of duty without blemish justified mitigation); Health Plus, Inc., 110 LA 618, 620 (Duff, 1998) (23 years with employer without any disciplinary suspension justifies mitigation); Mason & Hanger Corp., 109 LA 957, 965 (Jennings, 1998) (unblemished record for 12 years indicates event was "anomaly" and supports reinstatement); Bruce Hardwood Floors, 108 LA 115, 119 (Allen, Jr., 1997) (26 years without record of drug use or being observed or accused of being under influence of drugs while on job mitigates harsh penalty for drug-related offense); Kimberly-Clark Corp., 107 LA 554, 560 (Byars, 1996) (employee's "immaculate" record during 26-year tenure supports lesser penalty).

[92]Nabisco, Inc., 109 LA 547, 553 (Hayford, 1997) (20 years of satisfactory service without previous similar misconduct persuasive to determine that misconduct was one-time aberration unlikely to recur); Arvin Indus., 109 LA 539, 546 (Keenan, 1997) (12 years of employment with

C. Conditional Reinstatement

Various forms of conditional reinstatement have been used to remedy situations where there is just cause for discipline but circumstances or peculiar facts make discharge unreasonable. Reinstatement may be conditioned on the employee demonstrating that she or he is fit to work.[93]

IV. Review of Last-Chance Agreements

Last-chance agreements are used as a method for employers and unions to find mutually workable solutions to individual disciplinary problems.[94] Examination of disciplinary actions under last-chance agreements is often limited to interpreting the last-chance agreement in view of the facts presented.[95] Accordingly, once it is determined that an employee breached the last-chance agreement, the penalty specified within the agreement usually is enforced.[96] Specifically, in such cases there is no consideration of the proportionality of the discipline imposed to the misconduct involved, whether the discipline imposed is in keeping with that administered to other employees, or any mitigating factors relating to the employee's employment history.[97]

Last-chance agreements serve the useful social function of salvaging the employment of employees whose jobs would otherwise be lost and of potentially rehabilitating troubled employees. They operate "to everyone's advantage" so that employees may become valued members of the industrial community.[98]

A long-term employee who had been insubordinate to his supervisor but showed remorse for having done so was awarded reinstatement, but it was conditioned on the ground that future insubordination would constitute grounds for discharge.[99]

---

good record is mitigating factor in assessing degree of penalty to be imposed); J.L. Clark, 108 LA 1012, 1015 (Gordinier, 1997) (arbitrator's view of discharge influenced by 22 years of service without any disciplinary actions).

[93]Cross Oil Ref. Co., 111 LA 1013 (Bumpass, 1999) (employee reinstated conditioned on proof of mental and emotional fitness by jointly selected psychologist or psychiatrist); Mine Workers (UMW) Dist. No. 6, 110 LA 84 (Ruben, 1997) (reinstatement of depressed employee conditioned on employee submitting medical evidence of ability to return to work); Owens Brockway Plastic Prods., Inc., 109 LA 655 (Bailey, 1997) (mentally ill employee's reinstatement conditioned on obtaining authorization to return to work from psychiatrist authorized by company).

[94]Drummond Co., Inc., 106 LA 250, 253 (Sergent, 1996); Eaton Cutler-Hammer Corp., 110 LA 467, 471 (Franckiewicz, 1998).

[95]Hugo Bosca Co., Inc., 109 LA 533, 537 (Franckiewicz, 1997).

[96]Lenzing Fibers Corp., 105 LA 423, 428 (Sergent, 1995); Drummond Co., Inc., 106 LA 250, 253 (Sergent, 1996); ABTCO, Inc., 104 LA 551, 552 (Kanner, 1995).

[97]Eaton Cutler-Hammer Corp., 110 LA 467 (Franckiewicz, 1998).

[98]Drummond Co., Inc., 106 LA 250, 253 (Sergent, 1996); Appalachian Reg'l Healthcare, Inc., 112 LA 884, 888 (Murphy, 1999); ABTCO, Inc., 104 LA 551, 553 (Kanner, 1995).

[99]Bryan Foods, Inc., 109 LA 633 (Baroni, 1997).

However, last-chance agreements may not cause an employee to relinquish the basic procedural protections provided by the collective bargaining agreement.[100] The employer is obliged to prove that the last-chance agreement was violated, and the employee must be granted the opportunity to challenge the evidence and to present a defense.[101]

Sometimes equitable considerations are held to outweigh the specific provisions of such an agreement. In *Cross Oil Refining Co.*,[102] the arbitrator looked beyond the terms of the last-chance agreement, reinstating a discharge employee, in part, because of the lack of proportionality of the disciplinary action imposed by the agreement and, in part, because of other mitigating considerations.

Technical violations of last-chance agreements may be overlooked when mitigating medical conditions are present. In *LTV Steel Mining Co.*,[103] the arbitrator ordered reinstatement of an employee who had been discharged for an excessive rate of absenteeism. The employee had a mental condition that had been incorrectly diagnosed, resulting in the prescription of the wrong medication. While it was undisputed that the employee violated the last-chance agreement, the arbitrator held that there was no just cause for the discharge because the employee's misconduct may have been caused by the medical error.

Timeliness has also been held to be important to enforcement of last-chance agreements. In *Standard Products Co.*,[104] a technical violation of a last-chance agreement was found to be unenforceable after the employer had waited over 4 months to assert violation of the specific provision of the agreement. The arbitrator held that the employer has a duty to follow up and ensure that the employee is in compliance with the terms of the agreement.

In cases where reinstatement is ordered, the employee usually remains subject to the terms of the last-chance agreement.[105]

V. Other Remedies

A. Liquidated Damages

Provisions allowing liquidated damages in grievance awards are rare in collective bargaining agreements. When included, their enforceability has been held possible only if the damages are reasonably proportionate to the loss or injury actually sustained.[106]

---

[100]Lenzing Fibers Corp., 105 LA 423, 428 (Sergent, 1995).

[101]Drummond Co., Inc., 106 LA 250, 253 (Sergent, 1996).

[102]111 LA 1013 (Bumpass, 1999).

[103]110 LA 283, 286 (Doepken, 1997).

[104]112 LA 76 (Brodsky, 1999).

[105]GTE of Fla., Inc., 108 LA 1115, 1120 (Cohen, 1997).

[106]Retail Clerks v. Food Employers Council, 85 Cal. App.3d 286, 99 LRRM 3255 (Cal. Ct. App., 1978).

B. Punitive Damages

Generally, an award of damages is not designed to punish one party, but rather to compensate the injured party for damages actually suffered.[107] Inappropriate disciplinary actions are breaches of contract, not tortious acts meriting punitive damages.[108] For this reason, there is a reluctance to award punitive damages even when the nature of the conduct involved might support punitive damages in a court of law. In *Union Camp Corp.*,[109] the arbitrator refused to award punitive damages for sexual harassment violations. The arbitrator held that although the collective bargaining agreement contained a provision whereby the parties agreed to arbitrate sexual harassment disputes, the provision did not expressly vest the arbitrator with the power to award both compensatory and punitive damages. The arbitrator concluded that it would be improper for him to award punitive damages absent an express provision in the collective bargaining agreement granting him this authority.

VI. Ancillary Relief

A. Expungement of Records

Expungement of records is a remedy frequently granted to employees who successfully challenge, in whole or in part, an employer's disciplinary actions.[110] In *Township of East Lampeter*,[111] the arbitrator upheld a police officer's temporary demotion but ordered that documents relating to the incident could not remain in the officer's personnel file indefinitely. The arbitrator determined that, because the officer had been found innocent of the criminal charges brought against him and because the underlying domestic dispute had been resolved, it would be unfair to perpetually maintain documents in his file that would forever affect his chances at promotion.

[107]City of Fairbanks, 108 LA 674, 678 (Landau, 1997).

[108]Quaker Oats Co., 110 LA 204, 205 (Moreland, 1998).

[109]104 LA 295, 301 (Nolan, 1995).

[110]Everett Cmty. Coll., 110 LA 1102, 1106 (de Grasse, 1998) (expungement ordered because employer failed to prove just cause for employee's suspension); Snap-On Tools Corp., 104 LA 180, 185 (Cipolla, 1995) (expungement ordered because employer improperly disciplined employee for alleged misconduct that occurred while employee was off duty and off premises); York Wall Coverings, Inc., 110 LA 300, 305 (Duff, 1998) (letters of warnings expunged from employees personnel record where employer failed to provide specific allegations of employee's misconduct); Safeway Stores, Inc., 109 LA 817, 821 (Watkins, 1997).

[111]106 LA 133 (DiLauro, 1995).

Chapter 13

External Law

II. Title VII

A. General

Arbitrators may apply Title VII law in resolving grievances when the collective bargaining agreement (CBA) includes a clause explicitly barring discrimination. In *Owens-Brockway Glass Container, Inc.*,[1] under a clause providing that "the company and the union will comply with all laws preventing discrimination against any employee because of race, color, religion, sex, national origin, age, handicap, or veteran status,"[2] the arbitrator concluded that he was obligated to follow Title VII because the parties bargained for it. "The parties promised to follow laws designed to thwart gender discrimination, and it is the arbitrator's obligation to resolve this dispute within those legal-contractual parameters."[3] In this interpretation, Title VII includes the regulations promulgated thereunder.[4]

In the absence of an explicit contractual reference, reliance on Title VII law may be attributed to adherence to public policy. In *Conagra Frozen Foods*,[5] the arbitrator upheld the discharge of an alleged sexual harasser on the basis of Title VII, even though the

[1]1998 WL 1033371 (Snow, 1998).

[2]Id. at 5.

[3]Id. at 37. In so concluding, the arbitrator relied on a decision by the Eleventh Circuit, Montes v. Shearson Lehman Brothers, 128 F.3d 1456, 4 WH Cases 2d 385 (11th Cir., 1997) that said, "When a claim arises under specific laws, however, the arbitrators are bound to follow those laws in the absence of a valid and legal agreement not to do so." 128 F.3d at 1459.

[4]See Georgia Pac. Corp., 112 LA 317 (Caraway, 1999) (relying on burden of proof test set forth in McDonnell-Douglas Corp. v. Green, 411 U.S. 792, 5 FEP Cases 965 (1973)); Ralphs Grocery Co., 109 LA 1192 (Gentile, 1998) (relying, in part, on Equal Employment Opportunity Commission religious accommodation guidelines).

[5]113 LA 129 (Baroni, 1999).

parties did not have either an equal employment opportunity statement or a sexual harassment policy in their contract. The arbitrator relied on both external law and public policy:

> [F]ederal law makes sexual harassment in the workplace illegal * * * and federal law is binding on everyone, whether it is incorporated in company policy or not. * * * Based upon the strong "public policy" argument alone, widely established by courts and legislatures, Grievant was placed on notice of the legal prohibition against sexual harassment. Whether he actually was not aware of the prohibition (which the arbitrator does not believe), is not important. What is important is the fact that he should have known, given the strong public policy against sexual harassment.[6]

B. Awards Applying Title VII Provisions

1. Sex Discrimination and Sexual Harassment. In 1998, the U.S. Supreme Court rewrote a good deal of existing sexual harassment law when it decided *Faragher v. City of Boca Raton*[7] and *Burlington Industries, Inc. v. Ellerth.*[8] In *Faragher*, the Court rejected the concepts of both "quid pro quo" and "hostile environment" in the context of supervisory sexual harassment. It held that where a supervisor has taken a "tangible employment action" against an employee,[9] such as a termination, poor performance appraisal, or demotion, and that tangible employment action is connected to sexually harassing conduct, the employer will be held liable for the conduct of the supervisor regardless of whether the employer actually knew that the harassment was occurring or whether the plaintiff complained about it. In *Burlington*, the Court addressed sexual harassment situations where there had been no "tangible employment action." It said that in such instances the employer may raise an affirmative defense that (1) the employer exercised "reasonable care" to prevent and correct promptly any sexually harassing behavior, and (2) the employee "unreasonably failed to take advantage of any preventive or corrective opportunities provided by the employer or to avoid harm otherwise."[10] In another case, *Oncale v. Sundowner Offshore Services, Inc.*,[11] the Court held that same-sex sexual harassment is actionable under Title VII.

d. Arbitration Awards in Sex Discrimination. Sex discrimination continues to be a frequently arbitrated Title VII claim, and arbitrators often rely on the rules developed by the courts in resolving those claims. In cases where an employee is disciplined or discharged

---

[6]Id. at 133 (citations omitted).

[7]524 U.S. 775, 77 FEP Cases 14 (1998).

[8]524 U.S. 742, 77 FEP Cases 1 (1998).

[9]Faragher v. City of Boca Raton, 524 U.S. 775, 807.

[10]Burlington Indus., Inc. v. Ellerth, 524 U.S. 742, 765, 77 FEP Cases 1 (1998).

[11]523 U.S. 75, 76 FEP Cases 221 (1998).

for allegedly committing sexual harassment, arbitrators struggle with the issue of whether the conduct must rise to the level of actionable sexual harassment to justify a discharge, and even whether actionable sexual harassment constitutes sufficient just cause for a discharge. For example, in *Ralphs Grocery Co.*,[12] the employer discharged a male employee who twice kissed a female employee even though she indicated to him after the first kiss that it was unwelcome. The union argued that the employee should not have been fired because progressive discipline, as set forth in the CBA, was not followed. The arbitrator denied the grievance and upheld the discharge despite the employer's failure to follow progressive discipline. The arbitrator found that because the employer had adopted a policy against sexual harassment, allowing the individual to remain employed would expose the employer to significant potential liability.[13]

Similarly, in *Safeway, Inc.*,[14] a male employee made two sexually suggestive remarks to a 16-year-old female employee, who reported his remarks to management. The employee had made similar comments to a customer about a year earlier. On these facts the employer discharged the employee. The employer contended that because the employee violated its antiharassment policies, he was discharged for just cause. Upholding the employer's actions, the arbitrator rejected the union's contention that the employer had to show that the employee's conduct constituted severe and pervasive harassment in order to justify the discharge. The arbitrator reasoned that since the employee had been warned after the earlier incident, any similar conduct could lead to termination. His repeat of harassing conduct, therefore, justified his termination for cause.

By contrast, in *Fleming Companies*,[15] the employer did not have just cause to discharge a male grievant who made sexually offensive comments to a female co-employee even though the grievant had previously been written up for similar misconduct. Because there was evidence that the female co-employee had engaged in similar shop talk of her own, the single comment by the grievant did not rise to the level of sexual harassment. Therefore, the arbitrator held that the employer did not have just cause to discharge.[16]

2. Race Discrimination. In *Globe Furniture Rentals*,[17] the burden of proof was placed on the employee to establish that the basis

---

[12]112 LA 120 (Prayzich, 1999).

[13]See also Conagra Frozen Foods, 113 LA 129 (Baroni, 1999) (upholding discharge of alleged harasser where employer demonstrated by clear and convincing evidence that grievant sexually harassed co-employee).

[14]112 LA 1050 (Silver, 1999).

[15]112 LA 257 (Duff, 1999).

[16]See also City of Ada, 113 LA 422 (Goodman, 1999) (grievance sustained where grievant was demoted for harassment because he pulled bra strap of female co-employee, on finding that this single isolated incident did not constitute actionable sexual harassment).

[17]105 LA 888 (Heekin, 1995).

of the decision to discharge her was discriminatory. The employee was the employer's only African-American employee. Because her performance was substandard for at least 2 years prior to her discharge, even though she was replaced by a white employee, she could not meet her burden of showing that her discharge was racially motivated. Similarly, in *Lawrence Berkeley National Laboratory*,[18] in a reduction-in-force situation, an African-American employee claimed that his layoff was racially discriminatory. However, concluding that the grievant did not meet the burden of showing that the employer's stated reason for laying him off was merely a pretext for racial discrimination, the arbitrator denied the grievance.

In *Coca-Cola USA*,[19] a white employee discharged for making a single racially derogatory remark to an African-American co-employee was reinstated on a finding that a single remark does not rise to the level of actionable severe and pervasive harassment under federal law and that discharge for a single remark was too harsh a penalty. Similarly, in *Associated Wholesale Grocers*,[20] the employer discharged a white employee for violating its antiharassment policy after he wrote a single racially derogatory remark on an employer document. Noting that a single derogatory remark, although offensive, does not meet the federal legal definition of harassment, the arbitrator concluded that the employer did not have just cause to dismiss the individual. The discharge was reduced to a suspension without back pay.

3. Religious Discrimination. a. Scope of Protection. Religious discrimination and harassment cases involve the same questions raised by race, sex, and age discrimination cases: Was the employee subjected to an adverse employment action or was the employee harassed because of his or her religion? In *Venters v. City of Delphi*,[21] the plaintiff was discharged for failing to conform to her supervisor's religious beliefs. The Seventh Circuit noted that the reasonable accommodation theory was inapplicable in this instance. It said the employee had to show that her unwillingness to adopt her supervisor's religious beliefs played a motivating role in her discharge.

b. Reasonable Accommodation. What constitutes a reasonable accommodation or what is a de minimis cost are questions raised in disparate treatment cases. In *Ralphs Grocery Co.*,[22] the employer's discharge of a Seventh-Day Adventist was upheld after she refused to work on Saturdays, her Sabbath day. The contract contained a provision that the employer would not discriminate on the basis of religion to the extent required by federal law. Although the employer

---

[18] 108 LA 376 (Silver, 1996).

[19] 112 LA 193 (Rezler, 1999).

[20] 112 LA 1212 (Murphy, 1999).

[21] 123 F.3d 956, 74 FEP Cases 1095 (7th Cir., 1997).

[22] 109 LA 1192 (Gentile, 1998).

offered to accommodate the employee by giving her one Saturday a month off, the employee refused to work any Saturday on the basis that her religion required that she not perform any work on the Sabbath. She was then discharged for insubordination. The employee was the only full-time employee in her department. Following *Trans World Airlines v. Hardison*,[23] the arbitrator upheld the discharge, finding that because the grievant was the only full-time employee in her department and because her job required Saturday work, allowing her to have every Saturday off would result in an undue hardship on the employer, because it would cause serious operational and scheduling difficulties.

A grievance filed by a class of maintenance employees protesting their employer's decision to drop its longstanding policy of allowing employees to routinely have Sundays off was denied in *Goodyear Tire & Rubber*.[24] Also relying on *Hardison*, the arbitrator found that allowing the employees who were on a continuous shift to have Sundays off would result in considerable hardship. The arbitrator concluded that making the employer give Sundays off would be costly, because it would cause the employer to lose business or be forced to pay premium rates for replacement workers.

Even de minimis hardship was not found to exist in *Clallan County Public Hospital District No. 1*,[25] however. In that case the grievant, a member of the Worldwide Church of God, a sect that does not recognize Christmas as a holiday, requested to be relieved from having to assist in decorating the employer's Christmas tree on the basis of his religion. The employer refused his request, ordering him to assist with the decoration of the tree. Although the union advised him to comply with the order and grieve later, the employee simply refused to follow the order. He was then suspended without pay with a threat of discharge if he refused to cooperate in the future. Relying on the contract's nondiscrimination clause and federal case law, the arbitrator sustained the grievance on the basis that the employer made no attempt to accommodate the grievant's sincerely held belief that erecting the Christmas tree conflicted with his religion.

Discharge was upheld in *Bethlehem Structural Products*,[26] where a born-again Christian grievant claimed that a co-employee's use of foul language constituted religious harassment. The arbitrator found that because the co-employee used similar language in the presence of other employees and the grievant offered no evidence that the language was directed at him because of his religious beliefs, no religious harassment was involved.

---

[23] 432 U.S. 63, 14 FEP Cases 1697 (1977).

[24] 107 LA 193 (Sergent, 1996).

[25] 105 LA 609 (Calhoun, 1995).

[26] 105 LA 205 (Witt, 1995).

6. Awards Disregarding Title VII. In *Fulton Industries*,[27] after a female employee was disqualified from her position, she filed a grievance claiming sex discrimination. The CBA contained a generic nondiscrimination clause that prohibited discrimination on the basis of sex but did not specifically refer to Title VII. The arbitrator rejected the union's argument that relied on Title VII case law, stating that the contract did not require him to look to external law.

IV. Americans with Disabilities Act

A. Awards Applying ADA

Despite the absence of a specific reference to the Americans with Disabilities Act (ADA) in a CBA, in some cases the ADA has been applied anyway. In *Henkel Corp.*,[28] the arbitrator explained:

> The ultimate decision as to whether or not there is a violation of the ADA lies with the Equal Employment Opportunity Commission (herein EEOC) and the courts, and not the Arbitrator. However, there is no requirement that an Arbitrator wear blinders. The Arbitrator should consider the spirit and letter of the law when making a just cause determination involving a disabled individual.[29]

The arbitrator found that the grievant was not covered by the ADA because his heart condition did not constitute a "disability" within the meaning of the statute.

In *Interstate Brands Corp.*,[30] it was found that the CBA reference to a "duty to accommodate" provided a sufficient basis to apply the ADA to the employee's discrimination grievance. The arbitrator denied the grievance, however, finding that the employer did not need to accommodate the grievant's psychiatric problems where he refused to take his prescribed medication, the possibility of rehabilitation was remote, and the employer had legitimate safety concerns that provided just cause for the discharge. In *GTE North Inc.*,[31] the CBA contained a nondiscrimination clause that led to the arbitrator's conclusion that compliance with the ADA was a component of just cause. The arbitrator upheld the grievant's discharge, finding that he was not disabled because his leg and hip injuries did not substantially limit his major life activities. The arbitrator also found just cause because the grievant had turned down accommodations offered in the past by the employer without suggesting alternative accommodations

---

[27] 108 LA 1141 (Klein, 1997).
[28] 110 LA 1121 (West, 1998).
[29] Id. at 1125.
[30] 113 LA 161 (Howell, 1999).
[31] 113 LA 665 (Brodsky, 1999).

and because he was still unable to perform his job. In *Cramer, Inc.*,[32] the arbitrator not only applied the ADA, but deferred to the Equal Employment Opportunity Commission's (EEOC's) finding on the basis of its expertise in a collateral proceeding on a claim by the same employee about the same injury. Both the EEOC and the arbitrator found that rotator cuff injuries did not constitute disabilities under the ADA. The arbitrator found just cause for discharge, asserting that the only thing keeping the grievant from performing the assigned work was his refusal to attempt to do it.

In *Los Angeles Community College District*,[33] the arbitrator held that the employer had violated the ADA when it did not provide the grievant with appropriate accommodation. The grievant, a teacher, alleged that a foot and heel injury resulting from a serious auto accident was exacerbated by the hilly campus and the long drive to work. He asked to transfer to a community college that was less hilly and closer to his home. The point of his request was to relieve his pain, which affected his job performance—in other words, it was a question of personal safety. The arbitrator sustained the grievance, holding that the employer is not only required to accommodate an employee by creating a new job to sufficiently enable the employee to perform his or her duties, but also to enable the employee to live a healthier, more normal life, if possible. The job requirement in his case is peculiar to colleges that rely extensively on hourly (part-time) people to teach classes. In this instance, the grievant, a full-time faculty member, was bumping a number of part-time instructors, which was a common occurrence in that community college system, according to the testimony presented at the hearing. Neither his salary nor the financial burden on the system would be affected by the transfer he requested.

B. *Awards Not Applying ADA*

In *Shell Oil Co.*,[34] the arbitrator declined to apply the ADA in spite of a disability antidiscrimination provision in the CBA. The arbitrator asserted that the provision did not apply because the agreement "contains no specific language which incorporates the ADA."[35] However, the arbitrator upheld the grievant's discharge on the grounds that he was unable to perform his job and there was no reasonable accommodation available.

In *Jefferson Smurfit Corp.*,[36] it was held that the ADA did not apply because it was not specifically included in the CBA. The arbitrator also upheld the discharge because the employee could not perform

---

[32]110 LA 37 (O'Grady, 1998). See also City of Tampa, 111 LA 65 (Hoffman, 1998).
[33]112 LA 733 (Kaufman, 1999).
[34]109 LA 965 (Baroni, 1998).
[35]Id. at 968.
[36]103 LA 1041 (Canestraight, 1994).

his duties due to a disabling injury. He said that the CBA did not require the employer to accommodate the employee and therefore did not address the accommodation issue.

V. Family and Medical Leave Act

Arbitrators have applied the Family and Medical Leave Act (FMLA) where necessary to determine an employee's leave rights, even absent a CBA reference. In *Union Hospital*,[37] the arbitrator reviewed FMLA provisions governing the use of paid vacation or personal leave to determine whether the employer impermissibly reduced the employee's rights under the Act. In *Puget Sound Hospital*,[38] the arbitrator determined that the employer was not required to grant paid sick leave to an employee to care for her ailing mother during the FMLA leave period because of specific limitations on use of sick leave in the CBA.[39]

The FMLA was also considered in *Laidlaw Transit*[40] in determining the grievant's back pay entitlement when he was returned to work following a wrongful discharge. Applying the FMLA, the arbitrator found that the grievant had been on unpaid FMLA leave during part of the back pay period. His back pay was reduced accordingly.

In *City of Englewood, Ohio*,[41] it was held that the employer's discharge of the grievant when his FMLA leave expired violated the medical leave provision of the CBA. Although the additional leave was at the employer's discretion, the arbitrator said it could not be denied merely because the grievant's FMLA leave had expired.

VI. Title VII and ADEA Procedures and Remedies

In *Conagra Frozen Foods*,[42] the burden of proof requirements set forth in the U.S. Supreme Court's sexual harassment decisions of *Meritor Savings Bank v. Vinson*[43] and *Harris v. Forklift Systems*[44] were specifically applied. The arbitrator found a pervasive pattern

---

[37]108 LA 966 (Chattman, 1997) (employer did not have right to require that employees substitute paid leave for time used for FMLA leave where right of choice reserved to employees in collective bargaining agreement).

[38]109 LA 659 (Monat, 1997).

[39]See also Aerospace Ctr. Support, 112 LA 108 (Welch, 1999) (overturning discharge of employee for excessive absences when on FMLA leave caring for sick mother because employers have no discretion to deny legitimate FMLA leave).

[40]109 LA 647 (Landau, 1997).

[41]113 LA 624 (Kohler, 2000).

[42]113 LA 129 (Baroni, 1999).

[43]477 U.S. 57, 40 FEP Cases 1822 (1986).

[44]510 U.S. 17, 63 FEP Cases 225 (1993).

of conduct that "clearly and convincingly" established actions that justified the grievant's termination for harassing female co-workers.

VII. Forum Shopping: Court or Arbitration

In *Wright v. Universal Maritime Service Corp.*,[45] the U.S. Supreme Court held that an individual's right to a judicial forum for the adjudication of a statutory discrimination claim cannot be waived by a CBA absent a "clear and unmistakable" waiver.

Since that decision, courts have disagreed as to when an arbitration provision in an individual contract or employee handbook constitutes a waiver of the right to a judicial forum for the adjudication of statutory discrimination claims. In *Nelson v. Cypress Bagdad Cooper Corp.*,[46] the Ninth Circuit held that an employee's signed acknowledgment that she "has read and understands" the terms of an employee handbook, including its arbitration provision, does not constitute an agreement to arbitrate rather than litigate discrimination claims. In *Performance Contracting, Inc. v. Seaboard Surety Co.*,[47] the Sixth Circuit held that an agreement to resolve statutory claims outside the courts must be "made manifest by plain language."[48] Similarly, the First Circuit, in *Ramirez-de-Arellano v. American Airlines, Inc.*,[49] held that an arbitration provision in an employee handbook was not an agreement to arbitrate statutory claims in that it was not "voluntary and intentional." The court said that signing a "read and understood" form did not constitute a binding agreement. In *Paladino v. Avnet Computer Technologies, Inc.*,[50] the Eleventh Circuit held in pertinent part:

> In *Brisentine v. Stone & Webster Engineering Corp.*, 117 F.3d 519 (11th Cir. 1997), * * * we indicated that a mandatory arbitration clause does not bar litigation of a federal statutory claim, unless three requirements are met. First, the employee must have agreed individually to the contract containing the arbitration clause. Second, the agreement must authorize the arbitrator to resolve federal statutory claims—it is not enough that the arbitrator can resolve contract claims, even if factual issues arising from those claims overlap with the statutory claim issues. Third, the agreement must give the employee the right to insist on arbitration if the federal statutory claim is not resolved to his satisfaction in any grievance process.
>
> * * * To fall within the FAA's ambit, however, an arbitration agreement that purports to cover statutory claims must contain terms that generally and fairly inform the signatories that it covers statutory claims.

---

[45]525 U.S. 70, 159 LRRM 2769 (1998).

[46]119 F.3d 756, 6 AD Cases 1714 (9th Cir., 1997).

[47]163 F.3d 366 (6th Cir., 1998).

[48]Id. at 370.

[49]133 F.3d 89 (1st Cir., 1997).

[50]134 F.3d 1054, 76 FEP Cases 1315 (11th Cir., 1998).

> The arbitration agreement's terms regarding remedies must also be fully consistent with the purposes underlying any statutory claims subject to arbitration.[51]

In contrast, other courts have held that a general arbitration provision covering all employment disputes is sufficient to cover statutory discrimination claims.[52] Some courts have held that a clause mandating compulsory arbitration of statutory disputes as a condition of employment is unenforceable.[53]

In *Gibson v. Neighborhood Health Clinics, Inc.*,[54] the Seventh Circuit held that the arbitration provision in an employment manual was not enforceable for lack of consideration where the employee was not aware of and did not assent to the manual's terms. Where both parties agree to be bound by such an arbitration provision, however, the Fourth Circuit has determined consideration to be adequate and has enforced the provision.[55]

Some courts have held unenforceable an agreement to arbitrate statutory claims that does not allow for full statutory damages including attorneys' fees.[56] An arbitration provision has also been held to be unenforceable if the rules governing the arbitration process itself are unfair.[57]

VIII. Drug Testing

B. Arbitration and Public Policy

In *Alaska Department of Transportation*,[58] the discharge of an employee who tested positive to a random drug test was set aside. In reaching his decision, the arbitrator looked to department regulations, which do not support a mandatory discharge, in addition to the CBA. The CBA listed major offenses that could lead to discharge, such as

---

[51] Id. at 1059.

[52] See, e.g., Rojas v. TK Communications, Inc., 87 F.3d 745, 71 FEP Cases 664 (5th Cir., 1996); Arakawa v. Japan Network Group, 56 F. Supp. 2d 349, 83 FEP Cases 1097 (S.D.N.Y., 1999); Valdiviezo v. Phelps Dodge Hidalgo Smelter, Inc., 995 F. Supp. 1060 (D. Ariz., 1997); Topf v. Warnaco, Inc., 942 F. Supp. 762, 6 AD Cases 1315 (D. Conn., 1996); Walker v. MDM Servs. Corp., 997 F. Supp. 822, 76 FEP Cases 736 (W.D. Ky., 1998). See also Seus v. John Nuveen & Co., Inc., 146 F.3d 175, 77 FEP Cases 751 (3d Cir., 1998), cert. denied, 525 U.S. 1139 (1998) (declining to apply "knowing and voluntary" standard in determining whether agreement to arbitrate Title VII and Age Discrimination in Employment Act claims was enforceable under Federal Arbitration Act).

[53] See Shankle v. B-G Maint. Mgmt. of Colo., 163 F.3d 1230, 78 FEP Cases 1057 (10th Cir., 1999); Duffield v. Robertson Stephens & Co., 144 F.3d 1182, 76 FEP Cases 1450 (9th Cir.), cert. denied, 525 U.S. 982 (1998).

[54] 121 F.3d 1126 (7th Cir., 1997).

[55] Johnson v. Circuit City Stores, 148 F.3d 373, 77 FEP Cases 139 (4th Cir., 1998).

[56] See, e.g., Paladino v. Avnet Computer Techs., Inc., 134 F.3d 1054, 76 FEP Cases 1315 (11th Cir., 1998); Alcaraz v. Avnet, 933 F. Supp. 1025, 71 FEP Cases 68 (D.N.M., 1996).

[57] Hooters of Am., Inc. v. Phillips, 173 F.3d 933, 79 FEP Cases 629 (4th Cir., 1999).

[58] 108 LA 339 (Levak, 1997).

being intoxicated on the job. It did not list failing a random drug test as cause for immediate discharge. Therefore, the arbitrator said, there was insufficient cause to find that the grievant had committed a major offense, and the penalty was reduced to a 90-day suspension.

In *Hertz Corp.*,[59] the arbitrator upheld the employer's right to adopt policies that were more stringent than federal and state regulations. However, in applying the just cause standard, noting that the penalty under the federal regulations was much less severe, the arbitrator found that the penalty of discharge was too harsh given the grievant's long and favorable employment history. Reinstated without back pay, the grievant was required to pass an alcohol and drug test before coming back to work and was ordered to be subject to random testing thereafter for a period of 1 year.

In *Weyerhaeuser Forest Products*,[60] when the employer did not fully comply with department of transportation testing procedure rules in attempting to give a follow-up drug test to an employee whose original urine sample was thought to be the wrong temperature, the arbitrator held that the employer lacked just cause to terminate the grievant, and the penalty was reduced to a suspension.[61]

IX. Federal Antiretaliation Statutes

In *ITT Federal Services Corp.*,[62] a claim that the grievant was refused bumping rights after filing sexual harassment charges was denied. Although the union was able to establish a prima facie case of retaliation, the arbitrator found that the employer had a legitimate business reason for the layoff and that the grievant was not qualified for any other position. The arbitrator's opinion includes a detailed discussion of retaliation law.

XI. Lie Detectors and Monitoring

A. Lie Detectors

3. Arbitration Awards. c. Grievant's Request to Submit to Lie Detector Test. In *Potlatch Corp.*,[63] the arbitrator upheld the employer's right to refuse the grievant's request to take a lie detector test to

---

[59]108 LA 945 (Weckstein, 1997).

[60]108 LA 26 (Levak, 1997).

[61]See also Coca Cola Bottling Co., 110 LA 8 (Nadelbach, 1998) (grievant not discharged for just cause where employer's policies incorporated all department of transportation rules and regulations that required employer to notify grievant that he had right to request independent retest after testing positive for marijuana).

[62]105 LA 289 (Landau, 1995).

[63]104 LA 691 (Moore, 1995).

prove his innocence. Similarly, in *City of Youngstown*,[64] the arbitrator refused the city's request to introduce the results of a lie detector test as evidence of the employee's dishonesty.

B. Monitoring

3. Searches. An employer's right to conduct a search of an employee's property as well as his person was upheld in *Anheuser-Busch Inc.*[65] In so holding, the arbitrator found that "[t]he use of searches, including those involving the use of dogs, is an expected and reasonable application of the general authority to conduct searches and inspections, and has been so held in a number of arbitration and court cases."[66]

---

[64] 107 LA 588 (Skulina, 1996).

[65] 107 LA 1183 (Weckstein, 1996).

[66] Id. at 1191. See also Cleveland-Cliffs Iron Co., 110 LA 314 (Vonhof, 1997) (search of lunch buckets proper to prevent theft of company property).

Chapter 14

Finality of Awards and Court Actions

II. Resubmission and Clarification of Arbitration Awards

A. *The Doctrine of* Functus Officio *[New Topic]*

When there is dissatisfaction with an award or the award is unclear, the parties may agree to ask the arbitrator to reconsider or clarify the award. If both parties do not consent, however, the arbitrator may not have jurisdiction to review it because of the common law doctrine of "functus officio." This doctrine means that an arbitrator's jurisdiction ends when a final award is issued.[1]

There are three widely followed exceptions to the rule of functus officio: an arbitrator may (1) correct a mistake that is apparent on the face of the award, (2) finish an incomplete award, and (3) clarify an ambiguity.[2] The first exception allows an arbitrator to correct an award where there are "clerical mistakes or obvious errors of arithmetic computation," but not in cases of "alleged mistakes where extraneous facts must be considered."[3] The second exception applies

---

[1]The policies and limitations of the doctrine of functus officio are discussed in Markel, "*Functus Officio*: Does the Doctrine Apply in Labor Arbitration?" 1998 J. Disp. Resol. 53; Nicolau, "*O Functus Officio*: Is It Time to Go?" Proceedings of the 51st Annual Meeting, National Academy of Arbitrators (BNA Books, 1997); Tepstein, "Confirming an Amended Labor Arbitration Award in Federal Court: The Problem of *Functus Officio*," 8 Am. Rev. Int'l Arb. 65 (1997); Dunsford, "The Case for Retention of Remedial Jurisdiction in Labor Arbitration Awards," 31 Ga. L. Rev. 201 (1996).

[2]See Kennecott Utah Copper Corp. v. Steelworkers, 186 F.3d 1261, 162 LRRM 2010 (10th Cir., 1999) (upholding clarification of award in spite of ex parte contact).

[3]Teamsters Local 312 v. Matlack, Inc., 118 F.3d 985, 991, 155 LRRM 2738 (3d Cir., 1997). The National Academy of Arbitrators' Advisory Opinion No. 20 states that arbitrators are allowed to make corrections as to the identity of employees, back pay calculations, and "other corrections of similar evident clerical mistakes or computational errors." The opinion concludes that such corrections are consistent with common and statutory law and are necessary to avoid unfair burdens on the parties and misuse of the arbitration process.

"where the award does not adjudicate an issue which has been submitted," because if an arbitrator has not decided an issue, it remains open for adjudication.[4] The third exception applies if the award, "although seemingly complete, leaves doubt whether the submission has been fully executed."[5]

The Ninth Circuit recently compared the completion and ambiguity exceptions, finding that "the completion exception to the doctrine of *functus officio* applies when an arbitration award fails to resolve an issue or 'specify the remedy in definite terms.'"[6] In that case, the arbitrator had converted a discharge into a 3-day suspension. After the employer complied with the arbitrator's ruling, a dispute arose over whether the grievant was owed back pay for the period beyond the 3 days that he was out of work. The union asked the arbitrator to clarify whether she had intended to award back pay for that period. The employer objected on the grounds that the arbitrator was functus officio. The arbitrator then issued an amended award where she granted the employee back pay. The company refused to comply with the amended award, saying that the amendment amounted to a clarification without the consent of both parties. The court decided that "the arbitrator's clarification was permissible because it completed the award"[7] and, because the case fell within one of the three exceptions to the doctrine of functus officio, that consent of both parties was not necessary.

In *Teamsters Local 312 v. Matlack, Inc.*,[8] the employer claimed that it understood the arbitrator to say that he would rule on procedural questions but not on the merits, on the basis that the employer had not presented its substantive case. The arbitrator then issued an award in favor of the union on both the procedural issues and the merits. The district court vacated the award, sending it back for further hearing on the merits, after finding it to be incomplete. Because the arbitrator had not heard the merits of the case, that portion of the decision was held to be outside the arbitrator's jurisdiction, according to the doctrine of functus officio.[9]

In a 1999 case, the employer suspended the grievant for sexual harassment.[10] According to the terms of his agreement with the employer, he was to receive counseling from a particular therapist until the therapist believed the course of treatment was complete. If the grievant did not complete the treatment, he would be terminated.

---

[4]Colonial Penn Ins. Co. v. Omaha Indem. Co., 943 F.2d 327, 332 (3d Cir., 1991) (commercial arbitration case often cited by this court in its decisions in traditional labor cases).

[5]Id.

[6]Teamsters Local 631 v. Silver State Disposal Serv. Inc., 109 F.3d 1409, 1411, 154 LRRM 2865 (9th Cir., 1997).

[7]Id. at 1411.

[8]118 F.3d 985, 155 LRRM 2738 (3d Cir., 1997).

[9]Id. at 991.

[10]Office & Prof'l Employees Local 471 v. Brownsville Gen. Hosp., 186 F.3d 326, 161 LRRM 3057 (3d Cir., 1999).

The grievant and the therapist had a falling out, and the grievant did not attend therapy sessions for a week. When the company learned of this fact, they discharged the employee. The union filed a grievance.

The arbitrator ultimately reinstated the grievant on the condition that he complete a course of counseling with the therapist. The therapist, however, declined to see the grievant. The union asked the arbitrator to clarify whether the grievant could continue therapy with a second therapist, but the employer argued that the arbitrator was functus officio. Thus, the arbitrator said he would only clarify the award with consent of both parties.

The court held that the resignation of the first therapist created an unforeseen ambiguity in the award that should be resolved by the arbitrator. Although the arbitrator may not revisit the merits of the dispute, the court held that "a remand for clarification under such conditions is consistent with the policy of judicial restraint that is the thrust of federal arbitral jurisprudence. . . . Such a remand avoids the court's misinterpretation of the award and is therefore more likely to give the parties the award for which they bargained."[11]

A federal district court addressed the third exception to the doctrine of functus officio in a 1996 case.[12] The grievant and a co-worker fought, and the employer discharged the grievant. The arbitrator converted the discharge to a suspension, but the award mistakenly ordered reinstatement without pay. The arbitrator corrected the award 10 days after it was issued, but the employer refused to comply. The court enforced the award, stating that, in amending the award, the arbitrator had merely clarified his original intention.

In *Hotel Greystone*,[13] the employer argued that the impartial chairman of the arbitration board was functus officio when he reconsidered and then reopened an award. The court cited the language in the award, where the chairman noted that the parties' agreement had been interpreted to permit reconsideration "upon a showing that the previous award was 'clearly erroneous' or that there existed newly discovered evidence previously unavailable to the requesting party."[14] The court upheld the award, saying that the doctrine of functus officio did not apply.

B. Retaining Jurisdiction [New Topic]

Practitioners should know that it is difficult to anticipate if a court will return an ambiguous award to an arbitrator, because the

---

[11]Id. at 331–32.

[12]Cadillac Uniform & Linen Supply, Inc. v. Union de Tronquistas de P.R., Teamsters Local 901, 920 F. Supp. 19, 152 LRRM 2416 (D.P.R., 1996).

[13]Hotel Greystone Corp. v. New York Hotel & Motel Trades Council, AFL-CIO, 902 F. Supp. 482, 152 LRRM 2061 (S.D.N.Y., 1995).

[14]Id. at 484.

circuits vary in their interpretation of the term "make whole" in the context of an arbitral award.[15] One solution to avoid future litigation is for the arbitrator to retain jurisdiction in case questions arise regarding implementation of the award.[16] This action does not affect the finality of the award or prevent its enforcement. For example, a district court remanded a case involving a dispute over back pay where an arbitrator had expressly retained jurisdiction because it was impermissible for a court to investigate the merits of the dispute.[17]

III. Standards for the Review of Arbitration Awards

B. Deference to the Arbitration Award

Deferential standards of review of arbitral opinions continue to be the norm,[18] even when the suit is against the arbitrator for exceeding his authority.[19]

C. Exceptions to the Deference Standard

Over the years, courts have vacated arbitration awards on 2 broad grounds: (1) that the award does not draw its essence from the contract, or (2) that it violated public policy.[20] Courts continue to uphold awards even when they disagree with their findings as long as the award is squarely grounded in the contract.[21]

---

[15]Operating Eng'rs Local 841 v. Murphy Co., 82 F.3d 185, 152 LRRM 2315 (7th Cir., 1996) (award enforced despite ambiguity about damages because employer should have addressed question of damages during hearing).

[16]Dunsford, "The Case for Retention of Remedial Jurisdiction in Labor Arbitration Awards," 31 Ga. L. Rev. 201, 233–42 (1996). See Pathmark Stores, Inc. v. Local 1199, 160 LRRM 2346, 2349 (S.D.N.Y., 1999) ("an arbitrator may retain jurisdiction regarding issues that arise out of the rendering of an award, and the maintenance of jurisdiction does not require the award to be vacated"); Dean Foods Co. v. Steelworkers Local 5840, 911 F. Supp. 1116, 153 LRRM 2234 (N.D. Ind., 1995).

[17]Case-Hoyt Corp. v. Graphic Communications Local 503, 5 F. Supp. 2d 154, 158 LRRM 3016 (W.D.N.Y., 1998).

[18]See LLT Int'l Inc. v. MCI, 69 F. Supp. 2d 510 (S.D.N.Y., 1999).

[19]See Union Independiente de Trabajadores de Aeropuertos v. Cargo Servs. Corp., 52 F. Supp. 292, 162 LRRM 2441 (D.P.R., 1999).

[20]Judicial review, including the public policy exception and the "essence cases," is discussed generally in Feller, "Taft and Hartley Vindicated: The Curious History of Review of Labor Arbitration Awards," 19 Berkeley J. Emp. & Lab. L. 296 (1998); Barbakoff, "Application of the Public Policy Exception for the Enforcement of Arbitral Awards," 43 Vill. L. Rev. 829 (1998).

[21]See Kennecott Utah Copper Corp. v. Becker, 195 F.3d 1201, 162 LRRM 2641 (10th Cir., 1999); Tennessee Valley Auth. v. Tennessee Valley Trades & Labor Council, 184 F.3d 510, 161 LRRM 2844 (6th Cir., 1999); IMC-Agrico Co. v. Int'l Chem. Workers Council Local 35-C, 171 F.3d 1322, 160 LRRM 2961 (11th Cir., 1999). See generally Hodges, "Judicial Review of Arbitration Awards on Public Policy Grounds: Lessons From the Case Law," 16 Ohio St. J. on Disp. Resol. 91 (2000).

D. Public Policy Review

In November 2000, the U.S. Supreme Court reiterated the narrow scope of the public policy exception to enforcement of arbitration awards under collective bargaining agreements. In *Eastern Associated Coal Corp. v. Mine Workers (UMW) District 17*,[22] the Court upheld an arbitrator's decision to reinstate an employee who failed a second random drug test, on the ground that there was no explicit public policy that the award violated. On returning to work following an arbitral reinstatement upholding a grievance against being discharged, the employee was ordered to take regular drug tests. After 4 months back on the job, he again failed a random drug test. The subsequent discharge was grieved and went to arbitration. The arbitrator reinstated the grievant, finding no just cause for discharge because of the grievant's 17-year good work record and because of his personal plea of special circumstances that he asserted at the hearing.[23]

The grievant was a member of a road crew, a situation that required him to drive large vehicles on public highways and made him subject to department of transportation regulations relating to drug use and drug tests. For that reason, the employer had cited the federal Omnibus Transportation Employee Testing Act of 1991,[24] which includes policies against drug use and in favor of drug testing, as the statement of public policy that the arbitrator's award violated. The employer also asserted that this was the second time that the employee had failed a drug test, thus indicting the importance of upholding the employer's discharge at the second test failure for safety-sensitive positions. The Court found, however, that the statute alone was not a sufficient basis on which to claim a public policy exception, because the statute also emphasized rehabilitation of employees who use drugs and the arbitrator's reinstatement was not without a number of conditions intended to effect and check on the employee's rehabilitation. The Court said it could not find in the statute or in the regulations implementing it, "or [in] any other law or legal precedent," the explicit public policy statement that the arbitrator's award violated. In so finding, the Court specifically noted that the employer did not claim that the arbitrator's actions exceeded his authority under the collective bargaining agreement.

The U.S. Supreme Court granted certiorari because of a split in the circuits as to what constitutes public policy sufficient to warrant refusal to enforce an arbitrator's decision. The question was the approach used by the courts in evaluating the applicability of the public policy exception. The employer argued that the appropriate standard

---

[22]531 U.S. 57, 165 LRRM 2865 (2000).

[23]Id. at 60.

[24]105 Stat. 953

was whether the award was "contrary to public policy as ascertained by reference to positive law."[25] However, the Supreme Court adopted the alternative interpretation, whether the arbitral award "violates positive law," the one articulated by the district court in its decision to uphold the award.[26] In so doing, the Court explicitly limited the concept of an explicit, well-defined, dominant public policy, the criteria set forth in *Misco*[27] and its progeny, in favor of a direct violation of a statute, regulation, or other positive statement of law.[28]

Before this decision, the circuit courts interpreted the public policy exception in a variety of ways. The narrow view of upholding arbitration awards against challenges on public policy grounds generally prevailed,[29] although some courts interpreted arbitration awards more literally.[30] Courts continue to reaffirm judicial deference to an arbitrator's judgment.[31] Nevertheless, there have been a number of cases in which courts have found that the arbitrator's award did not draw its essence from the contract or that the arbitrator was dispensing "his own brand of industrial justice."[32] *Eastern Associated*

---

[25]Eastern Associated Coal Corp. v. Mine Workers (UMW) Dist. 17, 531 U.S. 57, 63, 165 LRRM 2865 (2000).

[26]66 F. Supp. 2d 796, 163 LRRM 2817 (S.D.W.V., 1998), aff'd, 188 F.3d 501, 165 LRRM 2864 (4th Cir., 1999).

[27]Misco, Inc. v. Paperworkers, 484 U.S. 29, 126 LRRM 3113 (1987).

[28]Eastern Associated Coal Corp. v. Mine Workers (UMW) Dist. 17, 531 U.S. 57, 63, 165 LRRM 2865 (2000).

[29]See St. Mary Home, Inc. v. Service Employees Dist. 1199, 116 F.3d 41, 46, 155 LRRM 2456 (2d Cir., 1997) (courts may invoke public policy to vacate arbitral award "only in those rare cases where enforcement of the award would be directly at odds with a well-defined and dominant public policy resting on clear law and legal precedent"); Electrical Workers (IBEW) Local 97 v. Niagara Mohawk Power Corp., 143 F.3d 704, 158 LRRM 2198 (2d Cir., 1998) (conditional reinstatement of nuclear power plant employee who falsified urine test did not violate public policy); Westvaco Corp. v. Paperworkers, 171 F.3d 971, 160 LRRM 2844 (4th Cir., 1999) (reversing district court's decision that reinstatement of employee terminated for sexual harassment violated public policy); Service Employees v. Local 1199 N.E., 70 F.3d 647, 150 LRRM 2911 (1st Cir., 1995) (court may not vacate arbitrator's award unless it violates well-defined and dominant policy).

[30]Exxon Corp. v. Baton Rouge Oil & Chem. Workers, 77 F.3d 850, 151 LRRM 2737 (5th Cir., 1996) (vacating award reinstating employee in safety-sensitive position who tested positive for cocaine because it violated public policy of drug-free society, although arbitrator found company's testing breached contract).

[31]See Mine Workers (UMW) Dist. 17 v. Island Creek Coal Co., 179 F.3d 133, 161 LRRM 2463 (4th Cir., 1999) (affirming award based on arbitrator's findings of fact); Kuhlman Elect. Corp. v. Auto Workers Local 1772, 144 F.3d 898, 158 LRRM 2331 (6th Cir., 1998) (upholding arbitrator's interpretation of side letter as part of collective bargaining agreement); Six Flags Over Texas v. Electrical Workers (IBEW) Local 116, 143 F.3d 213, 158 LRRM 2594 (5th Cir., 1998) (deferring to arbitrator's interpretation of contract provision requiring proof beyond reasonable doubt); Line Drivers, Pickup & Delivery Local 81 v. Roadway Express, Inc., 152 F.3d 1098, 158 LRRM 3082 (9th Cir., 1998) (affirming award construing contract requirement); Schrim v. Chicago & N.W. Transit, 156 LRRM 3092 (N.D. Iowa, 1997), aff'd sub nom. Schrim v. Union Pac. R.R., 156 LRRM 3120 (8th Cir., 1997), cert denied, 522 U.S. 981 (1997) (affirming award in which arbitrator went outside contract and considered parties' previous course of dealings); Cumberland Times-News Div. of Thomson Newspapers, Inc. v. Teamsters Local 453, 133 F.3d 914, 1998 WL 7932 (4th Cir., 1998) (unpublished) (affirming award because side letter agreement is part of collective bargaining agreement); Teamsters Local 957 v. Dayton Newspapers, Inc., 190 F.3d 434, 162 LRRM 2001 (6th Cir., 2000) (reversed district court and affirmed arbitrator's award that drew its essence from collective bargaining agreement).

[32]See Boise Cascade Corp. v. Association of Western Pulp & Paper Workers, 119 F.3d 5, 1997 WL 408068 (9th Cir., 1997) (unpublished) (vacating award that bore no relationship to contract); Logistics Personnel Corp. v. Truck Drivers Local Union 299, 6 F. Supp. 2d 650, 158 LRRM 2744 (E.D. Mich., 1998) (vacating award where arbitrator imposed additional evidentiary

Coal does not apply in such instances because it is specifically limited to cases where there is no contractual challenge to either the basis for the award or the arbitrator's authority.[33]

In *Alvey, Inc. v. Teamsters Local 688*,[34] authorities arrested and convicted the grievant for possession of cocaine in the company's parking lot. The company subsequently fired him. The arbitrator reinstated the grievant with back pay, finding that the company had not proved that he knowingly possessed cocaine in contravention of a plant rule.

The Eighth Circuit upheld the arbitrator's finding of no just cause for termination, because to overrule the decision would have improperly disturbed the arbitrator's view of the facts, but reversed and remanded on the ground that the arbitrator did not adequately consider the effect of a different plant rule allowing discharge on conviction of a felony.[35]

E. Procedural Grounds for Denying Enforcement: Arbitrator and Party Misconduct and Defects in Proceedings

An award may be challenged on the ground that an arbitrator may not review the manner in which a company imposes discipline. In *Bruce Hardwood Floors*,[36] a company dismissed an employee who told her supervisor that she needed to miss work to attend to her sick daughter. In reality, the employee used her time away from work to pay an overdue utility bill. The arbitrator found no just cause for dismissal and reinstated the grievant with a 10-day suspension. The Fifth Circuit vacated the award, holding that lying was "immoral conduct" and the employer's policy permitted immediate discharge for immoral conduct. Further, the court opined that there was nothing in the contract that provided for a suspension, so the parties had limited the arbitrator's authority to order such a remedy.

Conversely, when a New York U.S. district court vacated an award on similar grounds, the Second Circuit reversed.[37] It held that the district court judge had relied on its own interpretation of the

---

requirements on parties that specifically contradicted terms of collective bargaining agreement); National Hockey League Players' Ass'n v. National Hockey League, 30 F. Supp. 2d 1025, 159 LRRM 2161 (N.D. Ill., 1998) (vacating award where arbitrator exceeded scope of his authority by considering evidence that parties agreed to exclude); Champion Int'l Corp. v. Paperworkers, 168 F.3d 725, 160 LRRM 2513 (4th Cir., 1999) (vacating award and remanding grievance to de novo arbitration at parties' election where arbitrator mistakenly based findings and remedy on agreement other than collective bargaining agreement).

[33]Eastern Associated Coal Corp. v. Mine Workers (UMW) Dist. 17, 531 U.S. 57, 165 LRRM 2865 (2000).

[34]132 F.3d 1209, 157 LRRM 2018 (8th Cir., 1997).

[35]Id. at 1214.

[36]Bruce Hardwood Floors v. Carpenters Local 2713, 103 F.3d 449, 154 LRRM 2207 (5th Cir.), cert. denied, 522 U.S. 928 (1997).

[37]Hill v. Staten Island Zoological Soc'y, 147 F.3d 209, 158 LRRM 2709 (2d Cir., 1998).

contract when it found that lying was just cause for termination,[38] a violation of the basic tenets of judicial review of arbitration decisions.

The Fifth Circuit recently vacated an arbitration award in the context of a last-chance agreement.[39] In that case, the company discharged the grievant pursuant to its drug policy and a signed last-chance agreement previously accepted in lieu of termination. The arbitrator sustained the grievance, agreeing with the union that the grievant should not have been disciplined because he had no notice of the collective bargaining agreement's drug policy. The Fifth Circuit upheld the lower court's action vacating the award because the arbitrator ignored the plain language of the contract, holding that a last-chance agreement is considered to be a supplement to the collective bargaining agreement and is binding on the arbitrator.

Another basis for vacating an arbitration award is a determination that the arbitrator's decision has manifestly disregarded the law. Although it is applied predominantly in employment cases, this doctrine has migrated into some traditional labor cases where enforcement of federal statutes is not at issue.[40] The First, Second, and Tenth Circuits have used the manifest disregard standard to uphold arbitral decisions.[41]

The First Circuit has stated that a component of its standard of review in arbitration cases is whether the award is in manifest disregard of the law.[42] However, not all courts agree. In *Homestake Mining Co.*,[43] the grievant, a mine employee, was discharged for violating a federal safety rule. Using manifest disregard as a standard of review,

---

[38]See also Electrical Workers (IBEW) Local 97 v. Niagara Mohawk Power Corp., 143 F.3d 704, 158 LRRM 2198 (2d Cir., 1998) (vacating district court's determination that, where grievant was reinstated because he did not have sufficient notice of company's drug policy, reasonable person in employee's position would be on notice that his acts would result in termination). In another matter, the Eleventh Circuit observed that "if the collective bargaining agreement confers on the employer the absolute right to discharge employees for certain types of conduct, the inquiry of an arbitrator can be limited as to whether or not the disciplined employee did or did not engage in the specific conduct which resulted in the disciplinary action." If not, however, the reviewing court must defer to the arbitrator's interpretation of the scope and meaning of the just-cause provisions of the contract. IMC-Agrico Co. v. Chemical Workers (UFCW), 171 F.3d 1322, 1327, 160 LRRM 2961 (11th Cir., 1999).

[39]Operating Eng'rs Local 351 v. Cooper Natural Resources, Inc., 163 F.3d 916, 160 LRRM 2241 (5th Cir.), reh'g denied, 1999 U.S. App. LEXIS 4108 (5th Cir., Feb. 9, 1999), cert. denied, 528 U.S. 812 (1999).

[40]See Kiernan v. Piper Jaffray Co., Inc., 137 F.3d 588, 7 AD Cases 1499 (8th Cir., 1998) (statutory employment claim); Brennan v. King, 139 F.3d 258 (1st Cir., 1998); Halligan v. Piper Jaffray, Inc., 148 F.3d 197, 77 FEP Cases 182 (2d Cir., 1998); DiRussa v. Dean Witter Reynolds, Inc., 121 F.3d 818, 74 FEP Cases 726 (2d Cir., 1997); Weaver v. Florida Power & Light Co., 172 F.3d 771, 9 AD Cases 363 (11th Cir., 1999); Montes v. Shearson Lehman Bros., Inc., 128 F.3d 1456, 4 WH Cases 2d 385 (11th Cir., 1997) (Fair Labor Standards Act claim).

[41]Boston & Me. Corp. v. Maintenance of Way Employees, 94 F.3d 15, 153 LRRM 2281 (1st Cir., 1996) (dispute over seniority). See also ARN Exploration Corp. v. Aguirre, 45 F.3d 1455, 1463 (10th Cir., 1995) ("an arbitrator's erroneous interpretations or applications of the law are not reversible. Only manifest disregard of the law is subject to reversal.").

[42]See also Wheelabrator Envirotech Oper. Serv., Inc. v. Massachusetts Laborers Dist. Council Local 1144 & Laborers, 88 F.3d 40, 152 LRRM 2796 (1st Cir., 1996). See Electrical Workers (IBEW) Local 97 v. Niagara Mohawk Power Corp., 143 F.3d 704, 158 LRRM 2198 (2d Cir., 1998).

[43]Homestake Mining Co. v. Steelworkers Local 7044, 153 F.3d 678, 158 LRRM 3101 (8th Cir., 1998) (affirming award where no violation of well-defined public policy clearly shown).

the Eighth Circuit upheld the arbitrator's decision that interpreted the rule and reinstated the grievant.

IV. Statute of Limitations for Confirming and Vacating Arbitration Awards

A. Limitations Period for Unfair Representation Actions Under LMRA Section 301

Courts continue to hold that it is necessary to look to federal law for the applicable limitations period for suits under Section 301 of the Labor Management Relations Act (LMRA).[44] State law claims are preempted by the LMRA where they are based on an interpretation of a collective bargaining agreement.[45]

B. Court of Appeals Decisions in Actions to Confirm and Vacate Arbitration Awards

Efforts to enforce or vacate arbitration awards are covered by state law.[46]

VI. Deferral to Arbitration

E. Excluded Cases

The exception to deferral under Section 8(a)(2) of the National Labor Relations Act is still enforced. The Fifth Circuit recently upheld a National Labor Relations Board (NLRB) decision not to defer where it determined that the activity for which the discipline was given was organizing and was therefore a protected concerted activity under the law.[47] In that case, an employee was fired after speaking out against what he termed as collusion to defraud between the employer and officials of the recognized union. The company said it was looking into the matter; however, the employee continued to voice his concerns. He was subsequently fired for improper interference with the

---

[44]Bricklayers v. Excel Concrete, Inc., 2000 WL 1365904, 2000 U.S. Dist. LEXIS 13883 (N.D. Ill., 2000).

[45]Chapple v. National Starch & Chem. Co., 178 F.3d 501, 161 LRRM 2321 (7th Cir., 1999); Aguilera v. Pirelli Armstrong Tire Corp., 223 F.3d 1010, 165 LRRM 2203 (9th Cir., 2000).

[46]Premier Private Sec. Inc. v. Plant Guard Workers Local 796, 173 F.3d 864, 138 Lab. Cas. (CCH) ¶ 58,624 (10th Cir., 1999) (unpublished opinion).

[47]Mobil Exploration & Producing U.S. Inc. v. NLRB, 200 F.3d 230, 163 LRRM 2387 (5th Cir., 2000).

company's security investigation. In response to his unfair labor practice filing, the Board ordered him reinstated, finding that his statements were made in an attempt to generate support for a union to displace the existing exclusive bargaining representative and were not aimed at the investigation per se. The court challenge to the Board's action claimed that the agency should have deferred to arbitration. The court denied the claim, enforcing the Board's order, emphasizing the protected concerted activity interests that the Board cited as the rationale for its findings.

State public employee relations boards (PERBs) appear to follow the NLRB lead in determining when deferral is appropriate and when it is not. If there is an existing collective bargaining agreement that purports to cover the matter at issue, deferral is favored.[48]

[48]See Delaware State Univ. v. Delaware State Univ. Chapter of Univ. Professors, 165 LRRM 2084 (Del. Ch. Ct., 2000) (board's ruling requiring production of files by employer for use by union in grievance proceeding under contract was topic covered explicitly in contract language and deferral was required); Winchester v. Mountain Line, 294 Mont. 517, 161 LRRM 2694 (1999) (PERB's dismissal of complaint by employee fired for violating bus driver's handbook inappropriate for deferral where court found that contract language excluded statutory violations).

Listing of Back Matter

Appendices

Appendix A

Due Process Protocol for Mediation and Arbitration of Statutory Disputes Arising Out of the Employment Relationship

The Section of Labor and Employment Law, along with other organizations involved in employment relations, has endorsed A Due Process Protocol for Mediation and Arbitration of Statutory Disputes Arising Out of the Employment Relationship in order to assure some measure of fairness and due process to employer promulgated schemes for private resolution of statutory disputes. The organizations that have endorsed or support this protocol include the National Academy of Arbitrations, American Arbitration Association, Society of Professionals in Dispute Resolution, National Employment Lawyers Association, Federal Mediation and Conciliation Service, and the American Civil Liberties Union. Following is the text of the protocol:

The following protocol is offered by the undersigned individuals, members of the Task Force on Alternative Dispute Resolution in Employment, as a means of providing due process in the resolution by mediation and binding arbitration of employment disputes involving statutory rights. The signatories were designated by their respective organizations, but the protocol reflects their personal views and should not be construed as representing the policy of the designating organizations.

Genesis

This Task Force was created by individuals from diverse organizations involved in labor and employment law to examine questions of due process arising out of the use of mediation and arbitration for resolving employment disputes. In this protocol we confine ourselves to statutory disputes.

The members of the Task Force felt that mediation and arbitration of statutory disputes conducted under proper due process safeguards should be encouraged in order to provide expeditious, accessible, inexpensive and fair private enforcement of statutory employment disputes for the 100,000,000 members of the work force who might not otherwise have ready, effective access to administrative or judicial relief. They also hope that such as system will serve to reduce the delays which now arise out of the huge backlog of cases pending before administrative agencies and courts and that it will help forestall an even greater number of such cases.

A. *Pre- or Post-Dispute Arbitration*

The Task Force recognizes the dilemma inherent in the timing of an agreement to mediate and/or arbitrate statutory disputes. It did not achieve consensus on this difficult issue. The views in this spectrum are set forth randomly, as follows:

- Employers should be able to create mediation and/or arbitration systems to resolve statutory claims, but any agreement to mediate and/or arbitrate disputes should be informed, voluntary, and not a condition of initial or continued employment.
- Employers should have the right to insist on an agreement to mediate and/or arbitrate statutory disputes as a condition of initial or continued employment. Postponing such an agreement until a dispute actually arises, when there will likely exist a stronger predisposition to litigate, will result in very few agreements to mediate and/or arbitrate, thus negating the likelihood of effectively utilizing alternative dispute resolution and overcoming the problems of administrative and judicial delays which now plague the system.
- Employees should not be permitted to waive their right to judicial relief of statutory claims arising out of the employment relationship for any reason.
- Employers should be able to create mediation and/or arbitration systems to resolve statutory claims, but the decision to mediate and/or arbitrate individual cases should not be made until after the dispute arises.
- The Task Force takes no position on the timing of agreements to mediate and/or arbitrate statutory employment disputes, though it agrees that such agreements be knowingly made. The focus of this protocol is on standards of exemplary due process.

B. *Right of Representation*

1. Choice of Representative Employees considering the use of or, in fact, utilizing mediation and/or arbitration procedures should have the right to be represented by a spokesperson of their own choosing. The mediation and arbitration procedure should so specify and should include reference to institutions which might offer assistance, such as bar associations, legal service associations, civil rights organizations, trade unions, etc.

2. Fees for Representation The amount and method of payment for representation should be determined between the claimant and the representative. We recommend, however, a number of existing systems which provide employer reimbursement of at least a portion of the employee's attorney fees, especially for lower paid employees. The arbitrator should have the authority to provide for fee reimbursement, in whole or in part, as part of the remedy in accordance with applicable law or in the interests of justice.

3. Access to Information One of the advantages of arbitration is that there is usually less time and money spent in pre-trial discovery. Adequate but limited pre-trial discovery is to be encouraged and employees should have access to all information reasonably relevant to mediation and/or arbitration of their claims. The employees' representative should also have reasonable pre-hearing and hearing access to all such information and documentation. Necessary pre-hearing depositions consistent with the expedited nature of arbitration should be available.

We also recommend that prior to selection of an arbitrator, each side should be provided with the names, addresses and phone numbers of the representatives of the parties in that arbitrator's six most recent cases to aid them in selection.

C. Mediator and Arbitrator Qualification

1. Roster Membership Mediators and arbitrators selected for such cases should have skill in the conduct of hearings, knowledge of the statutory issues at stake in the dispute, and familiarity with the workplace and employment environment. The roster of available mediators and arbitrators should be established on a non-discriminatory basis, diverse by gender, ethnicity, background, experience, etc. to satisfy the parties that their interest and objectives will be respected and fully considered. Our recommendation is for selection if impartial arbitrators and mediators. We recognize the right of employers to jointly select as mediator and/or arbitrator one in whom both parties have requisite trust, even though not possessing the qualifications here recommended, as most promising to bring finality and to withstand judicial scrutiny.

The existing cadre of labor and employment mediators and arbitrators, some lawyers, some not, although skilled in conducting hearings and familiar with the employment milieu is unlikely, without special training, to consistently possess knowledge of the statutory environment in which these disputes arise and of the characteristics of the non-union workplace.

There is a manifest need for mediators and arbitrators with expertise in statutory requirements in the employment field who may, without special training, lack experience in the employment area and in the conduct of arbitration hearings and mediation sessions. Reexamination of rostering eligibility by designating agencies, such as the American Arbitration Association, may permit the expedited inclusion in the pool of this most valuable source of expertise. The roster of arbitrators and mediators should contain representatives with all such skills in order to meet the diverse needs of this caseload.

Regardless of their prior experience, mediators and arbitrators on the roster must be independent of bias toward either party. They should reject cases if they believe the procedure lacks requisite due process.

2. Training The creation of a roster containing the foregoing qualifications dictates the development of a training program to educate existing and potential labor and employment mediators and arbitrators as to the statutes, including substantive, procedural and remedial issues to be confronted and to train experts in the statutes as to employer procedures governing the employment relationship as well as due process and fairness in the conduct and control of arbitration hearings and mediation sessions.

Training in the statutory issues should be provided by the government agencies, bar associations, academic institutions, etc., administered perhaps by the designating agency, such as the AAA, at various locations throughout the country. Such training should be updated periodically and be required of all mediators and arbitrators. Training in the conduct of mediation and arbitration could be provided by a mentoring program with experienced panelists.

Successful completion of such training would be reflected in the resume or panel cards of the arbitrators supplied to the parties for their selection process.

3. Panel Selection Upon request of the parties, the designating agency should utilize a list procedure such as that of the AAA or select a panel composed of an odd number of mediators and arbitrators from its roster or pool. The panel cards for such individuals should be submitted to the parties for their perusal prior to alternate striking of the names on the list, resulting in the designation of the remaining mediator and/or arbitrator. The selection process could empower the designating agency to appoint a mediator and/or arbitrator if the striking procedure is unacceptable or unsuccessful. As noted above, subject to the consent of the parties, the designating agency should provide the names of the parties and their representatives in recent cases decided by the listed arbitrators.

4. Conflicts of Interest The mediator and arbitrator for a case has a duty to disclose any relationship which might reasonably constitute or be perceived as a conflict of interest. The designated mediator and/or arbitrator should be required to sign an oath provided by the designating agency, if any, affirming the absence of such present or preexisting ties.

5. *Authority of the Arbitrator* The arbitrator should be bound by applicable agreements, statutes, regulations and rules of procedure of the designating agency, including the authority to determine the time and place of the hearing, permit reasonable discovery, issue subpoenas, decide arbitrability issues, preserve order and privacy in the hearings, rule on evidentiary matters, determine the close of the hearing and procedures for post-hearing submissions, and issue an award resolving the submitted dispute. The arbitrator should be empowered to award whatever relief would be available in court under the law. The arbitrator should issue an opinion and award setting forth a summary of the issues, including the type(s) of dispute(s),the damages and/or other relief requested and awarded, a statement of any other issues resolved, and a statement regarding the disposition of any statutory claim(s).

6. *Compensation of the Mediator and Arbitrator* Impartiality is best assured by the parties sharing the fees and expenses of the mediator and arbitrator. In cases where the economic condition of a party does not permit equal sharing, the parties should make mutually acceptable arrangements to achieve that goal if at all possible. In the absence of such agreement, the arbitrator should determine allocation of fees. The designating agency, by negotiating the parties share of costs and collecting such fees, might be able to reduce the bias potential of disparate contributions by forwarding payment to the mediator and/or arbitrator without disclosing the parties share therein.

D. Scope of Review

The arbitrator's award should be final and binding and the scope of review should be limited.

Dated: May 9, 1995

Christopher A. Barreca, Co-Chair Partner Paul, Hastings, Janofsky & Walker Rep., Council of Labor & Employment Section American Bar Association	Max Zimny, Co-Chair General Counsel, International Ladies' Garment Workers' Union Rep., Council of Labor & Employment Section American Bar Association
Arnold Zack, Co-Chair President, National Academy of Arbitrators	

Carl E. VerBeek Partner Management Co-Chair Arbitration Committee of Labor & Employment Section, ABA	Robert D. Manning Angoff, Goldman, Manning, Payle, Wanger Varnum Riddering Schmidt & Howlett & Hiatt, P.C. Union Co-Chair Arbitration Committee of Labor & Employment Section, ABA
Charles F. Ipavec, Arbitrator Neutral Co-Chair Arbitration Committee of Labor & Employment Section, ABA	George H. Friedman Senior Vice President American Arbitration Association
Michael F. Hoellering General Counsel American Arbitration Association	W. Bruce Newman Rep., Society of Professionals in Dispute Resolution
Wilma Liebman Special Assistant to the Director Federal Mediation & Conciliation	Joseph Garrison, President National Employment Lawyers Association
Lewis Maltby Director, Workplace Rights Project American Civil Liberties Union	

American Bar Association 750 N. Lake Shore Dr., Chicago, IL 60611
312/988-5000
info@abanet.org

2001 Supplement Finding Aids

Table of Arbitration Decisions 2001 Supplement

*References are to Supplement chapter and footnote number (e.g., **12:** 86 refers to footnote 86 in chapter 12). Alphabetization is letter-by-letter (e.g., Bellevue precedes Bell Fed.).*

A

B

C

D

E

F

G

H

I

J

K

L

N

O

S

V

W

Y

Table of Arbitrators 2001 Supplement

This table lists the names of arbitrators from awards cited within the Supplement footnotes. No distinction is made between arbitrators with the same last name. This format may be useful to representatives in selecting arbitrators or in writing briefs; it may also be helpful to arbitrators in award preparation. References are to Supplement chapter and footnote number (e.g., ***11:*** *16 refers to footnote 16 in chapter 11).*

A

Abercrombie ***2:*** 89, 99; ***6:*** 20
Ables ***5:*** 19
Abrams ***8:*** 42
Allen ***2:*** 59, 85; ***3:*** 7; ***4:*** 27, 32; ***5:*** 7, 27; ***6:*** 135, 151, 152, 166; ***9:*** 18; ***12:*** 3, 27, 89
Allen, Jr. ***6:*** 27, 63, 80, 89; ***9:*** 5, 6; ***12:*** 43, 91
Alleyne ***5:*** 2, 21
Antoine ***5:*** 8
Archer ***6:*** 157

B

Babiskin ***3:*** 30, 43; ***4:*** 1, 10, 15
Bailey ***2:*** 28; ***3:*** 6, 38; ***5:*** 40; ***6:*** 49; ***8:*** 36; ***9:*** 1; ***12:*** 8, 9, 13, 27, 93
Bain ***2:*** 55; ***5:*** 40
Bankston ***2:*** 101; ***5:*** 11, 12; ***12:*** 56, 66, 83
Bankstown ***12:*** 53
Baroni ***2:*** 58; ***3:*** 8; ***5:*** 40, 46, 47; ***6:*** 20, 45, 50, 82, 95, 123, 161; ***8:*** 23; ***10:*** 2, 7; ***12:*** 2, 24, 37, 99; ***13:*** 5, 6, 13, 34, 35, 42
Barron ***12:*** 3
Beck ***6:*** 167
Beckjord ***7:*** 33
Bell ***6:*** 76
Belshaw ***6:*** 25
Berger ***3:*** 44, 48
Bernhardt ***8:*** 58; ***12:*** 21
Berquist ***12:*** 78
Bittel ***6:*** 77, 147
Block ***8:*** 17; ***12:*** 90
Bognanno ***2:*** 35
Bogue ***6:*** 6, 20, 138, 145; ***8:*** 34
Borland ***3:*** 9, 35; ***6:*** 12, 22, 60, 72; ***8:*** 67
Bressler ***4:*** 7
Briggs ***2:*** 31, 86; ***3:*** 45; ***6:*** 1, 35, 39, 43, 44, 46, 66; ***11:*** 7, 24; ***12:*** 42, 57, 59
Brisco ***8:*** 5, 8, 43; ***11:*** 16, 17, 18
Brodsky ***5:*** 11, 20; ***6:*** 21, 124, 126, 156, 164; ***10:*** 13; ***11:*** 32; ***12:*** 104; ***13:*** 31
Brookins ***2:*** 95; ***8:*** 38; ***10:*** 15
Brown ***5:*** 47; ***6:*** 134, 144; ***12:*** 12
Brunner ***12:*** 56, 63
Bumpass ***2:*** 43; ***6:*** 136, 155; ***12:*** 4, 13, 43, 87, 93, 102
Byars ***2:*** 44, 50; ***6:*** 10, 33; ***12:*** 91

C

Calhoun ***2:*** 93; ***6:*** 14, 22; ***13:*** 25
Canestraight ***13:*** 36
Cantor ***2:*** 92; ***8:*** 62
Caraway ***12:*** 43, 90; ***13:*** 4
Cayton ***5:*** 45
Cerone ***2:*** 20; ***6:*** 13, 117
Chandler ***5:*** 41; ***8:*** 63
Chattman ***6:*** 40; ***13:*** 37

D

E

F

G

H

Table of Court Cases 2001 Supplement

*References are to Supplement chapter and footnote number (e.g., **5:** 11 refers to footnote 11 in chapter 5).*

A

B

C

D

E

F

G

H

P

R

S

T

U

V

W

Index
2001 Supplement

This index is alphabetized word-by-word (e.g., Work slowdowns precedes Workplace misconduct). References are to page numbers in this Supplement.

I

J

L

S

Main Edition Finding Aids

Errata in Main Edition Notes

This table shows errors that appeared in the notes in the Main Edition. The incorrect information that appeared in the Main Edition appears in ~~strikethrough~~ format, while the corrected information appears in **boldface**. The corrected information reflected in this table was used for compiling the Table of Arbitration Decisions and Table of Arbitrators for the Main Edition, which follow this Table.

Chapter 2

n.1	United Tel. Co. of Fla., 61 LA 443 (~~Taylor,~~ **Murphy,** 1973)
n.40	United Tel. Co. of Fla., 61 LA 443 (Murphy, ~~1983~~**1973**)
n.69	Georgia Power Co., 93 LA 846 (Holley, **Jr.,** 1989)
n.73	ITT Continental Baking Co., ~~798~~ **79** LA 166 (Modjeska, 1982)
n.78	Stowe-Woodward Co., 78 LA 1038 (Thomson, **Jr.,** 1982)
n.106	Hyatt Hotels Palo Alto, 85 LA 11 (~~Oestereich,~~ **Oestreich,** 1985)
n.165	MacMillan Bloedel Containers, 92 LA 592 (Nicholas, ~~Jr.,~~ 1989)
n.172	Monarch Sidney Co., 96 LA 477 (~~Millous,~~ **Millious,** 1991)
n.194	Shop ~~N'~~ **'N** Save Warehouse Foods, Inc., 85 LA 494 (~~Neumark,~~ **Newmark,** 1985)
n.198	GATX Terminals Corp., 91 LA 1162 (~~Baron,~~ **Baroni,** 1988)
n.213	Curtis ~~Mathes,~~ **Mathis,** 74 LA 171 (Goodstein, 1979)
n.240	Fisher Foods, 88 LA ~~1984~~ **1084** (Richard, 1987)
n.249	~~Sime~~ **Simetco** & Co., 96 LA 193 (Odom, 1990)
n.259	International Harvester Co., 12 LA 1190 (McCoy, ~~1990~~**1949**)
n.259	~~Lukes~~ **Lukens** Steel Co., 101 LA 569 (Strongin, 1993)
n.261	~~Bistate~~ **Bi-State** Dev. Agency, 101 LA 427 (McGrady, 1993)
n.263	George Koch & Sons, 102 LA 737 (Brunner, 1994)
n.263	Schlage Lock Co., 88 LA 75 (Wyman, ~~1988~~**1986**)
n.269	~~Lukes~~ **Lukens** Steel Co., 101 LA 569 (Strongin, 1993)
n.269	New Haven, 101 LA ~~647~~ **646** (Stewart, 1993)
n.276	MacMillan Bloedel Containers, 92 LA 592 (Nicholas, ~~Jr.,~~ 1989)
n.281	Republic Steel Corp., **25** LA 733 (Platt, 1955)
n.285	Libby, ~~McNeil~~ **McNeill** & Libby of Canada, Ltd., 74 LA 991 (O'Shea, 1980)
n.286	Southwest Petro-Chem, Inc., 92 LA ~~493~~ **492** (Berger, 1988)
n.305	Bauer Bros., 48 LA ~~461~~ **861** (Kates, 1967)
n.306	Baltimore Transit Co., 47 LA 62 (**Duff,** 1966)
n.344	RMS Techs., Inc., 94 LA 297 (~~Nichols,~~**Nicholas,** 1990)
n.353	Bethlehem Steel, 12 LA 167 (~~Seleckman,~~ **Selekman,** 1949)
n.359	Eberele Tanning Co., 71 LA 302 (~~Sloan,~~ **Sloane,** 1978)
n.378	Florida Wire & Cable Co., 63 LA 335 (**McIntosh,** 1974)

n.380 Stockham Pipe ~~Fitting~~ **Fittings** Co., 1 LA 160 (McCoy, 1945)
n.387 Huntington Chair Corp., 24 LA ~~491~~ **490** (McCoy, 1955)
n.390 BHP Petroleum, 102 LA 321 (Najita, ~~1993~~**1994**)
n.391 Anchorage Hilton Hotel, 102 LA 55 (~~Landeau,~~ **Landau,** 1993)

Chapter 3

n.5 Burns Int'l Sec. ~~Sys.,~~**Serv.** Inc., 78 LA 1163 (Kelliher, 1982)
n.8 Lima Register Co., 76 LA 935 (~~Heinz,~~ **Heinsz,** 1981)
n.10 Primeline Indus., Inc., 88 LA 700 (Morgan, **Jr.,** 1986)
n.11 Burns Int'l Sec. ~~Sys.,~~**Serv.** Inc., 78 LA 1163 (Kelliher, 1982)
n.15 Nuodex, Inc., 87 LA 256 (~~Millous,~~ **Millious,** 1986)
n.18 North River Energy Co., 88 LA 447 (Witney, ~~1988~~**1987**)
n.20 Master Builders, Inc., ~~91???~~ **92** LA 1021 (Curry, 1989)
n.35 Southwest Detroit Hosp., 82 LA 491 (~~Ellman,~~ **Ellmann,** 1984)
n.38 Babcock & Wilcox Co., 72 LA 1073 (Mullin, **Jr.,** 1979) *3:* 38
n.52 Homestake Mining Co., 85 LA 29 (~~White,~~ **Gunderson,** 1985)
n.60 La Crosse Lutheran Hosp., 73 LA 722 (~~McCray,~~ **McCrary,** 1979)
n.64 Aeroquip Corp., 95 LA 31 (~~Steiber,~~ **Stieber,** 1990)
n.73 Cleveland Elec. Illuminating Co., 88 LA 781 (Morgan, **Jr.,** 1987)
n.74 Aeroquip Corp., 95 LA 31 (~~Steiber, 1991~~**Stieber,** 1990)
n.78 Warner-Lambert Co., 89 LA 265 (~~Sloan,~~ **Sloane,** 1987)
n.92 U.S. Steel Corp., 95 LA ~~???~~ **566** (Talarico, 1990)
n.95 Jones ~~Operating~~ **Operation** & Maintenance Co., 93 LA 239 (Schwartz, 1989)
n.122 ~~LaCrosse~~ **La Crosse** Lutheran Hosp., 73 LA 722 (McCrary, 1979)
n.122 Quaker Oats Co., 86 LA 673 (~~Peterson,~~ **Petersen,** 1986)
n.127 ~~McCarthy's~~ **McCartney's,** Inc., 84 LA 799 (Nelson, 1985)
n.127 ~~Redmar~~ **Redmer** Plastics, Inc., 79 LA 351 (Eagle, 1982)
n.132 Cleveland Elec. Illuminating Co., 88 LA 781 (Morgan, **Jr.,** 1987)
n.143 Redmer Plastics, Inc., ~~70~~ **79** LA 351 (Eagle, 1982)
n.168 Pacific ~~Air Motive~~ **Airmotive** Corp., 28 LA 761 (Jones, 1957)
n.184 ~~Tech. Cast.,~~ **Tech-Cast,** Inc., 74 LA 732 (Lewis, 1980)
n.207 Air Carrier Engine Serv., Inc., 81-2 ARB ¶ ~~8352~~ **8353** (Greene, 1980)
n.221 Gillette Co., 79 LA ~~943~~ **953** (Bard, 1982)

Chapter 4

n.18 KDFW-TV, ~~92~~ **94** LA 806 (Allen, 1990)
n.56 Curtis ~~Mathes~~ Mfg. Co., 56 LA 274 (Autrey, 1971)
n.85 Vons ~~Cons.~~**Cos.**, 100 LA 297 (Ross, 1992)
n.86 Hess Oil Virgin Islands, 91 LA 1284 (Hunter, **Jr.,** 1988)
n.90 Hess Oil Virgin Islands, 72 LA ~~181???~~ **81** (Berkman, 1978)
nn.93, 103 Curtis ~~Mathes~~ **Mathis** Co., 52 LA 145 (Merrill, 1968)
n.105, 116 Hess Oil Virgin Islands, 91 LA 1284 (Hunter, **Jr.,** 1988)
n.141 John ~~Brunner~~ **Bruener** Co., 75 LA 1292 (Craver, 1981)

Chapter 5

n.60 Ermanco, Inc., 101 LA 269 (~~Ellman,~~ **Ellmann,** 1993)
n.61 Day & ~~Zimmermann,~~**Zimmerman,** Inc., 44 LA 385 (Boles, 1965)
n.63 Federal Mogul Corp., 69 LA 919 (Morgan, **Jr.,** 1977)
n.64 Champion Int'l Corp., 73 LA 921 (Rimer, **Jr.,** 1979)
n.73 Beverly Enters., 100 LA ~~552~~ **522** (Berquist, 1993)
n.97 ~~Kimberley-Clark~~ **Kimberly-Clark** Corp., 55 LA 291 (Jaffee, 1970)
n.102 Robertshaw Controls Co., 55 LA 883 (~~Seinshemer,~~ **Seinsheimer,** 1970)
n.109 International Harvester Co., 16 LA 307 (McCoy, ~~1957~~**1951**)

n.118 ~~Rockhill~~ **Rock Hill** Printing & Finishing Co., 16 LA 722 (Jaffee, 1951)

n.122 Bronx-Lebanon Hosp. Ctr., 90 LA 1216 (~~Babishkin,~~ **Babiskin,** 1988)

n.127 Ralston Purina Co., 61 LA 14 (~~Kristov,~~ **Krislov,** 1973)

n.134 South Cent. Bell Tel. Co., 59 LA 134 (~~Steward,~~ **Seward,** 1972)

n.135 Signal Delivery Serv., Inc., 86 LA 75 (~~Weis,~~ **Wies,** 1985)

n.145 Reynolds ~~Metal~~ **Metals** Co., 17 LA 710 (Granoff, 1957)

n.158 Phillips 66 Co., 93 LA 707 (~~Goldstein,~~ **Goodstein,** 1989)

n.205 U.S. Dep't of Treasury, 82 LA 1209 (~~Kaplin,~~ **Kaplan,** 1984)

Chapter 6

n.2 National Car Rental Sys., Inc., 75 LA 518 (Zumas, ~~1989~~**1980**)

n.2 Warehouse Distrib. Ctrs., 90 LA 979 (Weiss, ~~1982~~**1987**)

n.5 Mississippi River Grain Elevator, 62 LA 200 (~~Zack,~~ **Marcus,** 1974)

n.6 Swift & Co., 72 LA 513 (~~Renfro,~~ **Rentfro,** 1979)

n.9 Mason & ~~Hangar-Silas~~ **Hanger-Silas** Mason Co., 103 LA 371 (Cipolla, 1994)

n.9 Union-Tribune Publ'g Co., 93 LA 617 (~~McBreaty,~~ **McBrearty,** 1989)

n.44 ~~Petibone~~ **Pettibone** Ohio Corp., 72 LA 1144 (Feldman, 1979)

n.49 Regional Transp. Dist., 94 LA ~~177~~ **117** (Hogler, 1989)

n.77 United Techs. ~~Ctr.~~**Carrier**, 92 LA 829 (Williams, 1989)

n.87 Koppers Co., 91 LA 363 (~~Yarwosky,~~ **Yarowsky,** 1988)

n.90 Swift & Co., 72 LA 513 (~~Renfro,~~ **Rentfro,** 1979)

n.93 Warehouse Distrib. Ctrs., 90 LA 979 (Weiss, ~~1982~~**1987**)

n.103 U.S. Plywood Corp., 88 LA 275 (~~Matthews,~~ **Mathews,** 1986)

n.120 Scott Paper Co., 100 LA 1113 (~~Carney,~~ **Caraway,** 1993)

n.124 Babcock & Wilcox Co., 102 LA 104 (~~Nicolas,~~ **Nicholas,** 1994)

n.136 ~~Growmar,~~ **Growmark,** Inc., 100 LA 785 (Ver Ploeg, 1993)

n.137 Phillip **Morris** U.S.A., 99 LA 1016 (Volz, 1992)

n.152 ~~Bistate~~ **Bi-State** Dev. Agency, 72 LA 198 (Newmark, 1979)

n.157 S.C. Elec. & Gas Co., ~~91 LA 1385 (Baroni, 1989)~~ **89 LA 845 (Boals, 1987)**

n.158 Texas City Ref., ~~89 LA 845 (Boals, 1987)~~ **89 LA 1159 (Milentz, 1987)**

n.166 Koppers Co., 91 LA 363 (~~Yarwosky,~~ **Yarowsky,** 1988)

n.174 Georgia Power Co., 93 LA 846 (Holley, **Jr.,** 1989)

n.176 Regional Transp. Dist., ~~92~~ **91** LA 213 (Goldstein, 1988)

n.180 Valvoline Oil Co., 89 LA 209 (Briscoe, ~~1989~~**1987**)

n.185 Delaware, 104 LA 845 (Gorman, ~~1995~~**1993**)

n.193 Mason & ~~Hangar-Silas~~ **Hanger-Silas** Mason Co., 103 LA 371 (Cipolla, 1994)

n.211 Crucible Materials Corp., 94 LA 540 (~~Harkness,~~ **Harkless,** 1989)

n.214 Thermo ~~Eng'g~~ **King** Corp., 102 LA 612 (Dworkin, 1993)

n.218 Allentown, 100 LA 592 (~~Di Lauro,~~ **DiLauro,** 1992)

n.219 Eaton Corp., 94 LA 971 (~~Eiselo,~~ **Eisele,** 1990)

n.224 Goodyear Tire & Rubber Co., 92 LA 91 (Dworkin, ~~1989~~1988)

n.251 Koppers Co., 91 LA 363 (~~Yarwosky,~~ **Yarowsky,** 1988)

n.284 Cleveland Elec. Illuminating Co., 88 LA 781 (Morgan, **Jr.,** 1987)

Chapter 7

n.38 ~~Carbide~~ **Carbidie** Corp., 100 LA 763 (Felice, 1993)

n.56 ~~Potlach~~ **Potlatch** Corp., 82 LA 445 (Kapsch, 1984)

n.61 ~~Carbide~~ **Carbidie** Corp., 100 LA 763 (Felice, 1993)

n.70 Arkansas Okla. Gas Corp., 96 LA 704 (Allen, ~~1989~~**1991**)

nn.70, 87 ~~Carbide~~ **Carbidie** Corp., 100 LA 763 (Felice, 1993)

n.96 Super Valu Stores, Inc., 74 LA 939 (~~Everson,~~ **Evenson,** 1980)

n.104 F. W. ~~Schumacker~~ **Schumacher** & Co., 87-2 ARB ¶ 8573 (Rocha, 1987)
n.112 ~~Bramer~~ **Brammer** Mfg. Co., 83-2 ARB ¶ 8541 (Talent, 1983)
n.137 ~~Brink's~~ **Brinks,** Inc., 79 LA 816 (Briggs, 1982)
nn.190, 191 San Diego Gas & Elec. Co., 82 LA 1039 (~~Johnson,~~ **Johnston,** 1983)

Chapter 8
n.7 Doe Run Co., 95 LA 705 (~~Heinz,~~ **Heinsz,** 1990)
n.38 ~~Von's~~ **Vons** Cos., 106 LA 740 (Darrow, 1996)
n.42 Enterprise Wire Co., 46 LA 359 (~~Dougherty,~~ **Daugherty,** 1966)
n.44, 79 Pet, Inc., 83 LA 468 (**Schedler, Jr.,** 1984)
n.90 Thorn Apple Valley, Inc., 98 LA 183 (Kanner, ~~1983~~**1991**)
n.102, 105 Suburban Mfg. Co., 77 LA 1200 (Rimer, **Jr.,** 1981)
n.106 General Elec. Co., 74 LA 115 (King, ~~1977 ???~~**1979**)
n.113 Essex Indus. Chems., Inc., 88 LA 991 (Cluster, ~~1991~~**1987**)
n.121 ~~Masillon,~~ **Massillon,** City of, 92 LA 1303 (Elkin, 1989)
n.126 Reynolds ~~Metal~~ **Metals** Co., 84 LA 367 (Gibson, 1985)
n.130 G. ~~Heilman~~ **Heileman** Brewing Co., 83 LA 829 (Hilgert, 1984)
n.135 Reynolds ~~Metal~~ **Metals** Co., 84 LA 367 (Gibson, 1985)
n.180 Burton Mfg. Co., 82 LA 1228 (~~Holly,~~ **Holley,** Jr., 1984)
n.181 ~~Keeble~~ **Keebler** Co., 92 LA 871 (Roumell, Jr., 1989)
n.182 ~~Hobard~~ **Hobart** Corp., 75 LA 907 (Curry, Jr., 1980)
n.184 Veterans Admin. Med. Ctr., 76 LA 412 (~~Pastone, Jr.,~~ **Pastore,** 1981)
n.188 GTE Cal., Inc., 103 LA 343 (~~Grabuski,~~ **Grabuskie,** 1994)
n.190 **Cumberland Lincoln Mercury,** 94 LA 521 (Chandler 1990)
n. 214 Owens-Corning ~~Fiberglas~~ **Fiberglass** Corp., 54 LA 419 (Reid, 1970)
n. 218 Curtis ~~Mathes~~ **Mathis** Mfg. Co., 70 LA 628 (Brown, 1978)
n.230 ~~Monsato~~ **Monsanto** Chem. Intermediates Co., 75 LA 592 (Penfield, 1980)
n.257 ~~RobertShaw~~ **Robertshaw** Controls, 55 LA 283 (Blak, 1970)
n.263 Southern Bell Tel. & Tel. Co., 74 LA ~~115~~ **1155** (Duff, 1980)
n.264 Arrow Redi-Mix Concrete, Inc., 56 LA 597 (~~Fleischi,~~ **Fleischli,** 1971)
nn.267, 270 Mister A's Restaurant, 80 LA 1104 (Christopher, ~~1980~~**1983**)
n.294 Hillhaven Corp., 91 LA 451 (McCurdy, ~~1981~~**1988**)

Chapter 9
n.10 Inland Container Corp., 28 LA 312 (Ferguson, ~~1951???~~**1957**)
nn.21, 22 ~~Ralphs~~ **Ralph's** Grocery Co., 77 LA 867 (Kaufman, 1981)

Chapter 10
n.36 ~~Phillip~~ **Philip** Morris U.S.A., 66 LA 626 (Beckman, 1976)
n.49 Reynolds ~~Metal~~ **Metals** Co., 84 LA 367 (Gibson, 1985)
n.88 E.A. Norris Plumbing Co., 90 LA ~~463~~ **462** (Christopher, 1987)
n.10 International Harvester Co., 16 LA 307 (McCoy, ~~1950~~**1951**)
n.95 E.A. Norris Plumbing Co., 90 LA ~~463~~ **462** (Christopher, 1987)
n.105 Hobart Corp., 75 LA 907 (Curry, **Jr.,** 1980)

Chapter 11
n.12 Armour-Dial, Inc., 76 LA 96 (Aaron, ~~1981~~**1980**)
n.27 Georgia Power Co., 93 LA 846 (Holley, **Jr.,** 1989)
n.33 Capital Area Transit Auth., 69 LA 811 (~~Ellman,~~ **Ellmann,** 1977)
n.36 Republic Airlines, Inc., ~~82~~ **83** LA 127 (Seidman, 1984)
n.69 Hess Oil Virgin Islands, 91 LA 1284 (Hunter, **Jr.,** 1988)
n.69 Mead Paper, 91 LA ~~53???~~ **52** (Curry, Jr., 1988)
n.115 Schlage Lock Co., 88 LA 75 (Wyman, ~~1975~~**1986**)

n.122 Soule Steel Co., ~~84~~ **85** LA 336 (Richman, 1985)
n.124 ~~Riley-Stoker~~ **Riley Stoker** Co., 63 LA 581 (Shister, 1974)
n.143 ~~Alden's,~~ **Aldens,** Inc., 61 LA 663 (Dolnick, 1973)
n.150 King Co., 89 LA 681 ~~???~~ **(Bard, 1987)**
n.167 Growmark, Inc., 100 LA 785 (~~VerPloeg,~~ **Ver Ploeg,** 1993)
n.174 Borden's Farm Prods., 3 LA 607 (~~???~~**Burke,** 1945)

Chapter 12
n.4 International Harvester Co., 15 LA 1 (~~Steward,~~ **Seward,** 1950)
n.45 Union Camp Corp., 104 LA 295 (Nolan, ~~1994~~**1995**)
n.107 Boston Edison Co., 92 LA ~~375~~ **374** (Nicolau, 1988)
n.114 Pepsi Cola Bottling Co., 93 LA 520 (~~Randell,~~ **Randall,** 1989)
nn.120, 121 Riverside Osteopathic Hosp., 98 LA 1044 (McDonald, ~~1991~~**1992**)
n.123 Firestone Tire & Rubber Co., ~~92~~ **93** LA 381 (Cohen, 1989)
n.123 J&L Specialty Prods. Corp., 94 LA ~~601~~ **600** (Duda, 1990)
n.124 Burton Mfg. Co., 82 LA 1228 (~~Holey,~~ **Holley, Jr.,** 1984)
n.126 ~~Stockholm~~ **Stockham** Pipe Fittings Co., 1 LA 160 (McCoy, 1945)
n.138 Liberal Mkt., Inc., 71 LA 148 (~~Layborne,~~ **Laybourne,** 1978)
n.248 ~~Mallincrodt~~ **Mallinckrodt** Chem. Works, 50 LA 933 (Goldberg, 1968)
n.256 Fort Pitt Bridge Works, 30 LA 633 (~~Lehoczy,~~ **Lehoczky,** 1958)

Chapter 13
n.227 Mason & ~~Hangar-Silas~~ **Hanger-Silas** Mason Co., 103 LA 371 (Cipolla, 1994)

Chapter 14
n.127 Todd Shipyards Corp., ~~16~~ **69** LA 27 (Jones, 1977)

Table of Arbitration Decisions Main Edition

*References are to Main Edition chapter and footnote number (e.g., **11:** 16 refers to footnote 16 in chapter 11). Alphabetization is letter-by-letter (e.g., "Northern" precedes "North Haven"). Numbers in party names are treated as if spelled out (e.g., "3M" is alphabetized as "ThreeM"). Some entries may not match precisely what appears in the Main Edition because corrected information, as reflected by the Errata table on page 191, was used to compile this table.*

A

B

C

Cerro Corp., 69 LA 965 (Griffin, 1977) ***6:*** 42
Certainteed Corp., 78 LA 1290 (Madden, 1982) ***8:*** 209
CGM Contractors, 93 LA 1159 (Duda, 1989) ***12:*** 70, 72
Chalfant Mfg. Co., 52 LA 51 (Nichols, 1968) ***5:*** 144
Challenge-Cook Bros., 55 LA 517 (Roberts, 1970) ***8:*** 277
Champion Dairypak, 105 LA 462 (Allen, 1995) ***4:*** 71
Champion Int'l Corp.
73 LA 921 (Rimer, Jr., 1979) ***5:*** 64
81-1 ARB ¶ 8218 (Johnson, Jr., 1981) ***11:*** 101
81 LA 1285 (Flannagan, 1983) ***3:*** 125
Champion Papers, Courtland Mill, 74 LA 623 (White, 1980) ***3:*** 31
Champion Spark Plug
68 LA 702 (Casselman, 1977) ***6:*** 9
77-1 ARB ¶ 8158 (Casselman, 1977) ***5:*** 228
93 LA 1277 (Dobry, 1989) ***2:*** 97, 179, 351; ***12:*** 13, 56, 143, 164, 258
Chanslor-Western Oil Co., 61 LA 113 (Meiners, 1973) ***7:*** 162
Chanute Mfg. Co.
92-2 ARB ¶ 8452 (Levy, 1991) ***8:*** 6
99 LA 20 (Levy, 1992) ***5:*** 62
Charles Todd Unif. Rental Serv. Co., 77 LA 144 (Hutcheson, 1981) ***8:*** 167, 314
Charlotte, 97 LA 1065 (Borland, 1991) ***12:*** 255
Charter Int'l Oil Co., 75 LA 929 (Milentz, 1980) ***10:*** 44
Chase Bag Co., 88 LA 441 (Straffhofer, 1986) ***6:*** 143
Chase Brass & Copper Co., 90 LA 916 (Bressler, 1988) ***2:*** 334; ***12:*** 111
Chatham Supermarkets, Inc., 71 LA 1084 (Roumell, 1978) ***8:*** 206, 207
Chattanooga Gas Co.
83 LA 48 (Mullin, 1984) ***3:*** 122
92-1 ARB ¶ 8180 (Howell, 1991) ***6:*** 276
Checker Cab Co., 62 LA 1107 (Fleischli, 1974) ***5:*** 38, 61
Checker Motors Corp.
61 LA 33 (Daniel, 1973) ***5:*** 73
95 LA 435 (Lipson, 1990) ***4:*** 125
Chevron, U.S.A., 95 LA 395 (Riker, 1990) ***6:*** 191
Cheyenne Pipeline Co., 59 LA 726 (Rentfro, 1972) ***4:*** 30
Chicago, 97 LA 20 (Goldstein, 1990) ***3:*** 260
Chicago Pneumatic Tool Co., 38 LA 891 (Duff, 1961) ***5:*** 196; ***9:*** 47, 50
Chicago Transit Auth.
84 LA 279 (Fletcher, 1985) ***11:*** 97
95 LA 753 (Goldstein, 1990) ***13:*** 166
97 LA 367 (Cox, 1991) ***8:*** 307
Chillicothe, Ohio, 96 LA 657 (DiLeone, 1991) ***2:*** 135
Chivas Prods., Ltd., 101 LA 546 (Kanner, 1993) ***12:*** 36
Choptank Elec. Coop., 87-2 ARB ¶ 8553 (Bernhardt, 1987) ***8:*** 9
Chromalloy Am. Corp.
61 LA 246 (Hon, 1973) ***10:*** 24
72 LA 838 (Cohen, 1979) ***10:*** 54
80 LA 720 (Woolf, 1983) ***3:*** 190
93 LA 828 (Woolf, 1989) ***2:*** 26, 110, 171; ***12:*** 13, 55, 57
Chromalloy Div.-Okla., 67 LA 1310 (Moore, 1977) ***5:*** 44
Chrome Deposit Corp., 102 LA 733 (Bethel, 1994) ***12:*** 89, 122
Chrysler Corp.
24 LA 549 (Wolff, 1955) ***7:*** 16
40 LA 935 (Alexander, 1963) ***6:*** 227; ***12:*** 23
63 LA 677 (Alexander, 1974) ***5:*** 89; ***10:*** 25
64 LA 700 (Alexander, 1975) ***2:*** 401
Cidcomm, Inc., 79-2 ARB ¶ 8534 (Barsamian, 1979) ***5:*** 176
Cincinnati, 80 LA 748 (Klein, 1983) ***2:*** 217, 243
Cincinnati Gas & Elec. Co., 90 LA 841 (Katz, 1988) ***8:*** 332
Cincinnati Paperboard Corp., 93 LA 505 (Dworkin, 1989) ***11:*** 125
Cissell Mfg. Co., 95 LA 937 (Kindig, 1990) ***2:*** 58, 71
Cities Serv. Oil Corp., 41 LA 1091 (Oppenheim, 1963) ***6:*** 108
City of. *See name of city*
Clagon Carbon Corp., 88 LA 347 (Tharp, 1987) ***12:*** 258
Claridge Prods. & Equip., 94 LA 1083 (Goodstein, 1990) ***11:*** 66
Clark Equip. Co., 61 LA 1301 (Kossoff, 1974) ***5:*** 42
Clark Grave Vault Co., 37 LA 860 (McCoy, 1961) ***2:*** 42
Clark Oil & Ref. Corp., 79 LA 1181 (Franke, 1982) ***7:*** 102
Clay Equip., 73 LA 817 (Carter, 1979) ***8:*** 230
Cleaners Hanger Co., 93 LA 526 (Miller, 1989) ***12:*** 160
Cleveland Bd. of Educ., 90-1 ARB ¶ 8070 (Van Pelt, 1988) ***6:*** 141
Cleveland, City of, 71 LA 1041 (Siegel, 1978) ***8:*** 65, 68, 71, 75

D

E

F

G

H

I

J

K

L

M

N

O

P

Q

R

82 LA 217 (Lawson, 1984) ***8:*** 324; ***12:*** 258
Rock Hill Printing & Finishing Co.
16 LA 722 (Jaffee, 1951) ***5:*** 17, 118
64 LA 856 (Whyte, 1975) ***12:*** 113
Rockwell Int'l Corp.
85 LA 246 (Feldman, 1985) ***13:*** 45
86 LA 120 (Feldman, 1985) ***3:*** 31, 39, 108
Rockwell Int'l Highway Brake & Trailer Axle Div., 88 LA 1092 (Morgan, 1987) ***3:*** 35, 73
Rocky Mountain Arsenal, 77 LA 229 (Rockwell, 1981) ***12:*** 172
Rocky Mountain News, 100 LA 1218 (Cohen, 1993) ***10:*** 74
Rodeway Inn, 102 LA 1003 (Goldberg, 1994) ***13:*** 10, 169, 247
Rohm & Haas Tex.
91 LA 339 (McDermott, 1988) ***3:*** 96; ***11:*** 20
92 LA 850 (Allen, 1989) ***4:*** 15, 82
106 LA 275 (Caraway, 1996) ***11:*** 139
Rohr Indus.
65 LA 982 (Lennard, 1975) ***4:*** 103
78 LA 978 (Sabo, 1982) ***8:*** 84
88 LA 703 (Ross, 1987) ***6:*** 2, 93
94 LA 1303 (Harkless, 1990) ***2:*** 244
Rolling Acres Care Ctr., 91 LA 795 (Dworkin, 1988) ***12:*** 70
Roskam Baking Co., 79 LA 993 (Beitner, 1982) ***8:*** 276, 340
Ross Clay Prods. Co., 64-1 ARB ¶ 8315 (Kabaker, 1963) ***11:*** 55
Ross Gear & Tool Co., 35 LA 293 (Schmidt, 1960) ***2:*** 131; ***8:*** 150
Ross Gear Tenn. Plant, 45 LA 959 (Sanders, 1965) ***2:*** 110
Ross-Meehan Foundries, 55 LA 1078 (King, 1970) ***8:*** 225
Roth Pump Mfg. Co., 82 LA 1199 (O'Reilly, 1984) ***5:*** 124; ***11:*** 85
The Round Dinner Playhouse, Inc., 55 LA 118 (Kamin, 1970) ***2:*** 107
Rubber Workers Fed. Credit Union, 80-1 ARB ¶ 8288 (Owen, 1980) ***3:*** 165, 169, 192, 193, 195
Rudin Mgmt. Co., 74 LA 189 (Talmadge, 1979) ***3:*** 219, 228
Russer Foods, 75 LA 305 (Grant, 1980) ***8:*** 229, 245
Rustco Prods. Co., 92 LA 1048 (Watkins, 1989) ***8:*** 327; ***11:*** 62; ***12:*** 29
Rust Eng'g Co.
85 LA 407 (Whyte, 1985) ***6:*** 22; ***11:*** 25
89 LA 1296 (Gallagher, 1987) ***10:*** 33, 35
Ryan Aeronautical Co., 29 LA 182 (Spaulding, 1957) ***7:*** 167, 168
Ryder Truck Rental, Inc.
78 LA 542 (Allen, 1982) ***2:*** 58
94 LA 7 (Bognanno, 1989) ***2:*** 174

S

Sacramento Air Logistics Ctr., 93 LA 470 (Hoh, 1989) ***2:*** 206
Safeway, Inc., 104 LA 102 (Nelson, 1994) ***11:*** 132
Safeway Stores, Inc.
45 LA 663 (McNaughton, 1965) ***5:*** 34, 59
51 LA 413 (Gillingham, 1967) ***5:*** 6
55 LA 1195 (Jacobs, 1971) ***7:*** 21
64 LA 563 (Gould, 1974) ***12:*** 13, 250
65 LA 1177 (J. Smith, 1975) ***2:*** 392
75 LA 430 (Winograd, 1980) ***3:*** 38
78 LA 394 (Jackson, 1982) ***5:*** 141
79 LA 742 (MacLean, 1982) ***3:*** 32
80 LA 735 (MacLean, 1983) ***3:*** 131
81 LA 657 (Wilmoth, 1983) ***3:*** 100, 125
85-1 ARB ¶ 8180 (Tilbury, 1985) ***6:*** 81
88 LA 1317 (Staudohar, 1987) ***6:*** 24
93 LA 1147 (Wilkinson, 1989) ***2:*** 115; ***3:*** 122
94 LA 983 (Knowlton, 1990) ***2:*** 231; ***8:*** 336
96 LA 304 (Coyle, 1990) ***11:*** 127
Saginaw Bd. of Educ., 101 LA 194 (McDonald, 1993) ***4:*** 6
Saginaw Mining Co.
81 LA 672 (Feldman, 1983) ***3:*** 3
83 LA 741 (Duda, Jr., 1984) ***3:*** 222, 258
Sahara-Nevada Corp., 80-2 ARB ¶ 8374 (Weiss, 1980) ***3:*** 149
St. Clair County, 80 LA 516 (Roumell, 1983) ***2:*** 58, 110
St. Francois County, 69 LA 102 (Elbert, 1977) ***10:*** 40
St. Joe Minerals Corp.
73 LA 1193 (McDermott, 1979) ***3:*** 64
76 LA 421 (Newmark, 1981) ***2:*** 83
St. Joseph, 102 LA 179 (Gordon, 1993) ***2:*** 392
St. Joseph Packaging, Inc., 68 LA 1366 (Moore, 1977) ***5:*** 150
St. Louis Paint Mfg. Co., 88 LA 1251 (Penfield, 1987) ***6:*** 9
St. Luke's Hosp., 93 LA 1241 (Johnson, 1989) ***4:*** 146
St. Paul, Minn.
100 LA 105 (Berquist, 1992) ***2:*** 95
101 LA 265 (Neigh, 1993) ***2:*** 390, 395; ***11:*** 150
St. Paul Pub. Sch. Indep. Sch. Dist. 625, 101 LA 503 (Imes, 1993) ***9:*** 5, 16

Shaefer's Ambulance Serv., 104 LA 481 (Calhoun, 1995) ***2:*** 171
Shaker Heights, Ohio, 96-1 ARB ¶ 6095 (Imundo, 1995) ***2:*** 233
Shamrock Indus. Inc., 84 LA 1203 (Reynolds, 1985) ***2:*** 172
Sharon Steel Corp, 71 LA 737 (Klein, 1978) ***3:*** 21
Sharples Coal Co., 91 LA 1317 (Volz, 1988) ***10:*** 74, 96, 99–102
Sharpless Coal Corp., 91 LA 1065 (Stoltenberg, 1988) ***6:*** 181, 189
Shawnee Local Bd. of Educ., 104 LA 682 (Weisheit, 1995) ***4:*** 119, 131
Shelby County Gov't, 100 LA 284 (Harvey, 1992) ***5:*** 106; ***10:*** 85
Sheller-Globe Corp., 60 LA 414 (Seidman, 1973) ***5:*** 74, 87
Sheller Mfg. Corp., 34 LA 689 (McCoy, 1960) ***5:*** 109, 115
Shell Oil Co.
81 LA 1205 (Brisco, 1983) ***5:*** 59, 224
83 LA 787 (Allen, 1984) ***3:*** 32
84 LA 562 (Milentz, 1985) ***2:*** 68, 83; ***5:*** 59
85-1 ARB ¶ 8290 (Bennett, 1985) ***5:*** 221
85 LA 769 (LeBaron, 1985) ***3:*** 21
87 LA 473 (Nicholas, 1986) ***6:*** 36; ***12:*** 53, 105
90 LA 286 (McDermott, 1988) ***3:*** 71, 76; ***6:*** 143
93 LA 273 (Allen, 1989) ***2:*** 244
Shop 'N Save Warehouse Foods, Inc., 85 LA 494 (Newmark, 1985) ***2:*** 194
Shuler Axle Co., 51 LA 210 (Dworkin, 1968) ***8:*** 116, 141
Shwayder Bros., 7 LA 552 (Whiting, 1947) ***12:*** 149
Sifco Indus., Steel Improvement & Forge Div., 97 LA 244 (Fullmer, 1991) ***13:*** 68
Signal Delivery Serv., Inc., 86 LA 75 (Wies, 1985) ***5:*** 135; ***6:*** 72
Simetco, Inc., 96 LA 193 (Odom, 1990) ***2:*** 249; ***6:*** 253
Sim-Kar Lighting Fixture Co., 99 LA 837 (Valentine, 1992) ***4:*** 100
Simoniz Co., 44 LA 658 (McGury, 1964) ***5:*** 206, 207
Simplex Prods. Div., 91 LA 356 (Byars, 1988) ***12:*** 75, 76
Simpson Paper Co., 86 LA 503 (Leach, 1985) ***3:*** 9
Singer Co., Link Simulation Sys. Div., 85 LA 152 (Yarowsky, 1985) ***2:*** 92
Sinternet Corp., 95 LA 978 (Richard, 1990) ***4:*** 146
Skenandoa Rayon Corp., 18 LA 239 (Justin, 1952) ***5:*** 16
SK Hand Tool Corp., 98 LA 643 (Hodgson, 1992) ***2:*** 26, 88, 110, 122, 123; ***12:*** 211
Smith-Blair, Inc., 100 LA 344 (Goodstein, 1992) ***5:*** 92; ***10:*** 2, 103
Smith Meter Co., 86 LA 1009 (Creo, 1986) ***3:*** 38
Smurfit Recycling Co., 103 LA 243 (Richman, 1994) ***8:*** 10
Snappy Air Distrib. Prods., 104 LA 184 (Jacobowski, 1995) ***2:*** 233
Snow Mountain Pine Co. & Tecton Laminates Corp., 94 LA 929 (Levak, 1990) ***2:*** 89, 120
Snyder Gen. Corp., 99 LA 1108 (Bard, 1992) ***7:*** 38
Social Sec. Admin.
79 LA 449 (Mittelman, 1982) ***13:*** 120, 121
80 LA 725 (Lubic, 1983) ***9:*** 74, 75
81 LA 1051 (Muessig, 1983) ***12:*** 174
89-2 ARB ¶ 8611 (Feigenbaum, 1989) ***3:*** 99
Social Sec. Admin., Office of Hearing & Appeals, 81 LA 1051 (Muessig, 1983) ***2:*** 67
Sohio Chem. Co., 44 LA 624 (Witney, 1964) ***2:*** 378
Soule Steel Co., 85 LA 336 (Richman, 1985) ***7:*** 25, 26; ***11:*** 122
South Cent. Bell Tel. Co.
59 LA 134 (Seward, 1972) ***5:*** 134, 215
71 LA 174 (Wolff, 1978) ***10:*** 8
Southeast Container Corp., 69 LA 884 (Seidenberg, 1977) ***8:*** 231, 251
Southeastern Pa. Transp. Auth.
88 LA 621 (Schwartz, 1986) ***4:*** 118
100 LA 767 (Goulet, 1992) ***14:*** 121
Southern Bakeries Co., 36 LA 440 (Dworet, 1960) ***5:*** 99
Southern Bell Tel. & Tel. Co.
25 LA 270 (McCoy, 1955) ***5:*** 210
74 LA 1115 (Duff, 1980) ***8:*** 260, 263
75 LA 409 (Seibel, 1980) ***2:*** 120; ***8:*** 320
Southern Bell Tel. Co., 27 LA 557 (Blair, 1956) ***5:*** 30
Southern Cal. Carton, 88 LA 591 (Scholtz, 1986) ***7:*** 38, 68
Southern Cal. Edison
61 LA 33 (Daniel, 1973) ***5:*** 91
61 LA 453 (Block, 1973) ***5:*** 97
61 LA 803 (Helbling, 1973) ***7:*** 5
89-1 ARB ¶ 8149 (Horowitz, 1989) ***3:*** 43, 44
89 LA 1129 (Collins, 1987) ***2:*** 351; ***7:*** 31
90 LA 960 (Draznin, 1988) ***6:*** 86
101 LA 201 (Prayzich, 1993) ***2:*** 272
Southern Cal. Gas Co.
89 LA 393 (Alleyne, 1987) ***6:*** 99

T

U

V

W

X

Y

Z

Table of Arbitrators Main Edition

This table lists the names of arbitrators from awards cited within the Main Edition footnotes. No distinction is made between arbitrators with the same last name. This format may be useful to representatives in selecting arbitrators or in writing briefs; it may also be helpful to arbitrators in award preparation. References are to Main Edition chapter and footnote number (e.g., ***11:*** *16 refers to footnote 16 in chapter 11). Some entries may not match precisely what appears in the Main Edition because corrected information, as reflected by the Errata table on page 191, was used to compile this table.*

A

B

C

D

E

F

G

H

I

J

K

L

M

N

O

P

Q

R

S

T

U

V

W

Y

Z